COLLECTED ESSAYS

VOLUME II

By Virginia Woolf

VOLUME II

COLLECTED
ESSAYS

VIRGINIA WOOLF

HARCOURT, BRACE & WORLD, INC., NEW YORK

KEY TO ABBREVIATIONS
OF VIRGINIA WOOLF'S WORKS
IN CONTENTS LIST

The Common Reader	C.R. I
The Moment	M.
The Common Reader II	C.R. II
The Death of the Moth	D.M.
The Captain's Death Bed	C.D.B.
Granite and Rainbow	G.R.

CONTENTS

COLLECTED ESSAYS

VOLUME II

How Should One Read a Book?[1]

IN the first place, I want to emphasise the note of interrogation at the end of my title. Even if I could answer the question for myself, the answer would apply only to me and not to you. The only advice, indeed, that one person can give another about reading is to take no advice, to follow your own instincts, to use your own reason, to come to your own conclusions. If this is agreed between us, then I feel at liberty to put forward a few ideas and suggestions because you will not allow them to fetter that independence which is the most important quality that a reader can possess. After all, what laws can be laid down about books? The battle of Waterloo was certainly fought on a certain day; but is *Hamlet* a better play than *Lear*? Nobody can say. Each must decide that question for himself. To admit authorities, however heavily furred and gowned, into our libraries and let them tell us how to read, what to read, what value to place upon what we read, is to destroy the spirit of freedom which is the breath of those sanctuaries. Everywhere else we may be bound by laws and conventions—there we have none.

But to enjoy freedom, if the platitude is pardonable, we have of course to control ourselves. We must not squander our powers, helplessly and ignorantly, squirting half the house in order to water a single rose-bush; we must train them, exactly and power-fully, here on the very spot. This, it may be, is one of the first difficulties that faces us in a library. What is 'the very spot'? There may well seem to be nothing but a conglomeration and huddle of confusion. Poems and novels, histories and memoirs, dictionaries and blue-books; books written in all languages by men and women of all tempers, races, and ages jostle each other on the shelf. And outside the donkey brays, the women gossip at the pump, the colts gallop across the fields. Where are we to begin? How are we to bring order into this multitudinous chaos and so get the deepest and widest pleasure from what we read?

It is simple enough to say that since books have classes—fiction, biography, poetry—we should separate them and take

[1] A paper read at a school

I

from each what it is right that each should give us. Yet few people ask from books what books can give us. Most commonly we come to books with blurred and divided minds, asking of fiction that it shall be true, of poetry that it shall be false, of biography that it shall be flattering, of history that it shall enforce our own prejudices. If we could banish all such preconceptions when we read, that would be an admirable beginning. Do not dictate to your author; try to become him. Be his fellow-worker and accomplice. If you hang back, and reserve and criticise at first, you are preventing yourself from getting the fullest possible value from what you read. But if you open your mind as widely as possible, then signs and hints of almost imperceptible fineness, from the twist and turn of the first sentences, will bring you into the presence of a human being unlike any other. Steep yourself in this, acquaint yourself with this, and soon you will find that your author is giving you, or attempting to give you, something far more definite. The thirty-two chapters of a novel—if we consider how to read a novel first—are an attempt to make something as formed and controlled as a building: but words are more impalpable than bricks; reading is a longer and more complicated process than seeing. Perhaps the quickest way to understand the elements of what a novelist is doing is not to read, but to write; to make your own experiment with the dangers and difficulties of words. Recall, then, some event that has left a distinct impression on you—how at the corner of the street, perhaps, you passed two people talking. A tree shook; an electric light danced; the tone of the talk was comic, but also tragic; a whole vision, an entire conception, seemed contained in that moment.

But when you attempt to reconstruct it in words, you will find that it breaks into a thousand conflicting impressions. Some must be subdued; others emphasised; in the process you will lose, probably, all grasp upon the emotion itself. Then turn from your blurred and littered pages to the opening pages of some great novelist—Defoe, Jane Austen, Hardy. Now you will be better able to appreciate their mastery. It is not merely that we are in the presence of a different person—Defoe, Jane Austen, or Thomas Hardy—but that we are living in a different world. Here, in *Robinson Crusoe*, we are trudging a plain high road; one thing happens after another; the fact and the order of the fact is enough.

But if the open air and adventure mean everything to Defoe they mean nothing to Jane Austen. Hers is the drawing-room, and people talking, and by the many mirrors of their talk revealing their characters. And if, when we have accustomed ourselves to the drawing-room and its reflections, we turn to Hardy, we are once more spun round. The moors are round us and the stars are above our heads. The other side of the mind is now exposed—the dark side that comes uppermost in solitude, not the light side that shows in company. Our relations are not towards people, but towards Nature and destiny. Yet different as these worlds are, each is consistent with itself. The maker of each is careful to observe the laws of his own perspective, and however great a strain they may put upon us they will never confuse us, as lesser writers so frequently do, by introducing two different kinds of reality into the same book. Thus to go from one great novelist to another—from Jane Austen to Hardy, from Peacock to Trollope, from Scott to Meredith—is to be wrenched and uprooted; to be thrown this way and then that. To read a novel is a difficult and complex art. You must be capable not only of great fineness of perception, but of great boldness of imagination if you are going to make use of all that the novelist—the great artist—gives you.

But a glance at the heterogeneous company on the shelf will show you that writers are very seldom 'great artists'; far more often a book makes no claim to be a work of art at all. These biographies and autobiographies, for example, lives of great men, of men long dead and forgotten, that stand cheek by jowl with the novels and poems, are we to refuse to read them because they are not 'art'? Or shall we read them, but read them in a different way, with a different aim? Shall we read them in the first place to satisfy that curiosity which possesses us sometimes when in the evening we linger in front of a house where the lights are lit and the blinds not yet drawn, and each floor of the house shows us a different section of human life in being? Then we are consumed with curiosity about the lives of these people—the servants gossiping, the gentlemen dining, the girl dressing for a party, the old woman at the window with her knitting. Who are they, what are they, what are their names, their occupations, their thoughts, and adventures?

Biographies and memoirs answer such questions, light up innumerable such houses; they show us people going about their daily affairs, toiling, failing, succeeding, eating, hating, loving, until they die. And sometimes as we watch, the house fades and the iron railings vanish and we are out at sea; we are hunting, sailing, fighting; we are among savages and soldiers; we are taking part in great campaigns. Or if we like to stay here in England, in London, still the scene changes; the street narrows; the house becomes small, cramped, diamond-paned, and malodorous. We see a poet, Donne, driven from such a house because the walls were so thin that when the children cried their voices cut through them. We can follow him, through the paths that lie in the pages of books, to Twickenham; to Lady Bedford's Park, a famous meeting-ground for nobles and poets; and then turn our steps to Wilton, the great house under the downs, and hear Sidney read the *Arcadia* to his sister; and ramble among the very marshes and see the very herons that figure in that famous romance; and then again travel north with that other Lady Pembroke, Anne Clifford, to her wild moors, or plunge into the city and control our merriment at the sight of Gabriel Harvey in his black velvet suit arguing about poetry with Spenser. Nothing is more fascinating than to grope and stumble in the alternate darkness and splendour of Elizabethan London. But there is no staying there. The Temples and the Swifts, the Harleys and the St. Johns beckon us on; hour upon hour can be spent disentangling their quarrels and deciphering their characters; and when we tire of them we can stroll on, past a lady in black wearing diamonds, to Samuel Johnson and Goldsmith and Garrick; or cross the channel, if we like, and meet Voltaire and Diderot, Madame du Deffand; and so back to England and Twickenham—how certain places repeat themselves and certain names!—where Lady Bedford had her Park once and Pope lived later, to Walpole's home at Strawberry Hill. But Walpole introduces us to such a swarm of new acquaintances, there are so many houses to visit and bells to ring that we may well hesitate for a moment, on the Miss Berrys' doorstep, for example, when behold, up comes Thackeray; he is the friend of the woman whom Walpole loved; so that merely by going from friend to friend, from garden to garden, from house to house, we have passed from one end of English literature to another and

4

wake to find ourselves here again in the present, if we can so differentiate this moment from all that have gone before. This, then, is one of the ways in which we can read these lives and letters; we can make them light up the many windows of the past; we can watch the famous dead in their familiar habits and fancy sometimes that we are very close and can surprise their secrets, and sometimes we may pull out a play or a poem that they have written and see whether it reads differently in the presence of the author. But this again rouses other questions. How far, we must ask ourselves, is a book influenced by its writer's life—how far is it safe to let the man interpret the writer? How far shall we resist or give way to the sympathies and antipathies that the man himself rouses in us—so sensitive are words, so receptive of the character of the author? These are questions that press upon us when we read lives and letters, and we must answer them for ourselves, for nothing can be more fatal than to be guided by the preferences of others in a matter so personal.

But also we can read such books with another aim, not to throw light on literature, not to become familiar with famous people, but to refresh and exercise our own creative powers. Is there not an open window on the right hand of the bookcase? How delightful to stop reading and look out! How stimulating the scene is, in its unconsciousness, its irrelevance, its perpetual movement—the colts galloping round the field, the woman filling her pail at the well, the donkey throwing back his head and emitting his long, acrid moan. The greater part of any library is nothing but the record of such fleeting moments in the lives of men, women, and donkeys. Every literature, as it grows old, has its rubbish-heap, its record of vanished moments and forgotten lives told in faltering and feeble accents that have perished. But if you give yourself up to the delight of rubbish-reading you will be surprised, indeed you will be overcome, by the relics of human life that have been cast out to moulder. It may be one letter—but what a vision it gives! It may be a few sentences—but what vistas they suggest! Sometimes a whole story will come together with such beautiful humour and pathos and completeness that it seems as if a great novelist had been at work, yet it is only an old actor, Tate Wilkinson, remembering the strange story of Captain Jones; it is only a young subaltern serving under Arthur

Wellesley and falling in love with a pretty girl at Lisbon; it is only Maria Allen letting fall her sewing in the empty drawing-room and sighing how she wishes she had taken Dr. Burney's good advice and had never eloped with her Rishy. None of this has any value; it is negligible in the extreme; yet how absorbing it is now and again to go through the rubbish-heaps and find rings and scissors and broken noses buried in the huge past and try to piece them together while the colt gallops round the field, the woman fills her pail at the well, and the donkey brays.

But we tire of rubbish-reading in the long run. We tire of searching for what is needed to complete the half-truth which is all that the Wilkinsons, the Bunburys, and the Maria Allens are able to offer us. They had not the artist's power of mastering and eliminating; they could not tell the whole truth even about their own lives; they have disfigured the story that might have been so shapely. Facts are all that they can offer us, and facts are a very inferior form of fiction. Thus the desire grows upon us to have done with half-statements and approximations; to cease from searching out the minute shades of human character, to enjoy the greater abstractness, the purer truth of fiction. Thus we create the mood, intense and generalised, unaware of detail, but stressed by some regular, recurrent beat, whose natural expression is poetry; and that is the time to read poetry . . . when we are almost able to write it.

> Western wind, when wilt thou blow?
> The small rain down can rain.
> Christ, if my love were in my arms,
> And I in my bed again!

The impact of poetry is so hard and direct that for the moment there is no other sensation except that of the poem itself. What profound depths we visit then—how sudden and complete is our immersion! There is nothing here to catch hold of; nothing to stay us in our flight. The illusion of fiction is gradual; its effects are prepared; but who when they read these four lines stops to ask who wrote them, or conjures up the thought of Donne's house or Sidney's secretary; or enmeshes them in the intricacy of the past and the succession of generations? The poet is always our contemporary. Our being for the moment is centred and constricted, as in any violent shock of personal emotion. Afterwards, it is true, the sensation begins to spread in wider rings through our minds; remoter senses are reached; these begin to sound and to comment and we are aware of echoes and reflections. The intensity of poetry covers an immense range of emotion. We have only to compare the force and directness of

> I shall fall like a tree, and find my grave,
> Only remembering that I grieve,

with the wavering modulation of

> Minutes are numbered by the fall of sands,
> As by an hour glass; the span of time
> Doth waste us to our graves, and we look on it;
> An age of pleasure, revelled out, comes home
> At last, and ends in sorrow; but the life,
> Weary of riot, numbers every sand,
> Wailing in sighs, until the last drop down,
> So to conclude calamity in rest,

or place the meditative calm of

> whether we be young or old,
> Our destiny, our being's heart and home,
> Is with infinitude, and only there;
> With hope it is, hope that can never die,
> Effort, and expectation, and desire,
> And something evermore about to be,

beside the complete and inexhaustible loveliness of

> The moving Moon went up the sky,
> And nowhere did abide:
> Softly she was going up,
> And a star or two beside—

7

or the splendid fantasy of

> And the woodland haunter
> Shall not cease to saunter
>   When, far down some glade,
> Of the great world's burning,
> One soft flame upturning
> Seems, to his discerning,
>   Crocus in the shade,

to bethink us of the varied art of the poet; his power to make us at once actors and spectators; his power to run his hand into character as if it were a glove, and be Falstaff or Lear; his power to condense, to widen, to state, once and for ever.

'We have only to compare'—with those words the cat is out of the bag, and the true complexity of reading is admitted. The first process, to receive impressions with the utmost understanding, is only half the process of reading; it must be completed, if we are to get the whole pleasure from a book, by another. We must pass judgment upon these multitudinous impressions; we must make of these fleeting shapes one that is hard and lasting. But not directly. Wait for the dust of reading to settle; for the conflict and the questioning to die down; walk, talk, pull the dead petals from a rose, or fall asleep. Then suddenly without our willing it, for it is thus that Nature undertakes these transitions, the book will return, but differently. It will float to the top of the mind as a whole. And the book as a whole is different from the book received currently in separate phrases. Details now fit themselves into their places. We see the shape from start to finish; it is a barn, a pigsty, or a cathedral. Now then we can compare book with book as we compare building with building. But this act of comparison means that our attitude has changed; we are no longer the friends of the writer, but his judges; and just as we cannot be too sympathetic as friends, so as judges we cannot be too severe. Are they not criminals, books that have wasted our time and sympathy; are they not the most insidious enemies of society, corrupters, defilers, the writers of false books, faked books, books that fill the air with decay and disease? Let us then be severe in our judgments; let us compare each book with the greatest of its kind. There they hang in the mind the shapes of the books we have read solidified by the judgments we have passed on them— *Robinson Crusoe, Emma, The Return of the Native*. Compare the novels with these—even the latest and least of novels has a right to be judged with the best. And so with poetry—when the intoxication of rhythm has died down and the splendour of words has faded, a visionary shape will return to us and this must be compared with *Lear*, with *Phèdre*, with *The Prelude*; or if not with these, with whatever is the best or seems to us to be the best in its own kind. And we may be sure that the newness of new poetry and fiction is its most superficial quality and that we have only to alter slightly, not to recast, the standards by which we have judged the old.

It would be foolish, then, to pretend that the second part of reading, to judge, to compare, is as simple as the first—to open the mind wide to the fast flocking of innumerable impressions. To continue reading without the book before you, to hold one shadow-shape against another, to have read widely enough and with enough understanding to make such comparisons alive and illuminating—that is difficult; it is still more difficult to press further and to say, 'Not only is the book of this sort, but it is of this value; here it fails; here it succeeds; this is bad; that is good'. To carry out this part of a reader's duty needs such imagination, insight, and learning that it is hard to conceive any one mind sufficiently endowed; impossible for the most self-confident to find more than the seeds of such powers in himself. Would it not be wiser, then, to remit this part of reading and to allow the critics, the gowned and furred authorities of the library, to decide the question of the book's absolute value for us? Yet how impossible! We may stress the value of sympathy; we may try to sink our identity as we read. But we know that we cannot sympathise wholly or immerse ourselves wholly; there is always a demon in us who whispers, 'I hate, I love', and we cannot silence him. Indeed, it is precisely because we hate and we love that our relation with the poets and novelists is so intimate that we find the presence of another person intolerable. And even if the results are abhorrent and our judgments are wrong, still our taste, the nerve of sensation that sends shocks through us, is our chief illuminant; we learn through feeling; we cannot suppress our own idiosyncrasy without impoverishing it. But as time goes on perhaps we can train our taste; perhaps we can make it submit to some control. When it has fed greedily and lavishly upon books of all sorts—poetry, fiction, history, biography—and has stopped reading and looked for long spaces upon the variety, the incongruity of the living world, we shall find that it is changing a little; it is not so greedy, it is more reflective. It will begin to bring us not merely judgments on particular books, but it will tell us that there is a quality common to certain books. Listen, it will say, what shall we call *this*? And it will read us perhaps *Lear* and then perhaps the *Agamemnon* in order to bring out that common quality. Thus, with our taste to guide us, we shall venture beyond the particular book in search of qualities that group books together; we shall give them names and thus frame a rule that brings order into our perceptions. We shall gain a further and a rarer pleasure from that discrimination. But as a rule only lives when it is perpetually broken by contact with the books themselves—nothing is easier and more stultifying than to make rules which exist out of touch with facts, in a vacuum—now at last, in order to steady ourselves in this difficult attempt, it may be well to turn to the very rare writers who are able to enlighten us upon literature as an art. Coleridge and Dryden and Johnson, in their considered criticism, the poets and novelists themselves in their considered sayings, are often surprisingly revelant; they light up and solidify the vague ideas that have been tumbling in the misty depths of our minds. But they are only able to help us if we come to them laden with questions and suggestions won honestly in the course of our own reading. They can do nothing for us if we herd ourselves under their authority and lie down like sheep in the shade of a hedge. We can only understand their ruling when it comes in conflict with our own and vanquishes it.

If this is so, if to read a book as it should be read calls for the rarest qualities of imagination, insight, and judgment, you may perhaps conclude that literature is a very complex art and that it is unlikely that we shall be able, even after a lifetime of reading, to make any valuable contribution to its criticism. We must remain readers; we shall not put on the further glory that belongs to those rare beings who are also critics. But still we have our responsibilities as readers and even our importance. The standards we raise and the judgments we pass steal into the air and become part of the atmosphere which writers breathe as they work. An influence is created which tells upon them even if it never finds its way into print. And that influence, if it were well instructed, vigorous and individual and sincere, might be of great value now when criticism is necessarily in abeyance; when books pass in review like the procession of animals in a shooting gallery, and the critic has only one second in which to load and aim and shoot and may well be pardoned if he mistakes rabbits for tigers, eagles for barndoor fowls, or misses altogether and wastes his shot upon some peaceful cow grazing in a further field. If behind the erratic gunfire of the press the author felt that there was another kind of criticism, the opinion of people reading for the love of reading, slowly and unprofessionally, and judging with great sympathy and yet with great severity, might this not improve the quality of his work? And if by our means books were to become stronger, richer, and more varied, that would be an end worth reaching.

Yet who reads to bring about an end, however desirable? Are there not some pursuits that we practise because they are good in themselves, and some pleasures that are final? And is not this among them? I have sometimes dreamt, at least, that when the Day of Judgment dawns and the great conquerors and lawyers and statesmen come to receive their rewards—their crowns, their laurels, their names carved indelibly upon imperishable marble—the Almighty will turn to Peter and will say, not without a certain envy when he sees us coming with our books under our arms, 'Look, these need no reward. We have nothing to give them here. They have loved reading.'

Reading

WHY did they choose this particular spot to build the house on? For the sake of the view perhaps. Not, I suppose, that they looked at views as we look at them, but rather as an incentive to ambition, as a proof of power. For in time they were lords of that valley, green with trees, and owned at least all that part of the moor that lies on the right-hand side of the road. At any rate the house was built here, here a stop was put to trees and ferns; here one room was laid upon another, and down some feet into the earth foundations were thrust and deep cool cellars hollowed out.

The house had its library; a long low room, lined with little burnished books, folios, and stout blocks of divinity. The cases were carved with birds pecking at clusters of wooden fruit. A sallow priest tended them, dusting the books and the carved birds at the same time. Here they all are; Homer and Euripides; Chaucer; then Shakespeare; and the Elizabethans, and following come the plays of the Restoration, more handled these, and greased as if from midnight reading, and so down to our time or very near it, Cowper, Burns, Scott, Wordsworth and the rest. I liked that room. I liked the view across country that one had from the window, and the blue line between the gap of the trees on the moor was the North Sea. I liked to read there. One drew the pale armchair to the window, and so the light fell over the shoulder upon the page. The shadow of the gardener mowing the lawn sometimes crossed it, as he led his pony in rubber shoes up and down, the machine giving a little creak, which seemed the very voice of summer, as it turned and drew another broad belt of green by the side of the one just cut. Like the wake of ships I used to think them, especially when they curved round the flower beds for islands, and the fuchsias might be lighthouses, and the geraniums, by some freak of fancy, were Gibraltar; there were the red coats of the invincible British soldiers upon the rock.

Then tall ladies used to come out of the house and go down the grass drives to be met by the gentlemen of those days, carrying racquets and white balls which I could just see, through the bushes that hid the tennis lawn, bounding over the net, and the figures of the players passed to and fro. But they did not distract me from my book; any more than the butterflies visiting the flowers, or the bees doing their more serious business on the same blossoms, or the thrushes hopping lightly from the low branches of the sycamore to the turf, taking two steps in the direction of some slug or fly, and then hopping, with light decision, back to the low branch again. None of these things distracted me in those days; and somehow or another, the windows being open, and the book held so that it rested upon a background of escalonia hedges and distant blue, instead of being a book it seemed as if what I read was laid upon the landscape, not printed, bound, or sewn up, but somehow the product of trees and fields and the hot summer sky, like the air which swam, on fine mornings, round the outlines of things.

These were circumstances, perhaps, to turn one's mind to the past. Always behind the voice, the figure, the fountain there seemed to stretch an immeasurable avenue, that ran to a point of other voices, figures, fountains which tapered out indistinguishably upon the furthest horizon. If I looked down at my book I could see Keats and Pope behind him, and then Dryden and Sir Thomas Browne—hosts of them merging in the mass of Shakespeare, behind whom, if one peered long enough, some shapes of men in pilgrims' dress emerged, Chaucer perhaps, and again—who was it? some uncouth poet scarcely able to syllable his words; and so they died away.

But, as I say, even the gardener leading his pony was part of the book, and, straying from the actual page, the eye rested upon his face, as if one reached it through a great depth of time. That accounted for the soft swarthy tint of the cheeks, and the lines of his body, scarcely disguised by the coarse brown stuff of his coat, might have belonged to any labouring man in any age, for the clothing of the field labourer has changed little since Saxon days, and a half-shut eye can people a field much as it was before the Norman conquest. This man took his place naturally by the side of those dead poets. He ploughed; he sowed; he drank; he marched in battle sometimes; he sang his song; he came courting and went underground raising only a green wave in the turf of the churchyard, but leaving boys and girls behind him to continue his name and lead the pony across the lawn, these hot summer mornings.

Through that same layer of time one could see, with equal clearness, the more splendid figures of knights and ladies. One could see them; that is true. The ripe apricot of the ladies' dress, the gilt crimson of the knights set floating coloured images in the dark ripples of the lake water. In the church too you see them laid out as if in triumphant repose, their hands folded, their eyes shut, their favourite hounds at their feet, and all the shields of their ancestors, faintly touched still with blue and red, supporting them. Thus garnished and made ready they seem to await, to expect in confidence. The Day of Judgment dawns. His eyes open, his hand seeks hers, he leads her forth through the opened doors and the lines of angels with their trumpets, to some smoother lawn, more regal residence and mansions of whiter masonry. Meanwhile, the silence is scarcely broken by a word. It is, after all, a question of seeing them.

For the art of speech came late to England. These Fanshawes and Leghs, Verneys, Pastons, and Hutchinsons, all well endowed by birth and nature and leaving behind them such a treasure of inlaid wood and old furniture, things curiously made and delicately figured, left with it only a very broken message or one so stiff that the ink seems to have dried as it traced the words. Did they, then, enjoy these possessions in silence, or was the business of life transacted in a stately way to match these stiff polysyllables and branching periods? Or, like children on a Sunday, did they compose themselves and cease their chatter when they sat down to write what would pass from hand to hand, serve for winter gossip round a dozen firesides, and be laid up at length with other documents of importance in the dry room above the kitchen fireplace?

'In October, as I told you', wrote Lady Fanshawe some time about the year 1601, 'my husband and I went into France by way of Portsmouth where, walking by the seaside . . . two ships of the Dutch shot bullets at us, so near that we heard them whiz by us: at which I called my husband to make haste back, and began to run. But he altered not his pace, saying, if we must be killed, it were as good to be killed walking as running.' There, surely, it is the spirit of dignity that controls her. The bullets whiz across the sand, but Sir Richard walks no faster, and summons up his idea of death—death visible, tangible, an enemy, but an enemy of flesh and blood to be met courageously with drawn sword like a gentleman—which temper she poor woman admires, though she cannot, on the beach at Portsmouth, altogether imitate. Dignity, loyalty, magnanimity—such are the virtues she would commend, and frame her speech to, checking it from its natural slips and trifles, and making believe that life for people of gentle birth and high morality was thus decorous and sublime. The pen, too, when the small shot of daily life came whizzing about her—eighteen children in twenty-one years she bore and buried the greater part—must curb itself to walk slowly, not to run. Writing is with them, as it can no longer be with us, making; making something that will endure and wear a brave face in the eyes of posterity. For posterity is the judge of these ideals, and it is for that distant and impartial public that Lady Fanshawe writes and Lucy Hutchinson, and not for John in London or Elizabeth married and gone to live in Sussex; there is no daily post for children and friends bringing to the breakfast table not only news of crops and servants, visitors and bad weather, but the subtler narrative of love and coldness, affection waning or carried on secure; there is no language it seems for that frail burden. Horace Walpole, Jane Carlyle, Edward Fitzgerald are ghosts on the very outskirts of time. Thus these ancestors of ours, though stately and fair to look upon, are silent; they move through galleries and parks in the midst of a little oasis of silence which holds the intruding modern spirit at bay. Here, again, are the Leghs; generations upon generations of them, all red haired, all living at Lyme, which has been building these three centuries and more, all men of education, character, and opportunity, and all, by modern standards, dumb. They will write of a fox hunt and how afterward 'a Bowle of Hott Punch with ye Fox's foot stew'd in it' was drunk, and how 'Sir Willm drunk pretty plentifully, and just at last perceive'd he should be fuddled, "but," quoth he, "I care not if I am, I have kill'd a fox today".' But having killed their fox, drunk their punch, raced their horses, fought their cocks, and toasted, discreetly, the King over the water, or, more openly, 'A Fresh Earth and High Metaled Terrier,' their lips shut, their eyes close; they have nothing more to say to us.

Taciturn or crass as we may think them, dull men inheriting their red hair and very little brain beneath it, nevertheless more business was discharged by them, more of life took its mould from them than we can measure, or, indeed, dispense with. If Lyme had been blotted out and the thousand other houses of equal importance which lay about England like little fortresses of civilization, where you could read books, act plays, make laws, meet your neighbours, and talk with strangers from abroad, if these spaces won from the encroaching barbarity had not persisted till the foothold was firm and the swamp withheld, how would our more delicate spirits have fared—our writers, thinkers, musicians, artists—without a wall to shelter under, or flowers upon which to sun their wings? Waging war year after year upon winter and rough weather, needing all their faculties to keep the roof sound, the larder full, the children taught and clothed, dependents cared for, naturally our ancestors appear in their spare time rather surly and silent—as ploughboys after a long day's work scrape the mud from their boots, stretch the cramped muscles of their backs, and stumble off to bed without thought of book or pen or evening paper. The little language of affection and intimacy which we seek in vain necessitates soft pillows, easy chairs, silver forks, private rooms; it must have at its command a store of little words, nimble and domesticated, coming at the call of the lightest occasion, refining themselves to the faintest shadow. Above all, perhaps, good roads and carriages, frequent meetings, partings, festivities, alliances, and ruptures are needed to break up the splendid sentences; easy chairs it may be were the death of English prose. The annals of an old and obscure family like the Leghs show clearly enough how the slow process of furnishing the bare rooms and taking coach for London, as a matter of course, abolish its isolation, merge the dialect of the district into the common speech of the land, and teach, by degrees, a uniform method of spelling. One can see in fancy the face itself changing, and the manner of father to son, mother to daughter, losing what must have been their tremendous formality, their unquestioned authority. But what dignity, what beauty broods over it all!

It's a hot summer morning. The sun has browned the outer-most leaves of the elm trees, and already, since the gale, one or two lie on the grass, having completed the whole range of exist-ence from bud to withered fibre and become nothing but leaves to be swept up for the autumn bonfires. Through the green arches the eye with a curious desire seeks the blue which it knows to be the blue of the sea; and knowing it can somehow set the mind off upon a voyage, can somehow encircle all this sub-stantial earth with the flowing and the unpossessed. The sea—the sea—I must drop my book, the pious Mrs. Hutchinson, and leave her to make what terms she can with Margaret, Duchess of Newcastle. There's a sweeter air outside—how spicy, even on a still day, after the house!—and bushes of verbena and southern-wood yield a leaf as one passes to be crushed and smelt. If we could see also what we can smell—if, at this moment crushing the southernwood, I could go back through the long corridor of sunny mornings, boring my way through hundreds of Augusts, I should come in the end, passing a host of less-important figures, to no less a person than Queen Elizabeth herself. Whether some tinted waxwork is the foundation of my view, I do not know; but she always appears very distinctly in the same guise. She flaunts across the terrace superbly and a little stiffly like the peacock spreading its tail. She seems slightly infirm, so that one is half inclined to smile; and then she raps out her favourite oath as Lord Herbert of Cherbury heard it, as he bowed his knee among the courtiers, when, far from being infirm, she shows a masculine and rather repulsive vigour. Perhaps, under all that stiff brocade, she has not washed her shrivelled old body? She breakfasts off beer and meat and handles the bones with fingers rough with rubies. It may be so, yet Elizabeth, of all our kings and queens, seems most fit for that gesture which bids the great sailors farewell, or welcomes them home to her presence again, her imagination still lusting for the strange tales they bring her, her imagination still young in its wrinkled and fantastic casket. It is their youth; it is their immense fund of credulity; their minds still unwritten over and capable of such enormous designs as the American forests cast upon them, or the Spanish ships, or the savages, or the soul of man—this is what makes it impossible, walking the terrace, not to look upon the blue sea line, and think of their ships. The ships, Froude says, were no bigger than a modern English yacht. As they shrink and assume the romantic proportions of the Elizabethan ship, so the sea runs enormously larger and freer and with bigger waves upon it than the sea of our time. The summons to explore, to bring back dyes and roots and oil, and find a market for wool and iron and cloth has been heard in the villages of the West. The little company gathers together somewhere off Greenwich. The courtiers come running to the palace windows; the Privy Councillors press their faces to the panes. The guns are shot off in salute, and then, as the ships swing down the tide, one sailor after another walks the hatches, climbs the shrouds, stands upon the mainyards to wave his friends a last farewell. For directly England and the coast of France are beneath the horizon, the ships swim into the unfamiliar, the air has its voices, the sea its lions and serpents, evaporations of fire and tumultuous whirlpools. The clouds but sparely hide the Divinity; the limbs of Satan are almost visible. Riding in company through the storm, suddenly one light disappears; Sir Humfrey Gilbert has gone beneath the waves: when morning comes they seek his ship in vain. Sir Hugh Willoughby sails to discover the North-West Passage, and makes no return. Sometimes, a ragged and worn out man comes knocking at the door, and claims to be the boy who went years ago to sea and is now come back to his father's house. 'Sir William his father and my lady his mother knew him not to be their son, until they found a secret mark, which was a wart upon one of his knees.' But he brings with him a black stone, veined with gold, or an ivory tusk, or a lamp of silver, and stories of how such stones are strewn about to be picked up off the ground as you will. What if the passage to the fabled land of uncounted riches lay only a little further up the coast? What if the known world was only the prelude to some more splendid panorama? When, after the long voyage, the ships dropped anchor in the great river of the Plate and the men went exploring through the undulating lands, startling the grazing herds of deer and glimpsing between the trees the dusky limbs of savages, they filled their pockets with pebbles that might be emeralds, or rubies, or sand that might be gold. Sometimes, rounding a headland, they saw far off a string of savages slowly descending to the beach bearing on their heads and linking their shoulders together with heavy burdens for the Spanish king.

These are the fine stories, used effectively all through the West Country to decoy the strong men lounging by the harbour-side to leave their nets and fish for gold. Less glorious but more urgent, considering the state of the country, was the summons of the more serious-minded to set on foot some intercourse between the merchants of England and the merchants of the East. For lack of work, this staid observer wrote, the poor of England were driven to crime and 'daily consumed with the gallows'. Wool they had in plenty, fine, soft, strong, and durable; but no market for it and few dyes. Gradually owing to the boldness of private travellers, the native stock had been improved and embellished. Beasts and plants had been imported; and along with them the seeds of all our roses. Gradually little groups of merchant men settled here and there on the borders of the unexplored, and through their fingers the precious stream of coloured and rare and curious things begins slowly and precariously to flow towards London; our fields are sown with new flowers. In the south and west, in America and the East Indies, the life was pleasanter and success more splendid; yet in the land of long winters and squat-faced savages the very darkness and strangeness draw the imagination. Here they are, three or four men from the west of England set down in the white landscape with only the huts of savages near them, and left to make what bargains they can and pick up what knowledge they can, until the little ships, no bigger than yachts, appear at the mouth of the bay next summer. Strange must have been their thoughts; strange the sense of the unknown; and of themselves, the isolated English, burning on the very rim of the dark, and the dark full of unseen splendours. One of them, carrying a charter from his company in London, went inland as far as Moscow, and there saw the Emperor, 'sitting in his chair of estate, with his crown on his head, and a staff of gold-smith work in his left hand.' All the ceremony that he saw is carefully written out, and the sight upon which the English merchant, the vanguard of civilization, first set eyes has the brilliancy still of a Roman vase or other shining ornament dug up and stood for a moment in the sun before, exposed to the air, seen by millions of eyes, it dulls and crumbles away. There, all these centuries, the glories of Moscow, the glories of Constantinople, have flowered unseen. Many are preserved as if under shades of glass. The Englishman, however, is bravely dressed for the occasion, leads in his hand, perhaps, 'three fair mastiffs in coats of red cloth' and carries a letter from Elizabeth 'the paper whereof did smell most fragrantly of camphor and ambergris, and the ink of perfect musk.'

Yet if by means of these old records, courts and palaces and Sultans' presence chambers are once more displayed, stranger still are the little disks of light calling out of obscurity for a second some unadorned savage, falling like lantern light upon moving figures. Here is a story of the savage caught somewhere off the coast of Labrador, taken to England and shown about like a wild beast. Next year they bring him back and fetch a woman savage on board to keep him company. When they see each other they blush; they blush profoundly; the sailor notices it but knows not why it is. And later the two savages set up house together on board ship, she attending to his wants, he nursing her in sickness, but living, as the sailors note, in perfect chastity. The erratic searchlight cast by these records falling for a second upon those blushing cheeks three hundred years ago, among the snow, sets up that sense of communication which we are apt to get only from fiction. We seem able to guess why they blushed; the Elizabethans would notice it, but it has waited over three hundred years for us to interpret it.

There are not perhaps enough blushes to keep the attention fixed upon the broad yellow-tinged pages of Hakluyt's book. The attention wanders. Still if it wanders, it wanders in the green shade of forests. It floats far out at sea. It is soothed almost to sleep by the sweet-toned voices of pious men talking the melodious language, much broader and more sonorous sounding than our own, of the Elizabethan age. They are men of fine limbs, arched brows, beneath which the oval eyes are full and luminous, and thin golden rings are in their ears. What need have they of blushes? What meeting would rouse such emotions in them? Why should they whittle down feelings and thoughts so as to cause embarrassment and bring lines between the eyes and perplex them, so that it is no longer a ship or a man that comes before them, but some thing doubtful as a phantom, and more of a symbol than a fact? If one tires of the long, dangerous, and memorable voyages of M. Ralph Fitch, M. Roger Bodenham, M. Anthony Jenkinson, M. John Lok, the Earl of Cumberland and others, to Pegu and Siam, Candia and Chio, Aleppo and Muscovy, it is for the perhaps unsatisfactory reason that they make no mention of oneself; seem altogether oblivious of such an organism; and manage to exist in comfort and opulence nevertheless. For simplicity of speech by no means implies rudeness or emptiness. Indeed this free-flowing, equable narrative, though now occupied merely with the toils and adventures of ordinary ships companies, has its own true balance, owing to the poise of brain and body arrived at by the union of adventure and physical exertion with minds still tranquil and unstirred as the summer sea.

In all this there is no doubt much exaggeration, much misunderstanding. One is tempted to impute to the dead the qualities we find lacking in ourselves. There is balm for our restlessness in conjuring up visions of Elizabethan magnanimity; the very flow and fall of the sentences lulls us asleep, or carries us along as upon the back of a large smooth-paced cart horse, through green pastures. It is the pleasantest atmosphere on a hot summer's day. They talk of their commodities and there you see them; more clearly and separately in bulk, colour, and variety than the goods brought by steamer and piled upon docks; they talk of fruit; the red and yellow globes hang unpicked on virgin trees; so with the lands they sight; the morning mist is only just now lifting and not a flower has been plucked. The grass has long whitened tracks upon it for the first time. With the towns too discovered for the first time it is the same thing. And so, as you read on across the broad pages with as many slips and somnolences as you like, the illusion rises and holds you of banks slipping by on either side, of glades opening out, of white towers revealed, of gilt domes and ivory minarets. It is, indeed, an atmosphere, not only soft and fine, but rich, too, with more than one can grasp at any single reading.

So that, if at last I shut the book, it was only that my mind was sated, not the treasure exhausted. Moreover, what with reading and ceasing to read, taking a few steps this way and then pausing to look at the view, that same view has lost its colours, and the yellow page was almost too dim to decipher. So the book must be stood in its place, to deepen the brown line of shadow which the folios made on the wall. The books gently swelled neath my hand as I drew it across them in the dark. Travels, histories, memoirs, the fruit of innumerable lives. The dusk was brown with them. Even the hand thus sliding seemed to feel beneath its palm fulness and ripeness. Standing at the window and looking out into the garden, the lives of all these books filled the room behind with a soft murmur. Truly, a deep sea, the past, a tide which will overtake and overflow us. Yes, the tennis players looked half transparent already, as they came up the grass lawn to the house, the game being over. The tall lady stooped and picked a pallid rose; and the balls which the gentleman kept dancing up and down upon his racquet, as he walked beside her, were dim little spheres against the deep green hedge. Then, as they passed inside, the moths came out, the swift grey moths of the dusk, that only visit flowers for a second, never settling, but hanging an inch or two above the yellow of the evening prim-roses, vibrating to a blur. It was, I supposed, nearly time to go into the woods.

About an hour previously, several pieces of flannel soaked in rum and sugar had been pinned to a number of trees. The business of dinner now engrossing the grown-up people we made ready our lantern, our poison jar, and took our butterfly nets in our hands. The road that skirted the wood was so pale that its hardness grated upon our boots unexpectedly. It was the last strip of reality, however, off which we stepped into the gloom of the unknown. The lantern shoved its wedge of light through the dark, as though the air were a fine black snow piling itself up in banks on either side of the yellow beam. The direction of the trees was known to the leader of the party, who walked ahead, and seemed to draw us, unheeding darkness or fear, further and further into the unknown world. Not only has the dark the power to extinguish light, but it also buries under it a great part of the human spirit. We hardly spoke, and then only in low voices which made little headway against the thoughts that filled us. The little irregular beam of light seemed the only thing that kept us together, and like a rope prevented us from falling asunder and being engulfed. It went on indefatigably all the time, making tree and bush stand forth, in their strange nightdress of paler green. Then we were told to halt while the leader went forward to ascertain which of the trees had been prepared, since it was necessary to approach gradually lest the moths should be startled by the light and fly off. We waited in a group, and the little circle of forest where we stood became as if we saw it through the lens of a very powerful magnifying glass. Every blade of grass looked larger than by day, and the crevices in the bark much more sharply cut. Our faces showed pale and as if detached in a circle. The lantern had not stood upon the ground for ten seconds before we heard (the sense of hearing too was much more acute) little crackling sounds which seemed connected with a slight waving and bending in the surrounding grass. Then there emerged here a grasshopper, there a beetle, and here again a daddylonglegs, awkwardly making his way from blade to blade. Their movements were all so awkward that they made one think of sea creatures crawling on the floor of the sea. They went straight, as if by common consent, to the lantern, and were beginning to slide or clamber up the glass panes when a shout from the leader told us to advance. The light was turned very cautiously towards the tree; first it rested upon the grass at the foot; then it mounted a few inches of the trunk; as it mounted our excitement became more and more intense; then it gradually enveloped the flannel and the cataracts of falling treacle. As it did so, several wings flitted round us. The light was covered. Once more it was cautiously turned on. There were no whirring wings this time, but here and there, dotted about on the veins of sweet stuff, were soft brown lumps. These lumps seemed unspeakably precious, too deeply attached to the liquid to be disturbed. Their probosces were deep plunged, and as they drew in the sweetness, their wings quivered slightly as if in ecstasy. Even when the light was full upon them they could not tear themselves away, but sat there, quivering a little more uneasily perhaps, but allowing us to examine the tracery on the upper wing, those stains, spots, and veinings by which we decided their fate. Now and again a large moth dashed through the light. This served to increase our excitement. After taking those we wanted and gently tapping the unneeded on the nose so that they dropped off and began crawling through the grass in the direction of their sugar, we went on to the next tree. Cautiously shielding the light, we saw from far off the glow of two red lamps which faded as the light turned upon them; and there emerged the splendid body which wore those two red lamps at its head. Great underwings of glowing crimson were displayed. He was almost still, as if he had alighted with his wing open and had fallen into a trance of pleasure. He seemed to stretch across the tree, and beside him other moths looked only like little lumps and knobs on the bark. He was splendid to look upon and so immobile that perhaps we were reluctant to end him; and yet when, as if guessing our intention and resuming a flight that had been temporarily interrupted, he roamed away, it seemed as if we had lost a possession of infinite value. Somebody cried out sharply. The lantern bearer flashed his light in the direction which the moth had taken. The space surrounding us seemed vast. Then we stood the light upon the ground, and once more after a few seconds, the grass bent, and the insects came scrambling from all quarters, greedy and yet awkward in their desire to partake of the light. Just as the eyes grow used to dimness and make out shapes where none were visible before, so sitting on the ground we felt we were surrounded by life, innumerable creatures were stirring among the trees; some creeping through the grass, others roaming through the air. It was a very still night, and the leaves intercepted any light from the young moon. Now and again a deep sigh seemed to breathe from somewhere near us, succeeded by sighs less deep, more wavering and in rapid succession, after which there was profound stillness. Perhaps it was alarming to have these evidences of unseen lives. It needed great resolution and the fear of appearing a coward to take up the light and penetrate still further into the depths of the wood. Somehow this world of night seemed hostile to us. Cold, alien, and unyielding, as if preoccupied with matters in which human beings could have no part. But the most distant tree still remained to be visited. The leader advanced unrelentingly. The white strip of road upon which our boots grated now seemed for ever lost. We had left that world of lights and homes hours ago. So we pressed on to this remote tree in the most dense part of the forest. It stood there as if upon the very verge of the world. No moth could have come as far as this. Yet as the trunk was revealed, what did we see?

The scarlet underwing was already there, immobile as before, astride a vein of sweetness, drinking deep. Without waiting a second this time the poison pot was uncovered and adroitly manœuvred so that as he sat there the moth was covered and escape cut off. There was a flash of scarlet within the glass. Then he composed himself with folded wings. He did not move again.

The glory of the moment was great. Our boldness in coming so far was rewarded, and at the same time it seemed as though we had proved our skill against the hostile and alien force. Now we could go back to bed and to the safe house. And then, standing there with the moth safely in our hands, suddenly a volley of shot rang out, a hollow rattle of sound in the deep silence of the wood which had I know not what of mournful and ominous about it. It waned and spread through the forest: it died away, then another of those deep sighs arose. An enormous silence succeeded. 'A tree,' we said at last. A tree had fallen.

What is it that happens between the hour of midnight and dawn, the little shock, the queer uneasy moment, as of eyes half open to the light, after which sleep is never so sound again? Is it experience, perhaps—repeated shocks, each unfelt at the time, suddenly loosening the fabric? breaking something away? Only this image suggests collapse and disintegration, whereas the process I have in mind is just the opposite. It is not destructive whatever it may be, one might say that it was rather of a creative character.

Something definitely happens. The garden, the butterflies, the morning sounds, trees, apples, human voices have emerged, stated themselves. As with a rod of light, order has been imposed upon tumult; form upon chaos. Perhaps it would be simpler to say that one wakes, after Heaven knows what internal process, with a sense of mastery. Familiar people approach all sharply outlined in morning light. Through the tremor and vibration of daily custom one discerns bone and form, endurance and permanence. Sorrow will have the power to effect this sudden arrest of the fluidity of life, and joy will have the same power. Or it may come without apparent cause, imperceptibly, much as some bud feels a sudden release in the night and is found in the morning with all its petals shaken free. At any rate the voyages and memoirs, all the lumber and wreckage and accumulation of time which has deposited itself so thickly upon our shelves and grows like a moss at the foot of literature, is no longer definite enough for our needs. Another sort of reading matches better with the morning hours. This is not the time for foraging and rummaging, for half-closed eyes and gliding voyages. We want something that has been shaped and clarified, cut to catch the light, hard as gem or rock with the seal of human experience in it, and yet sheltering as in a clear gem the flame which burns now so high and now sinks so low in our own hearts. We want what is timeless and contemporary. But one might exhaust all images, and run words through one's fingers like water and yet not say why it is that on such a morning one wakes with a desire for poetry.

There is no difficulty in finding poetry in England. Every English home is full of it. Even the Russians have not a deeper fountain of spiritual life. With us it is, of course, sunk very deep; hidden beneath the heaviest and dampest deposit of hymn books and ledgers. Yet equally familiar and strangely persistent, in the most diverse conditions of travel and climate, is the loveliness of the hurrying clouds, of the sun-stained ·green, of the rapid watery atmosphere, in which clouds have been crumbled with colour until the ocean of air is at once confused and profound. There will certainly be a copy of Shakespeare in such a house, another *Paradise Lost*, and a little volume of George Herbert. There may be almost as probably, though perhaps more strangely, *Vulgar Errors* and the *Religio Medici*. For some reason the folios of Sir Thomas Browne are to be found on the lowest shelf of libraries in other respects entirely humdrum and utilitarian. His popularity in the small country house rests perhaps chiefly upon the fact that the *Vulgar Errors* treats largely of animals. Books with pictures of malformed elephants, baboons of grotesque and indecent appearance, tigers, deer, and so on, all distorted and with a queer facial likeness to human beings, are always popular among people who care nothing for literature. The text of *Vulgar Errors* has something of the same fascination as these woodcuts. And then it may not be fanciful to suppose that even in the year nineteen hundred and nineteen a great number of minds are still only partially lit up by the cold light of knowledge. It is the most capricious illuminant. They are still apt to ruminate, without an overpowering bias to the truth, whether a kingfisher's body shows which way the wind blows; whether an ostrich digests iron; whether owls and ravens herald ill-fortune; and the spilling of salt bad luck; what the tingling of ears forebodes, and even to toy pleasantly with more curious speculations as to the joints of elephants and the politics of storks, which came within the province of the more fertile and better-informed brain of the author. The English mind is naturally prone to take its ease and pleasure in the loosest whimsies and humours. Sir Thomas ministers to the kind of wisdom that farmers talk over their ale, and housewives over their teacups, proving himself much more sagacious and better informed than the rest of the company, but still with the door of his mind wide open for any curious thing that chooses to enter in. For all his learning, the doctor will consider what we have to say seriously and in good faith. He will perhaps give our modest question a turn that sends it spinning among the stars. How charming, for example, to have found a flower on a walk, or a chip of pottery or a stone, that might equally well have been thunderbolt, or cannonball, and to have gone straightway to knock upon the doctor's door with a question. No business would have had precedence over such a matter as this, unless indeed someone had been dying or coming into the world. For the doctor was evidently a humane man, and one good to have at the bedside, imperturbable, yet sympathetic. His consolations must have been sublime; his presence full of composure; and then, if something took his fancy, what enlivening speculations he must have poured forth, talking, one guesses, mostly in soliloquy, with the strangest sequences, in a rapt pondering manner, as if not expecting an answer, and more to himself than to a second person.

What second person, indeed, could answer him? At Montpellier and Padua he had learnt, but learning, instead of settling his questions, had, it seems, greatly increased his capacity for asking them. The door of his mind opened more and more widely. In comparison with other men he was indeed learned; he knew six languages; he knew the laws, customs, and policies of several states, the names of all the constellations, and most of the plants of his country; and yet—must one not always break off thus?—'yet methinks, I do not know so many as when I did but know a hundred, and had scarcely ever simpled further than

Cheapside.' Suppose indeed that certainty had been attainable; it had been proved to be so, and so it must be; nothing would have been more intolerable to him. His imagination was made to carry pyramids. 'Methinks there be not impossibilities enough in religion for an active faith.' But then the grain of dust was a pyramid. There was nothing plain in a world of mystery. Consider the body. Some men are surprised by sickness. Sir Thomas can only 'wonder that we are not always so'; he sees the thousand doors that lead to death; and in addition—so he likes to speculate and fantastically accumulate considerations—'it is in the power of every hand to destroy us, and we are beholden unto everyone we meet, who doth not kill us'. What, one asks, as considerations accumulate, is ever to stop the course of such a mind, unroofed and open to the sky? Unfortunately, there was the Deity. His faith shut in his horizon. Sir Thomas himself resolutely drew that blind. His desire for knowledge, his eager ingenuity, his anticipations of truth must submit, shut their eyes, and go to sleep. Doubts he calls them. 'More of these no man hath known than myself; which I confess I conquered, not in a martial posture, but on my knees.' So lively a curiosity deserved a better fate. It would have delighted us to feed what Sir Thomas calls his doubts upon a liberal diet of modern certainties, but not if by so doing we had changed him, but that is the tribute of our gratitude. For is he not, among a variety of other things, one of the first of our writers to be definitely himself? His appearance has been recorded—his height moderate, his eyes large and luminous, his skin dark, and constantly suffused with blushes. But it is the more splendid picture of his soul that we feast upon. In that dark world, he was one of the explorers; the first to talk of himself, he broaches the subject with an immense gusto. He returns to it again and again, as if the soul were a wondrous disease and its symptoms not yet recorded. 'The world that I regard is myself; it is the microcosm of my own frame that I cast mine eye on: for the other I use it but like my globe, and turn it round sometimes for my recreation.' Sometimes, he notes, and he seems to take a pride in the strange gloomy confession, he has wished for death. 'I feel sometimes a hell within myself; Lucifer keeps his court in my breast; Legion is revived in me.' The strangest ideas and emotions have play in him, as he goes about his work, outwardly the most sober of mankind, and esteemed the greatest physician in Norwich. Yet, if his friends could see into his mind! But they cannot. 'I am in the dark to all the world, and my nearest friends behold me but in a cloud.' Strange beyond belief are the capacities that he detects in himself, profound the meditation into which the commonest sight will plunge him, while the rest of the world passes by and sees nothing to wonder at. The tavern music, the Ave Mary Bell, the broken pot that the workman has dug out of the field—at the sight and sound of them he stops dead, as if transfixed by the astonishing vista. 'And surely it is not a melancholy conceit to think we are all asleep in this world, and that the conceits of this life are as mere dreams——' No one so raises the vault of the mind, and, admitting conjecture after conjecture, positively makes us stand still in amazement, unable to bring ourselves to move on.

With such a conviction of the mystery and miracle of things, he is unable to reject, disposed to tolerate and contemplate without end. In the grossest superstition there is something of devotion; in tavern music something of divinity; in the little world of man something 'that was before the elements and owes no homage unto the sun'. He is hospitable to everything and tastes freely of whatever is set before him. For upon this sublime prospect of time and eternity, the cloudy vapours which his imagination conjures up, there is cast the figure of the author. It is not merely life in general that fills him with amazement, but his own life in particular, 'which to relate were not a history, but a piece of poetry, and would sound to common ears like a fable.' The littleness of egotism has not as yet attacked the health of his interest in himself. I am charitable, I am brave, I am averse from nothing, I am full of feeling for others, I am merciless upon myself, 'For my conversation, it is like the sun's, with all men, and with a friendly aspect to good and bad'; I, I, I—how we have lost the secret of saying that!

In short Sir Thomas Browne brings in the whole question, which is afterwards to become of such importance, of knowing one's author. Somewhere, everywhere, now hidden, now apparent in whatever is written down is the form of a human being. If we seek to know him, are we idly occupied, as when, listening to a speaker, we begin to speculate about his age and habits, whether he is married, has children, and lives in Hampstead? It is a question to be asked, and not one to be answered. It will be answered, that is to say, in an instinctive and irrational manner, as our disposition inclines us. Only one must note that Sir Thomas is the first English writer to rouse this particular confusion with any briskness. Chaucer—but Chaucer's spelling is against him. Marlowe then, Spenser, Webster, Ben Jonson? The truth is the question never presents itself quite so acutely in the case of a poet. It scarcely presents itself at all in the case of the Greeks and Latins. The poet gives us his essence, but prose takes the mould of the body and mind entire.

Could one not deduce from reading his books that Sir Thomas Browne, humane and tolerant in almost every respect, was nevertheless capable of a mood of dark superstition in which he would pronounce that two old women were witches and must be put to death? Some of his pedantries have the very clink of the thumbscrew: the heartless ingenuity of a spirit still cramped and fettered by the bonds of the Middle Ages. There were impulses of cruelty in him as in all people forced by their ignorance or weakness to live in a state of servility to man or nature. There were moments, brief but intense, in which his serene and magnanimous mind contracted in a spasm of terror. More often by far he is, as all great men are, a little dull. Yet the dullness of the great is distinct from the dullness of the little. It is perhaps more profound. We enter into their shades acquiescent and hopeful, convinced that if light is lacking the fault is ours. A sense of guilt, as the horror increases, mingles itself with our protest and increases the gloom. Surely, we must have missed the way? If one stitched together the passages in Wordsworth, Shakespeare, Milton, every great writer in short who has left more than a song or two behind him, where the light has failed us, and we have only gone on because of the habit of obedience, they would make a formidable volume —the dullest book in the world.

Don Quixote is very dull too. But his dullness, instead of having that lethargy as of a somnolent beast which is characteristic of great people's dullness—'After my enormous labours, I'm asleep and intend to snore if I like,' they seem to say—instead of this dullness Don Quixote has another variety. He is telling stories to children. There they sit round the fire on a winter's night, grown up children, women at their spinning, men relaxed and sleepy after the day's sport, 'Tell us a story—something to make us laugh—something gallant, too—about people like ourselves only more unhappy and a great deal happier.' Obedient to this demand, Cervantes, a kind accommodating man, spun them stories, about princesses lost and amorous knights, much to their taste, very tedious to ours. Let him but get back to Don Quixote and Sancho Panza and all is well, for him, we cannot help thinking, as for us. Yet what with our natural reverence and inevitable servility, we seldom make our position, as modern readers of old writers, plain. Undoubtedly all writers are immensely influenced by the people who read them. Thus, take Cervantes and his audience—we, coming four centuries later, have a sense of breaking into a happy family party. Compare that group with the group (only there are no groups now since we have become educated and isolated and read our books by our own firesides in our own copies), but compare the readers of Cera Cervantes with the readers of Thomas Hardy. Hardy whiles away no firelit hour with tales of lost princesses and amorous knights—refuses more and more sternly to make things up for our entertainment. As we read him separately so he speaks to us separately, as if we were individual men and women, rather than groups sharing the same tastes. That, too, must be taken into account. The reader of today, accustomed to find himself in direct communication with the writer, is constantly out of touch with Cervantes. How far did he himself know what he was about—how far again do we over-interpret, misinterpret, read into *Don Quixote* a meaning compounded of our own experience, as an elder person might read a meaning into a child's story and doubt whether the child himself was aware of it? If Cervantes had felt the tragedy and the satire as we feel them, could he have forborne as he does to stress them—could he have been as callous as he seems? Yet Shakespeare dismissed Falstaff callously enough. The great writers have this large way with them, nature's way; which we who are further from nature call cruel, since we suffer more from the effects of cruelty, or at any rate judge our suffering of greater importance, than they did. None of this, however, impairs the main pleasure of the jolly, delightful, plain-spoken book built up, foaming up, round the magnificent conception of the Knight and the world which, however people may change, must remain for ever an unassailable statement of man and the world. That will always be in existence. And as for knowing himself what he was about—perhaps great writers never do. Perhaps that is why later ages find what they seek.

But to return to the dullest book in the world. To this volume Sir Thomas has added certainly one or two pages. Yet should one desire a loophole to escape it is always possible to find one in the chance that the book is difficult, not dull. Accustomed as we are to strip a whole page of its sentences and crush their meaning out in one grasp, the obstinate resistance which a page of *Urne Burial* offers at first trips us and blinds us. 'Though if *Adam* were made out of an extract of the Earth, all parts might challenge a restitution, yet few have returned their bones farre lower than they might receive them'—We must stop, go back, try out this way and that, and proceed at a foot's pace. Reading has been made so easy in our days that to go back to these crabbed sentences is like mounting only a solemn and obstinate donkey instead of going up to town by an electric train. Dilatory, capricious, governed by no consideration save his own wish, Sir Thomas seems scarcely to be writing in the sense that Froude wrote or Matthew Arnold. A page of print now fulfils a different office. Is it not almost servile in the assiduity with which it helps us on our way, making only the standard charge on our attention and in return for that giving us the full measure, but not an ounce over or under our due? In Sir Thomas Browne's days weights and measures were in a primitive condition, if they had any existence at all. One is conscious all the time that Sir Thomas was never paid a penny for his prose. He is free since it is the offering of his own bounty to give us as little or as much as he chooses. He is an amateur; it is the work of his leisure and pleasure; he makes no bargain with us. Therefore, as Sir Thomas has no call to conciliate his reader, these short books of his are dull if he chooses, difficult if he likes, beautiful beyond measure if he has a mind that way. Here we approach the doubtful region—the region of beauty. Are we not already lost or sunk or enticed with the very first words? 'When the Funeral pyre was out, and the last valediction over, men took a lasting adieu to their interred Friends.' But why beauty should have the effect upon us that it does, the strange serene confidence that it inspires in us, none can say. Most people have tried and perhaps one of the invariable properties of beauty is that it leaves in the mind a desire to impart. Some offering we must make; some act we must dedicate, if only to move across the room and turn the rose in the jar, which, by the way, has dropped its petals.

Hours in a Library[1]

LET us begin by clearing up the old confusion between the man who loves learning and the man who loves reading, and point out that there is no connexion whatever between the two. A learned man is a sedentary, concentrated solitary enthusiast, who searches through books to discover some particular grain of truth upon which he has set his heart. If the passion for reading conquers him, his gains dwindle and vanish between his fingers. A reader, on the other hand, must check the desire for learning at the outset; if knowledge sticks to him well and good, but to go in pursuit of it, to read on a system, to become a specialist or an authority, is very apt to kill what it suits us to consider the more humane passion for pure and disinterested reading.

In spite of all this we can easily conjure up a picture which does service for the bookish man and raises a smile at his expense. We conceive a pale, attenuated figure in a dressing-gown, lost in speculation, unable to lift a kettle from the hob, or address a lady without blushing, ignorant of the daily news, though versed in the catalogues of the second-hand booksellers, in whose dark premises he spends the hours of sunlight—a delightful character, no doubt, in his crabbed simplicity, but not in the least resembling that other to whom we would direct attention. For the true reader is essentially young. He is a man of intense curiosity; of ideas; open-minded and communicative, to whom reading is more of the nature of brisk exercise in the open air than of sheltered study; he trudges the high road, he climbs higher and higher upon the hills until the atmosphere is almost too fine to breathe in; to him it is not a sedentary pursuit at all.

But, apart from general statements, it would not be hard to prove by an assembly of facts that the great season for reading is the season between the ages of eighteen and twenty-four. The bare list of what is read then fills the heart of older people with despair. It is not only that we read so many books, but that we had such books to read. If we wish to refresh our memories, let

---

[1] *Times Literary Supplement*, November 30, 1916

us take down one of those old notebooks which we have all, at one time or another, had a passion for beginning. Most of the pages are blank, it is true; but at the beginning we shall find a certain number very beautifully covered with a strikingly legible handwriting. Here we have written down the names of great writers in their order of merit; here we have copied out fine passages from the classics; here are lists of books to be read; and here, most interesting of all, lists of books that have actually been read, as the reader testifies with some youthful vanity by a dash of red ink. We will quote a list of the books that someone read in a past January at the age of twenty, most of them probably for the first time. 1. *Rhoda Fleming.* 2. *The Shaving of Shagpat.* 3. *Tom Jones.* 4. *The Laodicean.* 5. Dewey's *Psychology.* 6. *The Book of Job.* 7. Webbe's *Discourse of Poesie.* 8. *The Duchess of Malfi.* 9. *The Revenger's Tragedy.* And so he goes on from month to month, until, as such lists will, it suddenly stops in the month of June. But if we follow the reader through his months it is clear that he can have done practically nothing but read. Elizabethan literature is gone through with some thoroughness; he read a great deal of Webster, Browning, Shelley, Spenser, and Congreve; Peacock he read from start to finish; and most of Jane Austen's novels two or three times over. He read the whole of Meredith, the whole of Ibsen, and a little of Bernard Shaw. We may be fairly certain, too, that the time not spent in reading was spent in some stupendous argument in which the Greeks were pitted against the moderns, romance against realism, Racine against Shakespeare, until the lights were seen to have grown pale in the dawn.

The old lists are there to make us smile and perhaps to sigh a little, but we would give much to recall also the mood in which this orgy of reading was done. Happily, this reader was no prodigy, and with a little thought we can most of us recall the stages at least of our own initiation. The books we read in childhood, having purloined them from some shelf supposed to be inaccessible, have something of the unreality and awfulness of a stolen sight of the dawn coming over quiet fields when the household is asleep. Peeping between the curtains we see strange shapes of misty trees which we hardly recognize, though we may remember them all our lives; for children have a strange premonition of what is to come. But the later reading of which the above

35

list is an example is quite a different matter. For the first time, perhaps, all restrictions have been removed, we can read what we like; libraries are at our command, and, best of all, friends who find themselves in the same position. For days upon end we do nothing but read. It is a time of extraordinary excitement and exaltation. We seem to rush about recognizing heroes. There is a sort of wonderment in our minds that we ourselves are really doing this, and mixed with it an absurd arrogance and desire to show our familiarity with the greatest human beings who have ever lived in the world. The passion for knowledge is then at its keenest, or at least most confident, and we have, too, an intense singleness of mind which the great writers gratify by making it appear that they are at one with us in their estimate of what is good in life. And as it is necessary to hold one's own against some one who has adopted Pope, let us say, instead of Sir Thomas Browne, for a hero, we conceive a deep affection for these men, and feel that we know them not as other people know them, but privately by ourselves. We are fighting under their leadership, and almost in the light of their eyes. So we haunt the old book-shops and drag home folios and quartos, Euripides in wooden boards, and Voltaire in eighty-nine volumes octavo.

But these lists are curious documents, in that they seem to include scarcely any of the contemporary writers. Meredith and Hardy and Henry James were of course alive when this reader came to them, but they were already accepted among the classics. There is no man of his own generation who influences him as Carlyle, or Tennyson, or Ruskin influenced the young of their day. And this we believe to be very characteristic of youth, for unless there is some admitted giant he will have nothing to do with the smaller men, although they deal with the world he lives in. He will rather go back to the classics, and consort entirely with minds of the very first order. For the time being he holds himself aloof from all the activities of men, and, looking at them from a distance, judges them with superb severity.

Indeed, one of the signs of passing youth is the birth of a sense of fellowship with other human beings as we take our place among them. We should like to think that we keep our standard as high as ever; but we certainly take more interest in the writings of our contemporaries and pardon their lack of inspiration for the sake of something that brings them nearer to us. It is even arguable that we get actually more from the living, although they may be much inferior, than from the dead. In the first place there can be no secret vanity in reading our contemporaries, and the kind of admiration which they inspire is extremely warm and genuine because in order to give way to our belief in them we have often to sacrifice some very respectable prejudice which does us credit. We have also to find our own reasons for what we like and dislike, which acts as a spur to our attention, and is the best way of proving that we have read the classics with under- standing.

Thus to stand in a great bookshop crammed with books so new that their pages almost stick together, and the gilt on their backs is still fresh, has an excitement no less delightful than the old excite- ment of the second-hand bookstall. It it not perhaps so exalted. But the old hunger to know what the immortals thought has given place to a far more tolerant curiosity to know what our own generation is thinking. What do living men and women feel, what are their houses like and what clothes do they wear, what money have they and what food do they eat, what do they love and hate, what do they see of the surrounding world, and what is the dream that fills the spaces of their active lives? They tell us all these things in their books. In them we can see as much both of the mind and of the body of our time as we have eyes for seeing.

When such a spirit of curiosity has fully taken hold of us, the dust will soon lie thick upon the classics unless some necessity forces us to read them. For the living voices are, after all, the ones we understand the best. We can treat them as we treat our equals; they are guessing our riddles, and, what is perhaps more im- portant, we understand their jokes. And we soon develop another taste, unsatisfied by the great—not a valuable taste, perhaps, but certainly a very pleasant possession—the taste for bad books. Without committing the indiscretion of naming names we know which authors can be trusted to produce yearly (for happily they are prolific) a novel, a book of poems or essays, which affords us indescribable pleasure. We owe a great deal to bad books; indeed, we come to count their authors and their heroes among those figures who play so large a part in our silent life. Something of the same sort happens in the case of the memoir writers and autobiographers, who have created almost a fresh branch of literature in our age. They are not all of them important people, but strangely enough, only the most important, the dukes and the statesmen, are ever really dull. The men and women who set out, with no excuse except perhaps that they saw the Duke of Wellington once, to confide to us their opinions, their quarrels, their aspirations, and their diseases, generally end by becoming, for the time at least, actors in those private dramas with which we beguile our solitary walks and our sleepless hours. Refine all this out of our consciousness and we should be poor indeed. And then there are the books of facts and history, books about bees and wasps and industries and gold mines and Empresses and diplomatic intrigues, about rivers and savages, trade unions, and Acts of Parliament, which we always read and always, alas! forget. Perhaps we are not making out a good case for a bookshop when we have to confess that it gratifies so many desires which have apparently nothing to do with literature. But let us remember that here we have a literature in the making. From these new books our children will select the one or two by which we shall be known for ever. Here, if we could recognize it, lies some poem, or novel, or history which will stand up and speak with other ages about our age when we lie prone and silent as the crowd of Shakespeare's day is silent and lives for us only in the pages of his poetry.

This we believe to be true; and yet it is oddly difficult in the case of new books to know which are the real books and what it is that they are telling us, and which are the stuffed books which will come to pieces when they have lain about for a year or two. We can see that there are many books, and we are frequently told that everyone can write nowadays. That may be true; yet we do not doubt that at the heart of this immense volubility, this flood and foam of language, this irreticence and vulgarity and triviality, there lies the heat of some great passion which only needs the accident of a brain more happily turned than the rest to issue in a shape which will last from age to age. It should be our delight to watch this turmoil, to do battle with the ideas and visions of our own time, to seize what we can use, to kill what we consider worthless, and above all to realize that we must be generous to the people who are giving shape as best they can to the ideas within them. No age of literature is so little submissive to authority as ours, so free from the dominion of the great; none seems so way-ward with its gift of reverence, or so volatile in its experiments. It may well seem, even to the attentive, that there is no trace of school or aim in the work of our poets and novelists. But the pessimist is inevitable, and he shall not persuade us that our literature is dead, or prevent us from feeling how true and vivid a beauty flashes out as the young writers draw together to form their new vision, the ancient words of the most beautiful of living languages. Whatever we may have learnt from reading the classics we need now in order to judge the work of our contem-poraries, for whenever there is life in them they will be casting their net out over some unknown abyss to snare new shapes, and we must throw our imaginations after them if we are to accept with understanding the strange gifts they bring back to us.

But if we need all our knowledge of the old writers in order to follow what the new writers are attempting, it is certainly true that we come from adventuring among new books with a far keener eye for the old. It seems that we should now be able to surprise their secrets; to look deep down into their work and see the parts come together, because we have watched the making of new books, and with eyes clear of prejudice can judge more truly what it is that they are doing, and what is good and what bad. We shall find, probably, that some of the great are less vener-able than we thought them. Indeed, they are not so accomplished or so profound as some of our own time. But if in one or two cases this seems to be true, a kind of humiliation mixed with joy over-comes us in front of others. Take Shakespeare, or Milton, or Sir Thomas Browne. Our little knowledge of how things are done does not avail us much here, but it does lend an added zest to our enjoyment. Did we ever in our youngest days feel such amaze-ment at their achievement as that which fills us now that we have sifted myriads of words and gone along uncharted ways in search of new forms for our new sensations? New books may be more stimulating and in some ways more suggestive than the old, but they do not give us that absolute certainty of delight which breathes through us when we come back again to *Comus,* or *Lycidas, Urne Burial,* or *Antony and Cleopatra.* Far be it from us to hazard any theory as to the nature of art. It may be that we shall never know more about it than we know by nature, and our longer experience of it teaches us this only—that of all our pleasures those we get from the great artists are indisputably among the best; and more we may not know. But, advancing no theory, we shall find one or two qualities in such works as these which we can hardly expect to find in books made within the span of our lifetime. Age itself may have an alchemy of its own. But this is true: you can read them as often as you will without finding that they have yielded any virtue and left a meaningless husk of words; and there is a complete finality about them. No cloud of suggestions hangs about them teasing us with a multitude of irrelevant ideas. But all our faculties are summoned to the task, as in the great moments of our own experience; and some consecration descends upon us from their hands which we return to life, feeling it more keenly and understanding it more deeply than before.

The Modern Essay

AS Mr. Rhys truly says, it is unnecessary to go profoundly into the history and origin of the essay—whether it derives from Socrates or Siranney the Persian—since, like all living things, its present is more important than its past. Moreover, the family is widely spread; and while some of its representatives have risen in the world and wear their coronets with the best, others pick up a precarious living in the gutter near Fleet Street. The form, too, admits variety. The essay can be short or long, serious or trifling, about God and Spinoza, or about turtles and Cheapside. But as we turn over the pages of these five little volumes,[1] containing essays written between 1870 and 1920, certain principles appear to control the chaos, and we detect in the short period under review something like the progress of history.

Of all forms of literature, however, the essay is the one which least calls for the use of long words. The principle which controls it is simply that it should give pleasure; the desire which impels us when we take it from the shelf is simply to receive pleasure. Everything in an essay must be subdued to that end. It should lay us under a spell with its first word, and we should only wake, refreshed, with its last. In the interval we may pass through the most various experiences of amusement, surprise, interest, indignation; we may soar to the heights of fantasy with Lamb or plunge to the depths of wisdom with Bacon, but we must never be roused. The essay must lap us about and draw its curtain across the world.

So great a feat is seldom accomplished, though the fault may well be as much on the reader's side as on the writer's. Habit and lethargy have dulled his palate. A novel has a story, a poem rhyme; but what art can the essayist use in these short lengths of prose to sting us wide awake and fix us in a trance which is not sleep but rather an intensification of life—a basking, with every faculty alert, in the sun of pleasure? He must know—that is the first essential—how to write. His learning may be as profound as Mark Pattison's, but in an essay it must be so fused by the magic

[1] *Modern English Essays*, edited by Ernest Rhys. 5 vols.

of writing that not a fact juts out, not a dogma tears the surface of the texture. Macaulay in one way, Froude in another, did this superbly over and over again. They have blown more knowledge into us in the course of one essay than the innumerable chapters of a hundred text-books. But when Mark Pattison has to tell us, in the space of thirty-five little pages, about Montaigne, we feel that he had not previously assimilated M. Grün. M. Grün was a gentleman who once wrote a bad book. M. Grün and his book should have been embalmed for our perpetual delight in amber. But the process is fatiguing; it requires more time and perhaps more temper than Pattison had at his command. He served M. Grün up raw, and he remains a crude berry among the cooked meats, upon which our teeth must grate for ever. Something of the sort applies to Matthew Arnold and a certain translator of Spinoza. Literal truth-telling and finding fault with a culprit for his good are out of place in an essay, where everything should be for our good and rather for eternity than for the March number of the *Fortnightly Review*. But if the voice of the scold should never be heard in this narrow plot, there is another voice which is as a plague of locusts—the voice of a man stumbling drowsily among loose words, clutching aimlessly at vague ideas, the voice, for example, of Mr. Hutton in the following passage:

> Add to this that his married life was very brief, only seven years and a half, being unexpectedly cut short, and that his passionate reverence for his wife's memory and genius—in his own words, 'a religion'—was one which, as he must have been perfectly sensible, he could not make to appear otherwise than extravagant, not to say an hallucination, in the eyes of the rest of mankind, and yet that he was possessed by an irresistible yearning to attempt to embody it in all the tender and enthusiastic hyperbole of which it is so pathetic to find a man who gained his fame by his 'dry-light' a master, and it is impossible not to feel that the human incidents in Mr. Mill's career are very sad.

A book could take that blow, but it sinks an essay. A biography in two volumes is indeed the proper depository; for there, where the licence is so much wider, and hints and glimpses of outside things make part of the feast (we refer to the old type of Victorian volume), these yawns and stretches hardly matter, and have indeed some positive value of their own. But that value, which is contributed by the reader, perhaps illicitly, in his desire to get as much into the book from all possible sources as he can, must be ruled out here.

There is no room for the impurities of literature in an essay. Somehow or other, by dint of labour or bounty of nature, or both combined, the essay must be pure—pure like water or pure like wine, but pure from dullness, deadness, and deposits of extraneous matter. Of all writers in the first volume, Walter Pater best achieves this arduous task, because before setting out to write his essay ('Notes on Leonardo da Vinci') he has somehow contrived to get his material fused. He is a learned man, but it is not knowledge of Leonardo that remains with us, but a vision, such as we get in a good novel where everything contributes to bring the writer's conception as a whole before us. Only here, in the essay, where the bounds are so strict and facts have to be used in their nakedness, the true writer like Walter Pater makes these limitations yield their own quality. Truth will give it authority; from its narrow limits he will get shape and intensity; and then there is no more fitting place for some of those ornaments which the old writers loved and we, by calling them ornaments, presumably despise. Nowadays nobody would have the courage to embark on the once-famous description of Leonardo's lady who has

> learned the secrets of the grave; and has been a diver in deep seas and keeps their fallen day about her; and trafficked for strange webs with Eastern merchants; and, as Leda, was the mother of Helen of Troy, and, as Saint Anne, the mother of Mary . . .

The passage is too thumb-marked to slip naturally into the context. But when we come unexpectedly upon 'the smiling of women and the motion of great waters', or upon 'full of the refinement of the dead, in sad, earth-coloured raiment, set with pale stones', we suddenly remember that we have ears and we have eyes, and that the English language fills a long array of stout volumes with innumerable words, many of which are of more than one syllable.

The only living Englishman who ever looks into these volumes is, of course, a gentleman of Polish extraction. But doubtless our abstention saves us much gush, much rhetoric, much high-stepping and cloud-prancing, and for the sake of the prevailing sobriety and hard-headedness we should be willing to barter the splendour of Sir Thomas Browne and the vigour of Swift.

Yet, if the essay admits more properly than biography or fiction of sudden boldness and metaphor, and can be polished till every atom of its surface shines, there are dangers in that too. We are soon in sight of ornament. Soon the current, which is the life-blood of literature, runs slow; and instead of sparkling and flashing or moving with a quieter impulse which has a deeper excitement, words coagulate together in frozen sprays which, like the grapes on a Christmas tree, glitter for a single night, but are dusty and garish the day after. The temptation to decorate is great where the theme may be of the slightest. What is there to interest another in the fact that one has enjoyed a walking tour, or has amused oneself by rambling down Cheapside and looking at the turtles in Mr. Sweeting's shop window? Stevenson and Samuel Butler chose very different methods of exciting our interest in these domestic themes. Stevenson, of course, trimmed and polished and set out his matter in a traditional eighteenth-century form. It is admirably done, but we cannot help feeling anxious, as the essay proceeds, lest the material may give out under the craftsman's fingers. The ingot is so small, the manipulation so incessant. And perhaps that is why the peroration—

> To sit still and contemplate—to remember the faces of women without desire, to be pleased by the great deeds of men without envy, to be everything and everywhere in sympathy and yet content to remain where and what you are—

has the sort of insubstantiality which suggests that by the time he got to the end he had left himself nothing solid to work with. Butler adopted the very opposite method. Think your own thoughts, he seems to say, and speak them as plainly as you can. These turtles in the shop window which appear to leak out of their shells through heads and feet suggest a fatal faithfulness to a fixed idea. And so, striding unconcernedly from one idea to the next, we traverse a large stretch of ground; observe that a wound in the solicitor is a very serious thing; that Mary Queen of Scots wears surgical boots and is subject to fits near the Horse Shoe in Tottenham Court Road; take it for granted that no one really cares about Æschylus; and so, with many amusing anecdotes and some profound reflections, reach the peroration, which is that, as he had been told not to see more in Cheapside than he could get into twelve pages of the *Universal Review*, he had better stop. And yet obviously Butler is at least as careful of our pleasure as Stevenson; and to write like oneself and call it not writing is a much harder exercise in style than to write like Addison and call it writing well.

But, however much they differ individually, the Victorian essayists yet had something in common. They wrote at greater length than is now usual, and they wrote for a public which had not only time to sit down to its magazine seriously, but a high, if peculiarly Victorian, standard of culture by which to judge it. It was worth while to speak out upon serious matters in an essay; and there was nothing absurd in writing as well as one possibly could when, in a month or two, the same public which had welcomed the essay in a magazine would carefully read it once more in a book. But a change came from a small audience of cultivated people to a larger audience of people who were not quite so cultivated. The change was not altogether for the worse. In volume iii. we find Mr. Birrell and Mr. Beerbohm. It might even be said that there was a reversion to the classic type, and that the essay by losing its size and something of its sonority was approaching more nearly the essay of Addison and Lamb. At any rate, there is a great gulf between Mr. Birrell on Carlyle and the essay which one may suppose that Carlyle would have written upon Mr. Birrell. There is little similarity between *A Cloud of Pinafores*, by Max Beerbohm, and *A Cynic's Apology*, by Leslie Stephen. But the essay is alive; there is no reason to despair. As the conditions change so the essayist, most sensitive of all plants to public opinion, adapts himself, and if he is good makes the best of the change, and if he is bad the worst. Mr. Birrell is certainly good; and so we find that, though he has dropped a considerable amount of weight, his attack is much more direct and his movement more supple.

But what did Mr. Beerbohm give to the essay and what did he take from it? That is a much more complicated question, for here we have an essayist who has concentrated on the work and is without doubt the prince of his profession.

What Mr. Beerbohm gave was, of course, himself. This presence, which has haunted the essay fitfully from the time of Montaigne, had been in exile since the death of Charles Lamb. Matthew Arnold was never to his readers Matt, nor Walter Pater affectionately abbreviated in a thousand homes to Wat. They gave us much, but that they did not give. Thus, some time in the nineties, it must have surprised readers accustomed to exhortation, information, and denunciation to find themselves familiarly addressed by a voice which seemed to belong to a man no larger than themselves. He was affected by private joys and sorrows, and had no gospel to preach and no learning to impart. He was himself, simply and directly, and himself he has remained. Once again we have an essayist capable of using the essayist's most proper but most dangerous and delicate tool. He has brought personality into literature, not unconsciously and impurely, but so consciously and purely that we do not know whether there is any relation between Max the essayist and Mr. Beerbohm the man. We only know that the spirit of personality permeates every word that he writes. The triumph is the triumph of style. For it is only by knowing how to write that you can make use in literature of your self; that self which, while it is essential to literature, is also its most dangerous antagonist. Never to be yourself and yet always—that is the problem. Some of the essayists in Mr. Rhys' collection, to be frank, have not altogether succeeded in solving it. We are nauseated by the sight of trivial personalities decomposing in the eternity of print. As talk, no doubt, it was charming, and certainly the writer is a good fellow to meet over a bottle of beer. But literature is stern; it is no use being charming, virtuous, or even learned and brilliant into the bargain, unless, she seems to reiterate, you fulfil her first condition—to know how to write.

This art is possessed to perfection by Mr. Beerbohm. But he has not searched the dictionary for polysyllables. He has not moulded firm periods or seduced our ears with intricate cadences and strange melodies. Some of his companions—Henley and Stevenson, for example—are momentarily more impressive. But *A Cloud of Pinafores* has in it that indescribable inequality, stir, and final expressiveness which belong to life and to life alone. You have not finished with it because you have read it, any more than friendship is ended because it is time to part. Life wells up and alters and adds. Even things in a bookcase change if they are alive; we find ourselves wanting to meet them again; we find them altered. So we look back upon essay after essay by Mr. Beerbohm, knowing that, come September or May, we shall sit down with them and talk. Yet it is true that the essayist is the most sensitive of all writers to public opinion. The drawing-room is the place where a great deal of reading is done nowadays, and the essays of Mr. Beerbohm lie, with an exquisite appreciation of all that the position exacts, upon the drawing-room table. There is no gin about; no strong tobacco; no puns, drunkenness, or insanity. Ladies and gentlemen talk together, and some things, of course, are not said.

But if it would be foolish to attempt to confine Mr. Beerbohm to one room, it would be still more foolish, unhappily, to make him, the artist, the man who gives us only his best, the representative of our age. There are no essays by Mr. Beerbohm in the fourth or fifth volumes of the present collection. His age seems already a little distant, and the drawing-room table, as it recedes, begins to look rather like an altar where, once upon a time, people deposited offerings—fruit from their own orchards, gifts carved with their own hands. Now once more the conditions have changed. The public needs essays as much as ever, and perhaps even more. The demand for the light middle not exceeding fifteen hundred words, or in special cases seventeen hundred and fifty, much exceeds the supply. Where Lamb wrote one essay and Max perhaps writes two, Mr. Belloc at a rough computation produces three hundred and sixty-five. They are very short, it is true. Yet with what dexterity the practised essayist will utilize his space— beginning as close to the top of the sheet as possible, judging precisely how far to go, when to turn, and how, without sacrificing a hair's-breadth of paper, to wheel about and alight accurately upon the last word his editor allows! As a feat of skill it is well worth watching. But the personality upon which Mr. Belloc, like Mr. Beerbohm, depends suffers in the process. It comes to us not with the natural richness of the speaking voice, but strained and thin and full of mannerisms and affectations, like the voice of a man shouting through a megaphone to a crowd on a windy day. 'Little friends, my readers', he says in the essay called 'An Unknown Country', and he goes on to tell us how—

> There was a shepherd the other day at Findon Fair who had come from the east by Lewes with sheep, and who had in his eyes that reminiscence of horizons which makes the eyes of shepherds and of mountaineers different from the eyes of other men. . . . I went with him to hear what he had to say, for shepherds talk quite differently from other men.

Happily this shepherd had little to say, even under the stimulus of the inevitable mug of beer, about the Unknown Country, for the only remark that he did make proves him either a minor poet, unfit for the care of sheep, or Mr. Belloc himself masquerading with a fountain-pen. That is the penalty which the habitual essayist must now be prepared to face. He must masquerade. He cannot afford the time either to be himself or to be other people. He must skim the surface of thought and dilute the strength of personality. He must give us a worn weekly halfpenny instead of a solid sovereign once a year.

But it is not Mr. Belloc only who has suffered from the prevailing conditions. The essays which bring the collection to the year 1920 may not be the best of their authors' work, but, if we except writers like Mr. Conrad and Mr. Hudson, who have strayed into essay writing accidentally, and concentrate upon those who write essays habitually, we shall find them a good deal affected by the change in their circumstances. To write weekly, to write daily, to write shortly, to write for busy people catching trains in the morning or for tired people coming home in the evening, is a heart-breaking task for men who know good writing from bad. They do it, but instinctively draw out of harm's way anything precious that might be damaged by contact with the public, or anything sharp that might irritate its skin. And so, if one reads Mr. Lucas, Mr. Lynd, or Mr. Squire in the bulk, one feels that a common greyness silvers everything. They are as far removed from the extravagant beauty of Walter Pater as they are from the intemperate candour of Leslie Stephen. Beauty and courage are dangerous spirits to bottle in a column and a half; and thought, like a brown-paper parcel in a waistcoat pocket, has a way of spoiling the symmetry of an article. It is a kind, tired, apathetic world for which they write, and the marvel is that they never cease to attempt, at least, to write well.

But there is no need to pity Mr. Clutton Brock for this change in the essayist's conditions. He has clearly made the best of his circumstances and not the worst. One hesitates even to say that he has had to make any conscious effort in the matter, so naturally has he effected the transition from the private essayist to the public, from the drawing-room to the Albert Hall. Paradoxically enough, the shrinkage in size has brought about a corresponding expansion of individuality. We have no longer the 'I' of Max and of Lamb, but the 'we' of public bodies and other sublime personages. It is 'we' who go to hear the *Magic Flute*; 'we' who ought to profit by it; 'we', in some mysterious way, who, in our corporate capacity, once upon a time actually wrote it. For music and literature and art must submit to the same generalization or they will not carry to the farthest recesses of the Albert Hall. That the voice of Mr. Clutton Brock, so sincere and so disinterested, carries such a distance and reaches so many without pandering to the weakness of the mass or its passions must be a matter of legitimate satisfaction to us all. But while 'we' are gratified, 'I', that unruly partner in the human fellowship, is reduced to despair. 'I' must always think things for himself, and feel things for himself. To share them in a diluted form with the majority of well-educated and well-intentioned men and women is for him sheer agony; and while the rest of us listen intently and profit profoundly, 'I' slips off to the woods and the fields and rejoices in a single blade of grass or a solitary potato.

In the fifth volume of modern essays, it seems, we have got some way from pleasure and the art of writing. But in justice to the essayists of 1920 we must be sure that we are not praising the famous because they have been praised already and the dead because we shall never meet them wearing spats in Piccadilly. We must know what we mean when we say that they can write and give us pleasure. We must compare them; we must bring out the quality. We must point to this and say it is good because it is exact, truthful, and imaginative:

> Nay, retire men cannot when they would; neither will they, when it were Reason; but are impatient of Privateness, even in age and sickness, which require the shadow: like old Townsmen: that will still be sitting at their street door, though thereby they offer Age to Scorn . . .

and to this, and say it is bad because it is loose, plausible, and commonplace:

> With courteous and precise cynicism on his lips, he thought of quiet virginal chambers, of waters singing under the moon, of terraces where taintless music sobbed into the open night, of pure maternal mistresses with protecting arms and vigilant eyes, of fields slumbering in the sunlight, of leagues of ocean heaving under warm tremulous heavens, of hot ports, gorgeous and perfumed. . . .

It goes on, but already we are bemused with sound and neither feel nor hear. The comparison makes us suspect that the art of writing has for backbone some fierce attachment to an idea. It is on the back of an idea, something believed in with conviction or seen with precision and thus compelling words to its shape, that the diverse company which includes Lamb and Bacon, and Mr. Beerbohm and Hudson, and Vernon Lee and Mr. Conrad, and Leslie Stephen and Butler and Walter Pater reaches the farther shore. Very various talents have helped or hindered the passage of the idea into words. Some scrape through painfully; others fly with every wind favouring. But Mr. Belloc and Mr. Lucas and Mr. Squire are not fiercely attached to anything in itself. They share the contemporary dilemma—the lack of an obstinate conviction which lifts ephemeral sounds through the misty sphere of anybody's language to the land where there is a perpetual marriage, a perpetual union. Vague as all definitions are, a good essay must have this permanent quality about it; it must draw its curtain round us, but it must be a curtain that shuts us in, not out.

The Art of Fiction[1]

THAT fiction is a lady, and a lady who has somehow got herself into trouble, is a thought that must often have struck her
admirers. Many gallant gentlemen have ridden to her rescue,
chief among them Sir Walter Raleigh and Mr. Percy Lubbock.
But both were a little ceremonious in their approach; both, one
felt, had a great deal of knowledge of her, but not much intimacy
with her. Now comes Mr. Forster,[2] who disclaims knowledge but
cannot deny that he knows the lady well. If he lacks something
of the others' authority, he enjoys the privileges which are allowed
the lover. He knocks at the bedroom door and is admitted when
the lady is in slippers and dressing-gown. Drawing up their chairs
to the fire they talk easily, wittily, subtly, like old friends who
have no illusions, although in fact the bedroom is a lecture-room
and the place the highly austere city of Cambridge.

This informal attitude on Mr. Forster's part is of course
deliberate. He is not a scholar; he refuses to be a pseudo-scholar.
There remains a point of view which the lecturer can adopt use-
fully, if modestly. He can, as Mr. Forster puts it, 'visualize the
English novelists not as floating down that stream which bears all
its sons away unless they are careful, but as seated together in a
room, a circular room—a sort of British Museum reading-room—
all writing their novels simultaneously'. So simultaneous are they,
indeed, that they persist in writing out of their turn. Richardson
insists that he is contemporary with Henry James. Wells will write
a passage which might be written by Dickens. Being a novelist
himself, Mr. Forster is not annoyed at this discovery. He knows
from experience what a muddled and illogical machine the brain
of a writer is. He knows how little they think about methods; how
completely they forget their grandfathers; how absorbed they
tend to become in some vision of their own. Thus, though the
scholars have all his respect, his sympathies are with the untidy
and harassed people who are scribbling away at their books. And

---

[1] Written in 1927
[2] *Aspects of the Novel*, by E. M. Forster

51

looking down on them, not from any great height, but, as he says, over their shoulders, he makes out, as he passes, that certain shapes and ideas tend to recur in their minds whatever their period. Since story-telling began stories have always been made of much the same elements; and these, which he calls The Story, People, Plot, Fantasy, Prophecy, Pattern, and Rhythm, he now proceeds to examine.

Many are the judgments that we would willingly argue, many are the points over which we would willingly linger, as Mr. Forster passes lightly on his way. That Scott is a story-teller and nothing more; that a story is the lowest of literary organisms; that the novelist's unnatural preoccupation with love is largely a reflection of his own state of mind while he composes—every page has a hint or a suggestion which makes us stop to think or wish to contradict. Never raising his voice above the speaking level, Mr. Forster has the art of saying things which sink airily enough into the mind to stay there and unfurl like those Japanese flowers which open up in the depths of the water. But greatly though these sayings intrigue us, we want to call a halt at some definite stopping-place; we want to make Mr. Forster stand and deliver. For possibly, if fiction is, as we suggest, in difficulties, it may be because nobody grasps her firmly and defines her severely. She has had no rules drawn up for her, very little thinking done on her behalf. And though rules may be wrong and must be broken, they have this advantage—they confer dignity and order upon their subject; they admit her to a place in civilized society; they prove that she is worthy of consideration. But this part of his duty, if it is his duty, Mr. Forster expressly disowns. He is not going to theorize about fiction except incidentally; he doubts even whether she is to be approached by a critic, and if so, with what critical equipment. All we can do is to edge him into a position which is definite enough for us to see where he stands. And perhaps the best way to do this is to quote, much summarized, his estimates of three great figures—Meredith, Hardy, and Henry James. Meredith is an exploded philosopher. His vision of nature is 'fluffy and lush'. When he gets serious and noble he becomes a bully. 'And his novels; most of the social values are faked. The tailors are not tailors, the cricket matches are not cricket.' Hardy is a far greater writer. But he is not so successful as a novelist because his characters are 'required to contribute too much to the plot; except in their rustic humours their vitality has been impoverished, they have gone thin and dry—he has emphasized causality more strongly than his medium permits'. Henry James pursued the narrow path of aesthetic duty and was successful. But at what a sacrifice? 'Most of human life has to disappear before he can do us a novel. Maimed creatures can alone breathe in his novels. His characters are few in number and constructed on stingy lines.'

Now if we look at these judgments, and place beside them certain admissions and omissions, we shall see that if we cannot pin Mr. Forster to a creed we can commit him to a point of view. There is something—we hesitate to be more precise—which he calls 'life'. It is to this that he brings the books of Meredith, Hardy, or James for comparison. Always their failure is some failure in relation to life. It is the humane as opposed to the aesthetic view of fiction. It maintains that the novel is 'sogged with humanity'; that 'human beings have their great chance in the novel'; a triumph won at the expense of life is in fact a defeat. Thus we arrive at the notably harsh judgment of Henry James. For Henry James brought into the novel something besides human beings. He created patterns which, though beautiful in themselves, are hostile to humanity. And for his neglect of life, says Mr. Forster, he will perish.

But at this point the pertinacious pupil may demand: 'What is this "Life" that keeps on cropping up so mysteriously and so complacently in books about fiction? Why is it absent in a pattern and present in a tea party? Why is the pleasure that we get from the pattern in *The Golden Bowl* less valuable than the emotion which Trollope gives us when he describes a lady drinking tea in a parsonage? Surely the definition of life is too arbitrary, and requires to be expanded.' To all of this Mr. Forster would reply, presumably, that he lays down no laws; the novel somehow seems to him too soft a substance to be carved like the other arts; he is merely telling us what moves him and what leaves him cold. Indeed, there is no other criterion. So then we are back in the old bog; nobody knows anything about the laws of fiction; or what its relation is to life; or to what effects it can lend itself. We can only trust our instincts. If instinct leads one reader to call Scott a story-teller, another to call him a master of romance; if one reader is moved by art, another by life, each is right, and each can pile a card-house of theory on top of his opinion as high as he can go. But the assumption that fiction is more intimately and humbly attached to the service of human beings than the other arts leads to a further position which Mr. Forster's book again illustrates. It is unnecessary to dwell upon her aesthetic functions because they are so feeble that they can safely be ignored. Thus, though it is impossible to imagine a book on painting in which not a word should be said about the medium in which a painter works, a wise and brilliant book, like Mr. Forster's, can be written about fiction without saying more than a sentence or two about the medium in which a novelist works. Almost nothing is said about words. One might suppose, unless one had read them, that a sentence means the same thing and is used for the same purposes by Sterne and by Wells. One might conclude that *Tristram Shandy* gains nothing from the language in which it is written. So with the other aesthetic qualities. Pattern, as we have seen, is recognized, but savagely censured for her tendency to obscure the human features. Beauty occurs but she is suspect. She makes one furtive appearance— 'beauty at which a novelist should never aim, though he fails if he does not achieve it'—and the possibility that she may emerge again as rhythm is briefly discussed in a few interesting pages at the end. But for the rest fiction is treated as a parasite which draws sustenance from life and must in gratitude resemble life or perish. In poetry, in drama, words may excite and stimulate and deepen without this allegiance; but in fiction they must first and foremost hold themselves at the service of the teapot and the pug dog, and to be found wanting is to be found lacking.

Strange though this unaesthetic attitude would be in the critic of any other art, it does not surprise us in the critic of fiction. For one thing, the problem is extremely difficult. A book fades like a mist, like a dream. How are we to take a stick and point to that tone, that relation, in the vanishing pages, as Mr. Roger Fry points with his wand at a line or a colour in the picture displayed before him? Moreover, a novel in particular has roused a thousand ordinary human feelings in its progress. To drag in art in such a connection seems priggish and cold-hearted. It may well compromise the critic as a man of feeling and domestic ties. And so while the painter, the musician, and the poet come in for their

54

share of criticism, the novelist goes unscathed. His character will be discussed; his morality, it may be his genealogy, will be examined; but his writing will go scot-free. There is not a critic alive now who will say that a novel is a work of art and that as such he will judge it.

And perhaps, as Mr. Forster insinuates, the critics are right. In England at any rate the novel is not a work of art. There are none to be stood beside *War and Peace, The Brothers Karamazov,* or *A la Recherche du Temps Perdu.* But while we accept the fact, we cannot suppress one last conjecture. In France and Russia they take fiction seriously. Flaubert spends a month seeking a phrase to describe a cabbage. Tolstoy writes *War and Peace* seven times over. Something of their pre-eminence may be due to the pains they take, something to the severity with which they are judged. If the English critic were less domestic, less assiduous to protect the rights of what it pleases him to call life, the novelist might be bolder too. He might cut adrift from the eternal tea-table and the plausible and preposterous formulas which are supposed to represent the whole of our human adventure. But then the story might wobble; the plot might crumble; ruin might seize upon the characters. The novel, in short, might become a work of art.

Such are the dreams that Mr. Forster leads us to cherish. For his is a book to encourage dreaming. None more suggestive has been written about the poor lady whom, with perhaps mistaken chivalry, we still persist in calling the art of fiction.

Phases of Fiction[1]

THE following pages attempt to record the impressions made upon the mind by reading a certain number of novels in succession. In deciding which book to begin with and which book to go on with, the mind was not pressed to make a choice. It was allowed to read what it liked. It was not, that is to say, asked to read historically, nor was it asked to read critically. It was asked to read only for interest and pleasure, and, at the same time, to comment as it read upon the nature of the interest and the pleasure that it found. It went its way, therefore, independent of time and reputation. It read Trollope before it read Jane Austen and skipped, by chance or negligence, some of the most celebrated books in English fiction. Thus, there is little reference or none to Fielding, Richardson, or Thackeray.

Yet, if nobody save the professed historian and critic reads to understand a period or to revise a reputation, nobody reads simply by chance or without a definite scale of values. There is, to speak metaphorically, some design that has been traced upon our minds which reading brings to light. Desires, appetites, however we may come by them, fill it in, scoring now in this direction, now in that. Hence, an ordinary reader can often trace his course through literature with great exactness and can even think himself, from time to time, in possession of a whole world as inhabitable as the real world. Such a world, it may be urged against it, is always in process of creation. Such a world, it may be added, likewise against it, is a personal world, a world limited and unhabitable perhaps by other people, a world created in obedience to tastes that may be peculiar to one temperament and distasteful to another—indeed, any such record of reading, it will be concluded, is bound to be limited, personal, erratic.

In its defence, however, it may be claimed that if the critic and the historian speak a more universal language, a more learned language, they are also likely to miss the centre and to lose their way for the simple reason that they know so many things about a writer that a writer does not know about himself. Writers are

[1] *The Bookman*, April, May, and June, 1929

heard to complain that influences—education, heredity, theory—
are given weight of which they themselves are unconscious in the
act of creation. Is the author in question the son of an architect or
a bricklayer? Was he educated at home or at the university? Does
he come before or after Thomas Hardy? Yet not one of these
things is in his mind, perhaps, as he writes and the reader's
ignorance, narrowing and limiting as it is, has at least the advantage that it leaves unhampered what the reader has in common
with the writer, though much more feebly: the desire to create.

Here, then, very briefly and with inevitable simplifications, an
attempt is made to show the mind at work upon a shelf full of
novels and to watch it as it chooses and rejects, making itself a
dwelling-place in accordance with its own appetites. Of these appetites, perhaps, the simplest is the desire to believe wholly and
entirely in something which is fictitious. That appetite leads on all
the others in turn. There is no saying, for they change so much at
different ages, that one appetite is better than another. The common reader is, moreover, suspicious of fixed labels and settled
hierarchies. Still, since there must be an original impulse, let us
give the lead to this one and start upon the shelf full of novels in
order to gratify our wish to believe.

The Truth-tellers

In English fiction there are a number of writers who gratify our
sense of belief—Defoe, Swift, Trollope, Borrow, W. E. Norris, for
example; among the French, one thinks instantly of Maupassant.
Each of them assures us that things are precisely as they say they
are. What they describe happens actually before our eyes. We get
from their novels the same sort of refreshment and delight that we
get from seeing something actually happen in the street below. A
dustman, for example, by an awkward movement of his arm
knocks over a bottle apparently containing Condy's Fluid which
cracks upon the pavement. The dustman gets down; he picks up
the jagged fragments of the broken bottle; he turns to a man who is
passing in the street. We cannot take our eyes off him until we
have feasted our powers of belief to the full. It is as if a channel

were cut, into which suddenly and with great relief an emotion hitherto restrained rushes and pours. We forget whatever else we may be doing. This positive experience overpowers all the mixed and ambiguous feelings of which we may be possessed at the moment. The dustman has knocked over a bottle; the red stain is spreading on the pavement. It happens precisely so.

The novels of the great truth-tellers, of whom Defoe is easily the English chief, procure for us a refreshment of this kind. He tells us the story of Moll Flanders, of Robinson Crusoe, of Roxana, and we feel our powers of belief rush into the channel, thus cut, instantly, fertilizing and refreshing our entire being. To believe seems the greatest of all pleasures. It is impossible to glut our greed for truth, so rapacious is it. There is not a shadowy or insubstantial word in the whole book to startle our nervous sense of security. Three or four strong, direct strokes of the pen carve out Roxana's character. Her dinner is set indisputably on the table. It consists of veal and turnips. The day is fine or cloudy; the month is April or September. Persistently, naturally, with a curious, almost unconscious iteration, emphasis is laid upon the very facts that most reassure us of stability in real life, upon money, furniture, food, until we seem wedged among solid objects in a solid universe.

One element of our delight comes from the sense that this world, with all its circumstantiality, bright and round and hard as it is, is yet complete, so that in whatever direction we reach out for assurance we receive it. If we press on beyond the confines of each page, as it is our instinct to do, completing what the writer has left unsaid, we shall find that we can trace our way; that there are indications which let us realize them; there is an under side, a dark side to this world. Defoe presided over his universe with the omnipotence of a God, so that his world is perfectly in scale. Nothing is so large that it makes another thing too small; nothing so small that it makes another thing too large.

The name of God is often found on the lips of his people, but they invoke a deity only a little less substantial than they are themselves, a being seated solidly not so very far above them in the tree-tops. A divinity more mystical, could Defoe have made us believe in him, would so have discredited the landscape and cast doubt upon the substance of the men and women that our belief in them would have perished at the heart. Or, suppose that he let himself dwell upon the green shades of the forest depths or upon the sliding glass of the summer stream. Again, however much we were delighted by the description, we should have been uneasy because this other reality would have wronged the massive and monumental reality of Crusoe and Moll Flanders. As it is, saturated with the truth of his own universe, no such discrepancy is allowed to intrude. God, man, nature are all real, and they are all real with the same kind of reality—an astonishing feat, since it implies complete and perpetual submission on the writer's part to his conviction, an obdurate deafness to all the voices which seduce and tempt him to gratify other moods. We have only to reflect how seldom a book is carried through on the same impulse of belief, so that its perspective is harmonious throughout, to realize how great a writer Defoe was. One could number on one's fingers half a dozen novels which set out to be masterpieces and yet have failed because the belief flags; the realities are mixed: the perspective shifts and, instead of a final clarity, we get a baffling, if only a momentary, confusion.

Having, now, feasted our powers of belief to the full and so enjoyed the relief and rest of this positive world existing so palpably and completely outside of us, there begins to come over us that slackening of attention which means that the nerve in use is sated for the time being. We have absorbed as much of this literal truth as we can and we begin to crave for something to vary it that will yet be in harmony with it. We do not want, except in a flash or a hint, such truth as Roxana offers us when she tells us how her master, the Prince, would sit by their child and 'loved to look at it when it was asleep'. For that truth is hidden truth; it makes us dive beneath the surface to realize it and so holds up the action. It is, then, action that we want. One desire having run its course, another leaps forward to take up the burden and no sooner have we formulated our desire than Defoe has given it to us. 'On with the story'—that cry is forever on his lips. No sooner has he got his facts assembled than the burden is floated. Perpetually springing up, fresh and effortless, action and event, quickly succeeding each other, thus set in motion this dense accumulation of facts and keep the breeze blowing in our faces. It becomes obvious, then, that if his people are sparely equipped and bereft of certain affections, such as love of husband and child, which we expect of people at leisure, it is that they may move quicker. They must travel light since it is for adventure that they are made. They will need quick wits, strong muscles, and rocky common sense on the road they are to travel rather than sentiment, reflection, or the power of self-analysis.

Belief, then, is completely gratified by Defoe. Here, the reader can rest himself and enter into possession of a large part of his domain. He tests it; he tries it; he feels nothing give under him or fade before him. Still, belief seeks fresh sustenance as a sleeper seeks a fresh side of the pillow. He may turn, and this is likely, to someone closer to him in time than Defoe in order to gratify his desire for belief (for distance of time in a novel sets up pictur-esqueness, hence unfamiliarity). If he should take down, for example, some book of a prolific and once esteemed novelist, like W. E. Norris, he will find that the juxtaposition of the two books brings each out more clearly.

W. E. Norris was an industrious writer who is well worth singling out for inquiry if only because he represents that vast body of forgotten novelists by whose labours fiction is kept alive in the absence of the great masters. At first, we seem to be given all that we need: girls and boys, cricket, shooting, dancing, boating, love-making, marriage; a park here; a London drawing-room there; here, an English gentleman; there, a cad; dinners, tea-parties, canters in the Row; and, behind it all, green and grey, domestic and venerable, the fields and manor houses of England. Then, as one scene succeeds another, half-way through the book, we seem to have a great deal more belief on our hands than we know what to do with. We have exhausted the vividness of slang; the modernity, the adroit turn of mood. We loiter on the threshold of the scene, asking to be allowed to press a little further; we take some phrase, and look at it as if it ought to yield us more. Then, turning our eyes from the main figures, we try to sketch out some-thing in the background, to pursue these feelings and relations away from the present moment; not, needless to say, with a view to discovering some over-arching conception, something which we may call 'a reading of life'. No, our desire is otherwise: some shadow of depth appropriate to the bulk of the figures; some Providence such as Defoe provides or morality such as he suggests, so that we can go beyond the age itself without falling into inanity.

Then, we discover it is the mark of a second-rate writer that he cannot pause here or suggest there. All his powers are strained in keeping the scene before us, its brightness and its credibility. The surface is all; there is nothing beyond.

Our capacity for belief, however, is not in the least exhausted. It is only a question of finding something that will revive it for us. Not Shakespeare and not Shelley and not Hardy; perhaps Trollope, Swift, Maupassant. Above all, Maupassant is the most promising at the moment, for Maupassant enjoys the great advantage that he writes in French. Not from any merit of his own, he gives us that little fillip which we get from reading a language whose edges have not been smoothed for us by daily use. The very sentences shape themselves in a way that is definitely charming. The words tingle and sparkle. As for English, alas, it is *our* language—shop-worn, not so desirable, perhaps. Moreover, each of these compact little stories has its pinch of gunpowder, artfully placed so as to explode when we tread on its tail. The last words are always highly charged. Off they go, *bang*, in our faces and there is lit up for us in one uncompromising glare someone with his hand lifted, someone sneering, someone turning his back, someone catching an omnibus, as if this insignificant action, whatever it may be, summed up the whole situation forever.

The reality that Maupassant brings before us is always one of the body, of the senses—the ripe flesh of a servant girl, for example, or the succulence of food. 'Elle restait inerte, ne sentant plus son corps, et l'esprit dispersé, comme si quelqu'un l'eût déchiqueté avec un de ces instruments dont se servent les cardeurs pour effiloquer le laine des matelas.' Or her tears dried themselves upon her cheeks 'comme des gouttes d'eau sur du fer rouge'. It is all concrete; it is all visualized. It is a world, then, in which one can believe with one's eyes and one's nose and one's senses; nevertheless, it is a world which secretes perpetually a little drop of bitterness. Is this all? And, if this is all, is it enough? Must we, then, believe this? So we ask. Now that we are given truth unadorned, a disagreeable sensation seems attached to it, which we must analyse before we go further.

Suppose that one of the conditions of things as they are is that they are unpleasant, have we strength enough to support that unpleasantness for the sake of the delight of believing in it? Are we not shocked somehow by *Gulliver's Travels* and *Boule de suif* and *La Maison Tellier?* Shall we not always be trying to get round the obstacle of ugliness by saying that Maupassant and his like are narrow, cynical, and unimaginative when, in fact, it is their truthfulness that we resent—the fact that leeches suck the naked legs of servant girls, that there are brothels, that human nature is fundamentally cold, selfish, corrupt? This discomfort at the disagreeableness of truth is one of the first things that shakes very lightly our desire to believe. Our Anglo-Saxon blood, perhaps, has given us an instinct that truth is, if not exactly beautiful, at least pleasant or virtuous to behold. But let us look once more at truth and, this time, through the eyes of Anthony Trollope, 'a big, blustering, spectacled, loud-voiced hunting man . . . whose language in male society was, I believe, so lurid that I was not admitted to breakfast with him . . . who rode about the country establishing penny posts, and wrote, as the story goes, so many thousand words before breakfast every day of his life'.[1]

Certainly, the Barchester novels tell the truth, and the English truth, at first sight, is almost as plain of feature as the French truth, though with a difference. Mr. Slope is a hypocrite, with a 'pawing, greasy way with him'. Mrs. Proudie is a domineering bully. The Archdeacon is well-meaning but coarse-grained and thick-cut. Thanks to the vigour of the author, the world of which these are the most prominent inhabitants goes through its daily rigmarole of feeding and begetting children and worshipping with a thoroughness, a gusto, which leaves us no loophole of escape. We believe in Barchester as we believe in the reality of our own weekly bills. Nor, indeed, do we wish to escape from the consequences of our belief, for the truth of the Slopes and the Proudies, the truth of the evening party where Mrs. Proudie has her dress torn off her back under the light of eleven gas jets, is entirely acceptable.

At the top of his bent Trollope is a big, if not first-rate, novelist, and the top of his bent came when he drove his pen hard and fast after the humours of provincial life and scored, without cruelty but with hale and hearty common sense, the portraits of those

[1] *Vignettes of Memory*, by Lady Violet Greville, 1927

well-fed, black-coated, unimaginative men and women of the fifties. In his manner with them, and his manner is marked, there is an admirable shrewdness, like that of a family doctor or solicitor, too well acquainted with human foibles to judge them other than tolerantly and not above the human weakness of liking one person a great deal better than another for no good reason. Indeed, though he does his best to be severe and is at his best when most so, he could not hold himself aloof, but let us know that he loved the pretty girl and hated the oily humbug so vehemently that it is only by a great pull on his reins that he keeps himself straight. It is a family party over which he presides and the reader who becomes, as time goes on, one of Trollope's most intimate cronies has a seat at his right hand. Their relation becomes confidential.

All this, of course, complicates what was simple enough in Defoe and Maupassant. There, we were plainly and straightforwardly asked to believe. Here, we are asked to believe, but to believe through the medium of Trollope's temperament and, thus, a second relationship is set up with Trollope himself which, if it diverts us, distracts us also. The truth is no longer quite so true. The clear cold truth, which seems to lie before us unveiled in *Gulliver's Travels* and *Moll Flanders* and *La Maison Tellier*, is here garnished with a charming embroidery. But it is not from this attractive embellishment of Trollope's personality that the disease comes which in the end proves fatal to the huge, substantial, well buttressed, and authenticated truth of the Barchester novels. Truth itself, however unpleasant, is interesting always. But, unfortunately, the conditions of storytelling are harsh; they demand that scene shall follow scene; that party shall be supported by another party, one parsonage by another parsonage; that all shall be of the same calibre; that the same values shall prevail. If we are told here that the palace was lit by gas, we must be told there that the manor house was faithful to the oil lamp. But what will happen if, in process of solidifying the entire body of his story, the novelist finds himself out of facts or flagging in his invention? Must he then go on? Yes, for the story has to be finished: the intrigue discovered, the guilty punished, the lovers married in the end. The record, therefore, becomes at times merely a chronicle. Truth peters out into a thin-blooded catalogue. Better would it be, we feel, to leave a blank or even to outrage our sense of probability than to stuff the crevices with this makeshift substance: the wrong side of truth is a worn, dull fabric, unsteeped in the waters of imagination and scorched. But the novel has issued her orders; I consist, she says, of two and thirty chapters; and who am I, we seem to hear the sagacious and humble Trollope ask, with his usual good sense, that I should go disobeying the novel? And he manfully provides us with makeshifts.

If, then, we reckon up what we have got from the truth-tellers, we find that it is a world where our attention is always being drawn to things which can be seen, touched, and tasted, so that we get an acute sense of the reality of our physical existence. Having thus established our belief, the truth-tellers at once contrive that its solidity shall be broken before it becomes oppressive by action. Events happen; coincidence complicates the plain story. But their actions are all in keeping one with another and they are extremely careful not to discredit them or alter the emphasis in any way by making their characters other than such people as naturally express themselves to the full in active and adventurous careers. Then, again, they hold the three great powers which dominate fiction—God, Nature, and Man—in stable relation so that we look at a world in proper perspective; where, moreover, things hold good not only here at the moment in front of us, but there, behind that tree or among those unknown people far away in the shadow behind those hills. At the same time, truth-telling implies disagreeableness. It is part of truth—the sting and edge of it. We cannot deny that Swift, Defoe, and Maupassant all convince us that they reach a more profound depth in their ugliness than Trollope in his pleasantness. For this reason, truth-telling easily swerves a little to one side and becomes satiric. It walks beside the fact and apes it, like a shadow which is only a little more humped and angular than the object which casts it. Yet, in its perfect state, when we can believe absolutely, our satisfaction is complete. Then, we can say, though other states may exist which are better or more exalted, there is none that makes this unnecessary, none that supersedes it. But truth-telling carries in its breast a weakness which is apparent in the works of the lesser writers or in the masters themselves when they are exhausted. Truth-telling is liable to degenerate into perfunctory

64

fact-recording, the repetition of the statement that it was on Wednesday that the Vicar held his mothers' meeting which was often attended by Mrs. Brown and Miss Dobson in their pony carriage, a statement which, as the reader is quick to perceive, has nothing of truth in it but the respectable outside.

At length, then, taking into account the perfunctory fact-recording, the lack of metaphor, the plainness of the language, and the fact that we believe most when the truth is most painful to us, it is not strange that we should become aware of another desire welling up spontaneously and making its way into those cracks which the great monuments of the truth-tellers wear inevitably upon their solid bases. A desire for distance, for music, for shadow, for space, takes hold of us. The dustman has picked up his broken bottle; he has crossed the road; he begins to lose solidity and detail over there in the evening dusk.

The Romantics

'It was a November morning, and the cliffs which overlooked the ocean were hung with thick and heavy mist, when the portals of the ancient and half-ruinous tower, in which Lord Ravenswood had spent the last and troubled years of his life, opened, that his mortal remains might pass forward to an abode yet more dreary and lonely.'

No change could be more complete. The dustman has become a Lord; the present has become the past; homely Anglo-Saxon speech has become Latin and many syllabled; instead of pots and pans, gas jets and snug broughams, we have a half-ruinous tower and cliffs, the ocean and November, heavy in mist. This past and this ruin, this Lord and this autumn, this ocean and this cliff are as delightful to us as the change from a close room and voices to the night and the open air. The curious softness and remoteness of *The Bride of Lammermoor*, the atmosphere of rusty moorland and splashing waves, the dark and the distance actually seem to be adding themselves to that other more truthful scene which we still hold in mind, and to be giving it completeness. After that storm this peace, after that glare this coolness. The truth-tellers had very little love, it seems, of nature. They used nature almost entirely as an obstacle to overcome or as a background to complete, not aesthetically for contemplation or for any part it might play in the affairs of their characters. The town, after all, was their natural haunt. But let us compare them in more essential qualities: in their treatment of people. There comes towards us a girl tripping lightly and leaning on her father's arm:

. . . 'Lucy Ashton's exquisitely beautiful, yet somewhat girlish features, were formed to express peace of mind, serenity, and indifference to the tinsel of worldly pleasure. Her locks, which were of shadowy gold, divided on a brow of exquisite whiteness, like a gleam of broken and pallid sunshine upon a hill of snow. The expression of the countenance was in the last degree gentle, soft, timid and feminine, and seemed rather to shrink from the most casual look of a stranger than to court his admiration.'

Nobody could less resemble Moll Flanders or Mrs. Proudie. Lucy Ashton is incapable of action or of self-control. The bull runs at her and she sinks to the ground; the thunder peals and she faints. She falters out the strangest little language of ceremony and politeness, 'O if you be a man, if you be a gentleman assist me to find my father'. One might say that she has no character except the traditional; to her father she is filial; to her lover, modest; to the poor, benevolent. Compared with Moll Flanders, she is a doll with sawdust in her veins and wax in her cheeks. Yet we have read ourselves into the book and grow familiar with its proportions. We come, at length, to see that anything more individual or eccentric or marked would lay emphasis where we want none. This tapering wraith hovers over the landscape and is part of it. She and Edgar Ravenswood are needed to support this romantic world with their bare forms, to clasp it round with that theme of unhappy love which is needed to hold the rest together. But the world that they clasp has its own laws. It leaves out and eliminates no less drastically than the other. On the one hand, we have feelings of the utmost exaltation—love, hate, jealousy, remorse; on the other hand, raciness and simplicity in the extreme. The rhetoric of the Ashtons and Ravenswoods is completed by the humours of peasants and cackle of village women. The true romantic can swing us from earth to sky; and the great master of romantic fiction, who is undoubtedly Sir Walter Scott, uses his liberty to the full. At the same time, we retort upon this melancholy which he has called forth, as in *The Bride of Lammermoor*. We laugh at ourselves for having been so moved by machinery so absurd. However, before we impute this defect to romance itself, we must consider whether it is not Scott's fault. This lazy-minded man was quite capable when the cold fit was on him of filling a chapter or two currently, conventionally, from a fountain of empty, journalistic phrases which, for all that they have a charm of their own, let the slackened attention sag still further.

Carelessness has never been laid to the charge of Robert Louis Stevenson. He was careful, careful to a fault—a man who combined most strangely boy's psychology with the extreme sophistication of an artist. Yet, he obeyed no less implicitly than Walter Scott the laws of romance. He lays his scene in the past; he is always putting his characters to the sword's point with some desperate adventure; he caps his tragedy with homespun humour. Nor can there be any doubt that his conscience and his seriousness as a writer have stood him in good stead. Take any page of *The Master of Ballantrae* and it still stands wear and tear; but the fabric of *The Bride of Lammermoor* is full of holes and patches; it is scamped, botched, hastily flung together. Here, in Stevenson, romance is treated seriously and given all the advantages of the most refined literary art, with the result that we are never left to consider what an absurd situation this is or to reflect that we have no emotion left with which to meet the demand made upon us. We get, on the contrary, a firm, credible story, which never betrays us for a second, but is corroborated, substantiated, made good in every detail. With what precision and cunning a scene will be made visible to us as if the pen were a knife which sliced away the covering and left the core bare!

'It was as he said: there was no breath stirring; a windless stricture of frost had bound the air; and as we went forth in the shine of candles, the blackness was like a roof over our heads.' Or, again: 'All the 27th that rigorous weather endured; a stifling cold; folk passing about like smoking chimneys; the wide hearth in the hall piled high with fuel; some of the spring birds that had already blundered north into our neighbourhood besieging the windows of the house or trotting on the frozen turf like things distracted.'

'A windless stricture of frost . . . folk passing about like smoking chimneys'—one may search the Waverley Novels in vain for such close writing as this. Separately, these descriptions are lovely and brilliant. The fault lies elsewhere, in the whole of which they are a part. For in those critical minutes which decide a book's fate, when it is finished and the book swims up complete in the mind and lets us look at it, something seems lacking. Perhaps it is that the detail sticks out too prominently. The mind is caught up by this fine passage of description, by that curious exactitude of phrase; but the rhythm and sweep of emotion which the story has started in us are denied satisfaction. We are plucked back when we should be swinging free. Our attention is caught by some knot of ribbon or refinement of tracery when in fact we desire only a bare body against the sky.

Scott repels our taste in a thousand ways. But the crisis, that is the point where the accent falls and shapes the book under it, is right. Slouching, careless as he is, he will at the critical moment pull himself together and strike the one stroke needed, the stroke which gives the book its vividness in memory. Lucy sits gibbering 'couched like a hare upon its form'. 'So, you have ta'en up your bonnie bridegroom?' she says, dropping her fine lady's mincing speech for the vernacular. Ravenswood sinks beneath the quicksands. 'One only vestige of his fate appeared. A large sable feather had been detached from his hat, and the rippling waves of the rising tide wafted it to Caleb's feet. The old man took it up, dried it, and placed it in his bosom.' At both these points the writer's hand is on the book and it falls from him shaped. But in *The Master of Ballantrae*, though each detail is right and wrought so as separately to move our highest admiration, there is no such final consummation. What should have gone to help it seems, in retrospect, to stand apart from it. We remember the detail, but not the whole. Lord Durisdeer and the Master die together but we scarcely notice it. Our attention has been frittered away elsewhere.

It would seem that the romantic spirit is an exacting one; if it sees a man crossing the road in the lamplight and then lost in the gloom of the evening, it at once dictates what course the writer must pursue. We do not wish, it will say, to know much about him. We desire that he shall express our capacity for being noble and adventurous; that he shall dwell among wild places and suffer the extremes of fortune; that he be endowed with youth and distinction and allied with moors, winds, and wild birds. He is, moreover, to be a lover, not in a minute, introspective way, but largely and in outline. His feelings must be part of the landscape; the shallow browns and blues of distant woods and harvest fields are to enter into them; a tower, perhaps, and a castle where the snapdragon flowers. Above all, the romantic spirit demands here a crisis and there a crisis in which the wave that has swollen in the breast shall break. Such feelings Scott gratifies more completely than Stevenson, though with enough qualification to make us pursue the question of romance and its scope and its limitations a little further. Perhaps here it might be interesting to read *The Mysteries of Udolpho*.

The Mysteries of Udolpho have been so much laughed at as the type of Gothic absurdity that it is difficult to come at the book with a fresh eye. We come, expecting to ridicule. Then, when we find beauty, as we do, we go to the other extreme and rhapsodize. But the beauty and the absurdity of romance are both present and the book is a good test of the romantic attitude, since Mrs. Radcliffe pushes the liberties of romance to the extreme. Where Scott will go back a hundred years to get the effect of distance, Mrs. Radcliffe will go back three hundred. With one stroke, she frees herself from a host of disagreeables and enjoys her freedom lavishly.

As a novelist, it is her desire to describe scenery and it is there that her great gift lies. Like every true writer, she shoulders her way past every obstacle to her goal. She brings us into a huge, empty, airy world. A few ladies and gentlemen, who are purely eighteenth century in mind, manner, and speech, wander about in vast champaigns, listen to nightingales singing amorously in midnight woods; see the sun set over the lagoon of Venice; and watch the distant Alps turn pink and blue from the turrets of an Italian castle. These people, when they are well born, are of the same blood as Scott's gentry; attenuated and formal silhouettes who have the same curious power of being in themselves negligible and insipid but of merging harmoniously in the design.

Again, we feel the force which the romantic acquires by obliterating facts. With the sinking of the lights, the solidity of the foreground disappears, other shapes become apparent and other senses are roused. We become aware of the danger and darkness of our existence; comfortable reality has proved itself a phantom too. Outside our little shelter we hear the wind raging and the waves breaking. In this mood our senses are strained and apprehensive. Noises are audible which we should not hear normally. Curtains rustle. Something in the semi-darkness seems to move. Is it alive? And what is it? And what is it seeking here? Mrs. Radcliffe succeeds in making us feel all this, largely because she is able to make us aware of the landscape and, thus, induces a detached mood favourable to romance; but in her, more plainly than in Scott or Stevenson, the absurdity is evident, the wheels of the machine are visible and the grinding is heard. She lets us see more clearly than they do what demands the romantic writer makes upon us.

Both Scott and Stevenson, with the true instinct of the imagination, introduced rustic comedy and broad Scots dialect. It is in that direction, as they rightly divined, that the mind will unbend when it relaxes. Mrs. Radcliffe, on the other hand, having climbed to the top of her pinnacle, finds it impossible to come down. She tries to solace us with comic passages, put naturally into the mouths of Annette and Ludovico who are servants. But the break is too steep for her limited and ladylike mind and she pieces out her high moments and her beautiful atmosphere with a pale reflection of romance which is more tedious than any ribaldry. Mysteries abound. Murdered bodies multiply; but she is incapable of creating the emotion to feel them by, with the result that they lie there, unbelieved in; hence, ridiculous. The veil is drawn; there is the concealed figure; there is the decayed face; there are the writhing worms—and we laugh.

Directly the power which lives in a book sinks, the whole fabric of the book, its sentences, the length and shape of them, its inflections, its mannerisms, all that it wore proudly and naturally under the impulse of a true emotion become stale, forced, unappetizing. Mrs. Radcliffe slips limply into the faded Scott manner and reels off page after page in a style illustrated by this example:

> Emily, who had always endeavoured to regulate her conduct by the nicest laws, and whose mind was finely sensible, not only of what is just in morals, but of whatever is beautiful in the feminine character, was shocked by these words.

And so it slips along and so we sink and drown in the pale tide. Nevertheless, *Udolpho* passes this test: it gives us an emotion which is both distinct and unique, however high or low we rate the emotion itself.

If we see now where the danger of romance lies: how difficult the mood is to sustain; how it needs the relief of comedy; how the very distance from common human experience and strangeness of its elements become ridiculous—if we see these things, we see also that these emotions are in themselves priceless jewels. The romantic novel realizes for us an emotion which is deep and genuine. Scott, Stevenson, Mrs. Radcliffe, all in their different ways, unveil another country of the land of fiction; and it is not the least proof of their power that they breed in us a keen desire for something different.

The Character-mongers and Comedians

The novels which make us live imaginatively, with the whole of the body as well as the mind, produce in us the physical sensations of heat and cold, noise and silence, one reason perhaps why we desire change and why our reactions to them vary so much at different times. Only, of course, the change must not be violent. It is rather that we need a new scene; a return to human faces; a sense of walls and towns about us, with their lights and their characters after the silence of the wind-blown heath.

After reading the romances of Scott and Stevenson and Mrs. Radcliffe, our eyes seem stretched, their sight a little blurred, as if they had been gazing into the distance and it would be a relief to turn for contrast to a strongly marked human face, to characters of extravagant force and character in keeping with our romantic mood. Such figures are most easily to be found in Dickens, of course, and particularly in *Bleak House* where, as Dickens said, 'I have purposely dwelt upon the romantic side of familiar things'. They are found there with peculiar aptness—for if the characters satisfy us by their eccentricity and vigour, London and the land-scape of the Dedlocks' place at Chesney Wold are in the mood of the moor, only more luridly lit up and more sharply dark and bright because in Dickens the character-making power is so pro-digious that the very houses and streets and fields are strongly featured in sympathy with the people. The character-making power is so prodigious, indeed, that it has little need to make use of observation, and a great part of the delight of Dickens lies in the sense we have of wantoning with human beings twice or ten times their natural size or smallness who retain only enough human likeness to make us refer their feelings very broadly, not to our own, but to those of odd figures seen casually through the half-opened doors of public houses, lounging on quays, slinking mysteriously down little alleys which lie about Holborn and the Law Courts. We enter at once into the spirit of exaggeration.

Who, in the course of a long life, has met Mr. Chadband or Mr. Turveydrop or Miss Flite? Who has met anybody who, whatever the day or the occasion, can be trusted to say the same phrase, to repeat the same action? This perpetual repetition has, of course, an enormous power to drive these characters home, to stabilize them. Mr. Vholes, with his three dear girls at home and his father to support in the Vale of Taunton, Mrs. Jellyby and the natives of Borrioboola-Gha, Mr. Turveydrop and his deportment, all serve as stationary points in the flow and confusion of the narrative; they have a decorative effect as if they were gargoyles carved, motionless, at the corner of a composition. Wherever we may have wandered, we shall come back and find them there. They uphold the extraordinary intricacy of the plot in whose confusion we are often sunk up to our lips. For it is impossible to imagine that the Jellybys and the Turveydrops are ever affected by human emotions or that their habitual routine is disturbed by the astonishing events which blow through the pages of the book, from so many quarters at the same time. Thus they have a force, a sublimity, which the slighter and more idiosyncratic characters miss.

After all, is not life itself, with its coincidences and its convolutions, astonishingly queer? 'What connexion,' Dickens himself exclaims, 'can there have been between many people in the innumerable histories of this world, who, from opposite sides of great gulfs, have, nevertheless, been very curiously brought together!' One after another his characters come into being, called into existence by an eye which has only to glance into a room to take in every object, human or inanimate, that is there; by an eye which sees once and for all; which snatches at a woman's steel hair-curlers, a pair of red-rimmed eyes, a white scar and makes them somehow reveal the essence of a character; an eye gluttonous, restless, insatiable, creating more than it can use. Thus, the prevailing impression is one of movement, of the endless ebb and flow of life round one or two stationary points.

Often we cease to worry about the plot and wander off down some strange avenue of suggestion stirred in this vast and mobile world by a casual movement, a word, a glance. 'Still, very steadfastly and quietly walking towards it, a peaceful figure, too, in the landscape, went Mademoiselle Hortense, shoeless, through the wet grass.' She goes and she leaves a strange wake of emotion behind her. Or, again, a door is flung open in the misty purlieus of London; there is Mr. Tulkinghorn's friend, who appears once and once only—'a man of the same mould and a lawyer too, who lived the same kind of life until he was seventy-five years old, and then, suddenly conceiving (as it is supposed) an impression that it was too monotonous, gave his gold watch to his hairdresser one summer evening, and walked leisurely home to the Temple, and hanged himself'.

This sense that the meaning goes on after the words are spoken, that doors open and let us look through them, is full of romance. But romance in Dickens is impressed on us through characters, through extreme types of human beings, not through castles or banners, not through the violence of action, adventure, or nature. Human faces, scowling, grinning, malignant, benevolent, are projected at us from every corner. Everything is unmitigated and extreme.

But at last, among all these characters who are so static and so extreme, we come upon one—Inspector Bucket, the detective—which is not, as the others are, of a piece, but made up of contrasts and discrepancies. The romantic power of the single-piece character is lost. For the character is no longer fixed and part of the design; it is in itself of interest. Its movements and changes compel us to watch it. We try to understand this many-sided man who has brushed his hair, which is thin, with a wet brush; who has his bombastic, official side, yet with it combines, as we see when the mine is sprung, ability, conscience, even compassion—for all these qualities are displayed by turns in the astonishingly vivid account of the drive through the night and the storm, in pursuit of Esther's mother. If much more were added, so that Inspector Bucket drew more of our attention to him and diverted it from the story, we should begin with his new scale of values in our eyes to find the glaring opposites in use elsewhere too violent to be tolerable. But Dickens committed no such sin against his readers. He uses this clear-cut, many-faced figure to sharpen his final scenes and, then, letting Inspector Bucket of the detective force disappear, gathers the loose folds of the story into one prodigious armful and makes an end. But he has sharpened our curiosity and made us dissatisfied with the limitations and even with the exuberance of his genius. The scene becomes too elastic, too voluminous, too cloud-like in its contours. The very abundance of it tires us, as well as the impossibility of holding it all together. We are always straying down bypaths and into alleys where we lose our way and cannot remember where we were going.

Though the heart of Dickens burned with indignation for public wrongs, he lacked sensitiveness privately, so that his attempts at intimacy failed. His great figures are on too large a scale to fit nicely into each other. They do not interlock. They need company to show them off and action to bring out their humours. They are often out of touch with each other. In Tolstoy, in the scenes between Princess Marya and her father, the old Prince, the pressure of character upon character is never relaxed. The tension is perpetual, every nerve in the character is alive. It may be for this reason that Tolstoy is the greatest of novelists. In Dickens the characters are impressive in themselves but not in their personal relations. Often, indeed, when they talk to each other they are vapid in the extreme or sentimental beyond belief. One thinks of them as independent, existing forever, unchanged, like monoliths looking up into the sky. So it is that we begin to want something smaller, more intense, more intricate. Dickens has, himself, given us a taste of the pleasure we derive from looking curiously and intently into another character. He has made us instinctively reduce the size of the scene in proportion to the figure of a normal man, and now we seek this intensification, this reduction, carried out more perfectly and more completely, we shall find, in the novels of Jane Austen.

At once, when we open *Pride and Prejudice*, we are aware that the sentence has taken on a different character. Dickens, of course, at full stride is as free-paced and far-stretched as possible. But in comparison with this nervous style, how large-limbed and how loose. The sentence here runs like a knife, in and out, cutting a shape clear. It is done in a drawing-room. It is done by the use of dialogue. Half a dozen people come together after dinner and begin, as they so well might, to discuss letter-writing. Mr. Darcy writes slowly and 'studies too much for words of four syllables'. Mr. Bingley, on the other hand (for it is necessary that we should get to know them both and they can be quickest shown if they are opposed), 'leaves out half his words and blots the rest'. But such is only the first rough shaping that gives the outline of the face. We go on to define and distinguish. Bingley, says Darcy, is really boasting, when he calls himself a careless letter-writer because he thinks the defect interesting. It was a boast when he told Mrs. Bennet that if he left Nethfield he would be gone in five minutes. And this little passage of analysis on Darcy's part, besides proving his astuteness and his cool observant temper, rouses Bingley to show us a vivacious picture of Darcy at home. 'I don't know a more awful object than Darcy, on particular occasions, and in particular places; at his own house especially, and of a Sunday evening, when he has nothing to do.'

So, by means of perfectly natural question and answer, every-one is defined and, as they talk, they become not only more clearly seen, but each stroke of the dialogue brings them together or moves them apart, so that the group is no longer casual but interlocked. The talk is not mere talk; it has an emotional in-tensity which gives it more than brilliance. Light, landscape—everything that lies outside the drawing-room is arranged to illumine it. Distances are made exact; arrangements accurate. It is one mile from Meryton; it is Sunday and not Monday. We want all suspicions and questions laid at rest. It is necessary that the characters should lie before us in as clear and quiet a light as possible since every flicker and tremor is to be observed. Nothing happens, as things so often happen in Dickens, for its own oddity or curiosity, but with relation to something else. No avenues of suggestion are opened up, no doors are suddenly flung wide; the ropes which tighten the structure, since they are all rooted in the heart, are so held firmly and tightly. For, in order to develop personal relations to the utmost, it is important to keep out of the range of the abstract, the impersonal; and to suggest that there is anything that lies outside men and women would be to cast the shadow of doubt upon the comedy of their relationships and its sufficiency. So with edged phrases where often one word, set against the current of the phrase, serves to fledge it (thus: 'and whenever any of the cottagers were disposed to be quarrelsome, discontented, or *too poor*') we go down to the depths, for deep they are, for all their clarity.

But personal relations have limits, as Jane Austen seems to realize by stressing their comedy. Everything, she seems to say, has, if we could discover it, a reasonable summing up; and it is extremely amusing and interesting to see the efforts of people to upset the reasonable order, defeated as they invariably are. But if, complaining of the lack of poetry or the lack of tragedy, we are about to frame the familiar statement that this is a world which is too small to satisfy us, a prosaic world, a world of inches and blades of grass, we are brought to a pause by another impression which requires a moment further of analysis. Among all the elements which play upon us in reading fiction there has always been, though in different degrees, some voice, accent, or temperament clearly heard, though behind the scenes of the book. 'Trollope, the novelist, a big, blustering, spectacled, loud-voiced, hunting man'; Scott, the ruined country gentleman, whose very pigs trotted after him, so gracious was the sound of his voice—both come to us with the gesture of hosts, welcoming us, and we fall under the spell of their charm or the interest of their characters.

We cannot say this of Jane Austen, and her absence has the effect of making us detached from her work and of giving it, for all its sparkle and animation, a certain aloofness and completeness. Her genius compelled her to absent herself. So truthful, so clear, so sane a vision would not tolerate distraction, even if it came from her own claims, nor allow the actual experience of a transitory woman to colour what should be unstained by personality. For this reason, then, though we may be less swayed by her, we are less dissatisfied. It may be the very idiosyncrasy of a writer that tires us of him. Jane Austen, who has so little that is peculiar, does not tire us, nor does she breed in us a desire for those writers whose method and style differ altogether from hers. Thus, instead of being urged as the last page is finished to start in search of something that contrasts and completes, we pause when we have read *Pride and Prejudice*.

The pause is the result of a satisfaction which turns our minds back upon what we have just read, rather than forward to something fresh. Satisfaction is, by its nature, removed from analysis, for the quality which satisfies us is the sum of many different parts, so that if we begin praising *Pride and Prejudice* for the qualities that compose it—its wit, its truth, its profound comic power—we shall still not praise it for the quality which is the sum of all these. At this point, then, the mind, brought to bay, escapes the dilemma and has recourse to images. We compare *Pride and Prejudice* to something else because, since satisfaction can be defined no further, all the mind can do is to make a likeness of the thing, and, by giving it another shape, cherish the illusion that it is explaining it, whereas it is, in fact, only looking at it afresh. To say that *Pride and Prejudice* is like a shell, a gem, a crystal, whatever image we may choose, is to see the same thing under a different guise. Yet, perhaps, if we compare *Pride and Prejudice* to something concrete, it is because we are trying to express the sense we have in other novels imperfectly, here with distinctness, of a quality which is not in the story but above it, not in the things themselves but in their arrangement.

Pride and Prejudice, one says, has form; *Bleak House* has not. The eye (so active always in fiction) gives its own interpretation of impressions that the mind has been receiving in different terms. The mind has been conscious in *Pride and Prejudice* that things are said, for all their naturalness, with a purpose; one emotion has been contrasted with another; one scene has been short, the next long; so that all the time, instead of reading at random, without control, snatching at this and that, stressing one thing or another, as the mood takes us, we have been aware of check and stimulus, of spectral architecture built up behind the animation and variety of the scene. It is a quality so precise it is not to be found either in what is said or in what is done; that is, it escapes analysis. It is a quality, too, that is much at the mercy of fiction. Its control is invariably weak there, much weaker than in poetry or in drama because fiction runs so close to life the two are always coming into collision. That this architectural quality can be possessed by a novelist, Jane Austen proves. And she proves, too, that far from chilling the interest or withdrawing the attention from the characters, it seems on the contrary to focus it and add an extra pleasure to the book, a significance. It makes it seem that here is something good in itself, quite apart from our personal feelings.

Not to seek contrast but to start afresh—this is the impulse which urges us on after finishing *Pride and Prejudice*. We must make a fresh start altogether. Personal relations, we recall, have limits. In order to keep their edges sharp, the mysterious, the unknown, the accidental, the strange subside; their intervention would be confusing and distressing. The writer adopts an ironic attitude to her creatures, because she has denied them so many adventures and experiences. A suitable marriage is, after all, the upshot of all this coming together and drawing apart. A world which so often ends in a suitable marriage is not a world to wring one's hands over. On the contrary, it is a world about which we can be sarcastic; into which we can peer endlessly, as we fit the jagged pieces one into another. Thus, it is possible to ask not that her world shall be improved or altered (that our satisfaction forbids) but that another shall be struck off, whose constitution shall be different and shall allow of the other relations. People's relations shall be with God or nature. They shall think. They shall sit, like Dorothea Casaubon in *Middlemarch*, drawing plans for other people's houses; they shall suffer like Gissing's characters in solitude; they shall be alone. *Pride and Prejudice*, because it has such integrity of its own, never for an instant encroaches on other provinces, and, thus, leaves them more clearly defined.

Nothing could be more complete than the difference between *Pride and Prejudice* and *Silas Marner*. Between us and the scene which was so near, so distinct, is now cast a shadow. Something intervenes. The character of Silas Marner is removed from us. It is held in relation to other men and his life compared with human life. This comparison is perpetually made and illustrated by somebody not implicit in the book but inside it, somebody who at once reveals herself as 'I', so that there can be no doubt from the first that we are not going to get the relations of people together, but the spectacle of life so fas as 'I' can show it to us. 'I' will do my best to illumine these particular examples of men and women with all the knowledge, all the reflections that 'I' can offer you.

'I', we at once perceive, has access to many more experiences and reflections than can have come the way of the rustics themselves. She discovers what a simple weaver's emotions on leaving his native village are, by comparing them with those of other people. 'People whose lives have been made various by learning, sometimes find it hard to keep a fast hold on their habitual views of life, on their faith in the Invisible. . . .' It is the observer speaking and we are at once in communication with a grave mind—a mind which it is part of our business to understand. This, of course, darkens and thickens the atmosphere, for we see through so many temperaments; so many sidelights from knowledge, from reflection, play upon what we see; often, even as we are watching the weaver, our minds circle round him and we observe him with an amusement, compassion, or interest which it is impossible that he should feel himself.

Raveloe is not simply a town like Meryton now in existence with certain shops and assembly room; it has a past and therefore the present becomes fleeting, and we enjoy, among other things, the feeling that this is a world in process of change and decay, whose charm is due partly to the fact that it is past. Perhaps we compare it in our own minds with the England of today and the Napoleonic Wars with those of our own time. All this, if it serves to enlarge the horizon, also makes the village and the people in it who are placed against so wide a view smaller and their impact on each other less sharp. The novelist who believes that personal relations are enough, intensifies them and sharpens them and devotes his power to their investigation. But if the end of life is not to meet, to part, to love, to laugh, if we are at the mercy of other forces, some of them unknown, all of them beyond our power, the urgency of these meetings and partings is blurred and lessened. The edges of the coming together are blunted and the comedy tends to widen itself into a larger sphere and so to modulate into something melancholy, tolerant, and perhaps resigned. George Eliot has removed herself too far from her characters to dissect them keenly or finely, but she has gained the use of her own mind upon these same characters. Jane Austen went in and out of her people's minds like the blood in their veins.

George Eliot has kept the engine of her clumsy and powerful mind at her own disposal. She can use it, when she has created enough matter to use it upon, freely. She can stop at any moment to reason out the motives of the mind that has created it. When Silas Marner discovers that his gold has been stolen, he has recourse to 'that sort of refuge which always comes with the prostration of thought under an overpowering passion; it was that expectation of impossibilities, that belief in contradictory images, which is still distinct from madness, because it is capable of being dissipated by the external fact'. Such analysis is unthinkable in Dickens or in Jane Austen. But it adds something to the character which the character lacked before. It makes us feel not only that the working of the mind is interesting but that we shall get a much truer and subtler understanding of what is actually said and done if we so observe it. We shall perceive that often an action has only a slight relation to a feeling and, thus, that the truth-tellers, who are content to record accurately what is said and done are often ludicrously deceived and out in their estimate. In other directions there are changes. The use of dialogue is limited; for people can say very little directly. Much more can be said for them or about them by the writer himself. Then, the writer's mind, his knowledge, his skill, not merely the colour of his temperament, become means for bringing out the disposition of the character and also for relating it to other times and places. There is thus revealed underneath a state of mind which often runs counter to the action and the speech.

It is in this direction that George Eliot turns her characters and her scenes. Shadows checker them. All sorts of influences of history, or time, or reflection play upon them. If we consult our own difficult and mixed emotions as we read, it becomes clear that we are fast moving out of the range of pure character-mongering, of comedy, into a far more dubious region.

The Psychologists

Indeed, we have a strange sense of having left every world when we take up *What Maisie Knew*; of being without some support which, even if it impeded us in Dickens and George Eliot, upheld us and controlled us. The visual sense which has hitherto been so active, perpetually sketching fields and farmhouses and faces, seems now to fail or to use its powers to illumine the mind within rather than the world without. Henry James has to find an equivalent for the processes of the mind, to make concrete a mental state. He says, she was 'a ready vessel for bitterness, a deep little porcelain cup in which biting acids could be mixed'. He is forever using this intellectual imagery. The usual supports, the props and struts of the conventions, expressed or observed by the writer, are removed. Everything seems aloof from interference, thrown open to discussion and light, though resting on no visible support. For the minds of which this world is composed seem oddly freed from the pressure of the old encumbrances and raised above the stress of circumstances.

Crises cannot be precipitated by any of the old devices which Dickens and George Eliot used. Murders, rapes, seductions, sudden deaths have no power over this high, aloof world. Here the people are the sport only of delicate influences: of thoughts that people think, but hardly state, about each other; of judgments which people whose time is unoccupied have leisure to devise and apply. In consequence, these characters seem held in a vacuum at a great remove from the substantial, lumbering worlds of Dickens and George Eliot or from the precise crisscross of convention which metes out the world of Jane Austen. They live in a cocoon, spun from the finest shades of meaning, which a society, completely unoccupied by the business of getting its living, has time to spin round and about itself. Hence, we are at once conscious of using faculties hitherto dormant, ingenuity and skill, a mental nimbleness and dexterity such as serve to solve a puzzle ingeniously; our pleasure becomes split up, refined, its substance infinitely divided instead of being served to us in one lump.

Maisie, the little girl who is the bone of contention between two parents, each of them claiming her for six months, each of them finally marrying a second husband or wife, lies sunk beneath the depths of suggestion, hint, and conjecture, so that she can only affect us very indirectly, each feeling of hers being deflected and reaching us after glancing off the mind of some other person. Therefore she rouses in us no simple and direct emotion. We always have time to watch it coming and to calculate its pathway, now to the right, now to the left. Cool, amused, intrigued, at every second trying to refine our senses still further and to marshal all

that we have of sophisticated intelligence into one section of ourselves, we hang suspended over this aloof little world and watch
with intellectual curiosity for the event.

In spite of the fact that our pleasure is less direct, less the result
of feeling strongly in sympathy with some pleasure or sorrow, it has
a fineness, a sweetness, which the more direct writers fail to give
us. This comes in part from the fact that a thousand emotional
veins and streaks are perceptible in this twilight or dawn which
are lost in the full light of midday.

Besides this fineness and sweetness we get another pleasure
which comes when the mind is freed from the perpetual demand
of the novelist that we shall feel with his characters. By cutting off
the responses which are called out in the actual life, the novelist
frees us to take delight, as we do when ill or travelling, in things in
themselves. We can see the strangeness of them only when habit
has ceased to immerse us in them, and we stand outside watching
what has no power over us one way or the other. Then we see the
mind at work; we are amused by its power to make patterns; by
its power to bring out relations in things and disparities which are
covered over when we are acting by habit or driven on by the
ordinary impulses. It is a pleasure somewhat akin, perhaps, to
the pleasure of mathematics or the pleasure of music. Only, of
course, since the novelist is using men and women as his subjects,
he is perpetually exciting feelings which are opposed to the impersonality of numbers and sound; he seems, in fact, to ignore and
to repress their natural feelings, to be coercing them into a plan
which we call with vague resentment 'artificial' though it is
probable that we are not so foolish as to resent artifice in art.
Either through a feeling of timidity or prudery or through a lack
of imaginative audacity, Henry James diminishes the interest and
importance of his subject in order to bring about a symmetry
which is dear to him. This his readers resent. We feel him there,
as the suave showman, skilfully manipulating his characters;
nipping, repressing; dexterously evading and ignoring, where a
writer of greater depth or natural spirits would have taken the
risk which his material imposes, let his sails blow full and so,
perhaps, achieved symmetry and pattern, in themselves so
delightful, all the same.

But it is the measure of Henry James's greatness that he has given us so definite a world, so distinct and peculiar a beauty that we cannot rest satisfied but want to experiment further with these extraordinary perceptions, to understand more and more, but to be free from the perpetual tutelage of the author's presence, his arrangements, his anxieties. To gratify this desire, naturally, we turn to the work of Proust, where we find at once an expansion of sympathy so great that it almost defeats its own object. If we are going to become conscious of everything, how shall we realize anything? Yet if Henry James's world, after the worlds of Dickens and George Eliot, seemed without material boundaries, if everything was pervious to thought and susceptible of twenty shades of meaning, here illumination and analysis are carried far beyond those bounds. For one thing, Henry James himself, the American, ill at ease for all his magnificent urbanity in a strange civilization, was an obstacle never perfectly assimilated even by the juices of his own art. Proust, the product of the civilization which he describes, is so porous, so pliable, so perfectly receptive that we realize him only as an envelope, thin but elastic, which stretches wider and wider and serves not to enforce a view but to enclose a world. His whole universe is steeped in the light of intelligence. The commonest object, such as the telephone, loses its simplicity, its solidity, and becomes a part of life and transparent. The commonest actions, such as going up in an elevator or eating cake, instead of being discharged automatically, rake up in their progress a whole series of thoughts, sensations, ideas, memories which were apparently sleeping on the walls of the mind.

What are we to do with it all? we cannot help asking, as these trophies are piled up round us. The mind cannot be content with holding sensation after sensation passively to itself; something must be done with them; their abundance must be shaped. Yet at first it would seem as if this vitalizing power has become so fertile that it cumbers the way and trips us up, even when we have need to go quickest, by putting some curious object enticingly in our way. We have to stop and look even against our will.

Thus, when his mother calls him to come to his grandmother's deathbed, the author says, ' "I was not asleep," I answered as I awoke'. Then, even in this crisis, he pauses to explain carefully and subtly why at that moment of waking we so often think for a second that we have not been to sleep. The pause, which is all the more marked because the reflection is not made by 'I' himself but is supplied impersonally by the narrator and therefore, from a different angle, lays a great strain upon the mind, stretched by the urgency of the situation to focus itself upon the dying woman in the next room.

Much of the difficulty of reading Proust comes from this content obliquity. In Proust, the accumulation of objects which surround any central point is so vast and they are often so remote, so difficult of approach and of apprehension that this drawing-together process is gradual, tortuous, and the final relation difficult in the extreme. There is so much more to think about them than one had supposed. One's relations are not only with another person but with the weather, food, clothes, smells, with art and religion and science and history and a thousand other influences.

If one begins to analyse consciousness, it will be found that it is stirred by thousands of small, irrelevant ideas stuffed with odds and ends of knowledge. When, therefore, we come to say something so usual as 'I kissed her', we may well have to explain also how a girl jumped over a man in a deck-chair on the beach before we come tortuously and gradually to the difficult process of describing what a kiss means. In any crisis, such as the death of the grandmother or that moment when the Duchess learns as she steps into her carriage that her old friend Swann is fatally ill, the number of emotions that compose each of these scenes is immensely larger, and they are themselves much more incongruous and difficult of relation than any other scene laid before us by a novelist.

Moreover, if we ask for help in finding our way, it does not come through any of the usual channels. We are never told, as the English novelists so frequently tell us, that one way is right and the other wrong. Every way is thrown open without reserve and without prejudice. Everything that can be felt can be said. The mind of Proust lies open with the sympathy of a poet and the detachment of a scientist to everything that it has the power to feel. Direction or emphasis, to be told that that is right, to be nudged and bidden to attend to that, would fall like a shadow on this profound luminosity and cut off some section of it from our view. The common stuff of the book is made of this deep reservoir of perception. It is from these depths that his characters rise, like waves forming, then break and sink again into the moving sea of thought and comment and analysis which gave them birth.

In retrospect, thus, though as dominant as any characters in fiction, the characters of Proust seem made of a different substance. Thoughts, dreams, knowledge are part of them. They have grown to their full stature, and their actions have met with no rebuff. If we look for direction to help us put them in their places in the universe, we find it negatively in an absence of direction— perhaps sympathy is of more value than interference, understanding than judgment. As a consequence of the union of the thinker and the poet, often, on the heel of some fanatically precise observation, we come upon a flight of imagery—beautiful, coloured, visual, as if the mind, having carried its powers as far as possible in analysis, suddenly rose in the air and from a station high up gave us a different view of the same object in terms of metaphor. This dual vision makes the great characters in Proust and the whole world from which they spring more like a globe, of which one side is always hidden, than a scene laid flat before us, the whole of which we can take in at one glance.

To make this more precise, it might be well to choose another writer, of foreign birth also, who has the same power of illuminating the consciousness from its roots to the surface. Directly we step from the world of Proust to the world of Dostoevsky, we are startled by differences which for a time absorb all our attention. How positive the Russian is, in comparison with the Frenchman. He strikes out a character or a scene by the use of glaring oppositions which are left unbridged. Extreme terms like 'love' and 'hate' are used so lavishly that we must race our imaginations to cover the ground between them. One feels that the mesh of civilization here is made of a coarse netting and the holes are wide apart. Men and women have escaped, compared with the imprisonment that they suffer in Paris. They are free to throw themselves from side to side, to gesticulate, to hiss, to rant, to fall into paroxysms of rage and excitement. They are free, with the freedom that violent emotion gives, from hesitation, from scruple, from analysis. At first we are amazed by the emptiness and the crudity of this world compared with the other. But when we have arranged our perspective a little, it is clear that we are still in the same world—that it is the mind which entices us and the adventures of the mind that concern us. Other worlds, such as Scott's or Defoe's, are incredible. Of this we are assured when we begin to encounter those curious contradictions of which Dostoevsky is so prolific. There is a simplicity in violence which we find nowhere in Proust, but violence also lays bare regions deep down in the mind where contradiction prevails. That contrast which marked Stavrogin's appearance, so that he was at once 'a paragon of beauty, yet at the same time there seemed something repellent about him', is but the crude outer sign of the vice and virtue we meet, at full tilt, in the same breast. The simplification is only on the surface; when the bold and ruthless process, which seems to punch out characters, then to group them together and then to set them all in violent motion, so energetically, so impatiently, is complete, we are shown how, beneath this crude surface, all is chaos and complication. We feel at first that we are in a savage society where the emotions are much simpler and stronger and more impressive than any we encounter in *A la Recherche du Temps perdu*.

Since there are so few conventions, so few barriers (Stavrogin, for instance, passes easily from the depths to the heights of society) the complexity would appear to lie deeper, and these strange contradictions and anomalies which make a man at once divine and bestial would seem to be deep in the heart and not superimposed. Hence, the strange, emotional effect of *The Possessed*. It appears to be written by a fanatic ready to sacrifice skill and artifice in order to reveal the soul's difficulties and confusions. The novels of Dostoevsky are pervaded with mysticism; he speaks not as a writer but as a sage, sitting by the roadside in a blanket, with infinite knowledge and infinite patience.

> 'Yes,' she answered, 'the mother of God is the great mother— the damp earth, and therein lies great joy for men. And every earthly woe and every earthly fear is a joy for us; and when you water the earth with your tears a foot deep, you will rejoice at everything at once, and your sorrow will be no more, such is the prophecy.' That word sank into my heart at the time. Since then when I bow down to the ground at my prayers, I've taken to kissing the earth. I kiss it and weep.

Such is a characteristic passage. But in a novel the voice of the teacher, however exalted, is not enough. We have too many interests to consider, too many problems to face. Consider a scene like that extraordinary party to which Varvara Petrovna has brought Marya, the lame idiot, whom Stavrogin has married 'from a passion for martyrdom, from a craving for remorse, through moral sensuality'. We cannot read to the end without feeling as if a thumb were pressing on a button in us, when we have no emotion left to answer the call. It is a day of surprises, a day of startling revelations, a day of strange coincidences. For several of the people there (and they come flocking to the room from all quarters) the scene has the greatest emotional importance. Everything is done to suggest the intensity of their emotions. They turn pale; they shake with terror; they go into hysterics. They are thus brought before us in flashes of extreme brilliance—the mad woman with the paper rose in her hat; the young man whose words patter out 'like smooth big grains. . . . One somehow began to imagine that he must have a tongue of special shape, somehow exceptionally long and thin, and extremely red, with a very sharp everlastingly active little tip.'

Yet though they stamp and scream, we hear the sound as if it went on next door. Perhaps the truth is that hate, surprise, anger, horror, are all too strong to be felt continuously. This emptiness and noise lead us to wonder whether the novel of psychology, which projects its drama in the mind, should not, as the truth-tellers showed us, vary and diversify its emotions, lest we shall become numb with exhaustion. To brush aside civilization and plunge into the depths of the soul is not really to enrich. We have, if we turn to Proust, more emotion in a scene which is not supposed to be remarkable, like that in the restaurant in the fog. There we live along a thread of observation which is always going in and out of this mind and that mind; which gathers information from different social levels, which makes us now feel with a prince, now with a restaurant keeper, and brings us into touch with different physical experiences such as light after darkness, safety after danger, so that the imagination is being stimulated on all sides to close slowly, gradually, without being goaded by screams or violence, completely round the object. Proust is determined to bring before the reader every piece of evidence upon which any state of mind is founded; so convinced is Dostoevsky of some point of truth that he sees before him, he will skip and leap to his conclusion with a spontaneity that is in itself stimulating.

By this distortion the psychologist reveals himself. The intellect, which analyses and discriminates, is always and almost at once overpowered by the rush to feeling; whether it is sympathy or anger. Hence, there is something illogical and contradictory often in the characters, perhaps because they are exposed to so much more than the usual current of emotional force. Why does he act like this? we ask again and again, and answer rather doubtfully, that so perhaps madmen act. In Proust, on the other hand, the approach is equally indirect, but it is through what people think and what is thought about them, through the knowledge and thoughts of the author himself, that we come to understand them very slowly and laboriously, but with the whole of our minds.

The books, however, with all these dissimilarities, are alike in this; both are permeated with unhappiness. And this would seem to be inevitable when the mind is not given a direct grasp of whatever it may be. Dickens is in many ways like Dostoevsky; he is prodigiously fertile and he has immense powers of caricature. But Micawber, David Copperfield, and Mrs. Gamp are placed directly before us, as if the author saw them from the same angle, and had nothing to do, and no conclusion to draw, except direct amusement or interest. The mind of the author is nothing but a glass between us, or, at most, serves to put a frame round them. All the author's emotional power has gone into them. The surplus of thought and feeling which remained after the characters had been created in George Eliot, to cloud and darken her page, has been used up in the characters of Dickens. Nothing of importance remains over.

But in Proust and Dostoevsky, in Henry James, too, and in all those who set themselves to follow feelings and thoughts, there is always an overflow of emotion from the author as if characters of such subtlety and complexity could be treated only when the rest of the book is a deep reservoir of thought and emotion. Thus, though the author himself is not present, characters like Stephen Trofimovitch and Charlus can exist only in a world made of the same stuff as they are, though left unformulated. The effect of

this brooding and analysing mind is always to produce an atmosphere of doubt, of questioning, of pain, perhaps of despair. At
least, such would seem to be the result of reading *A la Recherche
du Temps perdu* and *The Possessed*.

The Satirists and Fantastics

The confused feelings which the psychologists have roused in us,
the extraordinary intricacy which they have revealed to us, the
network of fine and scarcely intelligible yet profoundly interesting
emotions in which they have involved us, set up a craving for
relief, at first so primitive that it is almost a physical sensation.
The mind feels like a sponge saturated full with sympathy and
understanding; it needs to dry itself, to contract upon something
hard. Satire and the sense that the satirist gives us that he has the
world well within his grasp, so that it is at the mercy of his pen,
precisely fulfil our needs.

A further instinct will lead us to pass over such famous satirists
as Voltaire and Anatole France in favour of someone writing in
our own tongue, writing English. For without any disrespect to
the translator we have grown intolerably weary in reading
Dostoevsky, as if we were reading with the wrong spectacles or as
if a mist had formed between us and the page. We come to feel
that every idea is slipping about in a suit badly cut and many
sizes too large for it. For a translation makes us understand more
clearly than the lectures of any professor the difference between
raw words and written words; the nature and importance of what
we call style. Even an inferior writer, using his own tongue upon
his own ideas, works a change at once which is agreeable and remarkable. Under his pen the sentence shrinks and wraps itself
firmly round the meaning, if it be but a little one. The loose, the
baggy, shrivels up. And while a writer of passable English will do
this, a writer like Peacock does infinitely more.

When we open *Crotchet Castle* and read that first very long
sentence which begins, 'In one of those beautiful valleys, through
which the Thames (not yet polluted by the tide, the scouring of
cities or even the minor defilement of the sandy streams of
Surrey)', it would be difficult to describe the relief it gives us,
except metaphorically. First there is the shape which recalls something visually delightful, like a flowing wave or the lash of a whip

vigorously flung; then as phrase joins phrase and one parenthesis after another pours in its tributary, we have a sense of the whole swimming stream gliding beneath old walls with the shadows of ancient buildings and the glow of green lawns reflected in it. And what is even more delightful after the immensities and obscurities in which we have been living, we are in a world so manageable in scale that we can take its measure, tease it and ridicule it. It is like stepping out into the garden on a perfect September morning when every shadow is sharp and every colour bright after a night of storm and thunder. Nature has submitted to the direction of man. Man himself is dominated by his intelligence. Instead of being many-sided, complicated, elusive, people possess one idiosyncrasy apiece, which crystallizes them into sharp separate characters, colliding briskly when they meet. They seem ridiculously and grotesquely simplified out of all knowledge. Dr. Folliott, Mr. Firedamp, Mr. Skionar, Mr. Chainmail, and the rest seem after the tremendous thickness and bulk of the Guermantes and the Stavrogins nothing but agreeable caricatures which a clever old scholar has cut out of a sheet of black paper with a pair of scissors. But on looking closer we find that though it would be absurd to credit Peacock with any desire or perhaps capacity to explore the depths of the soul, his reticence is not empty but suggestive. The character of Dr. Folliott is drawn in three strokes of the pen. What lies between is left out. But each stroke indicates the mass behind it, so that the reader can make it out for himself; while it has, because of this apparent simplicity, all the sharpness of a carica-ture. The world so happily constituted that there is always trout for breakfast, wine in the cellar, and some amusing contretemps, such as the cook setting herself alight and being put out by the footman, to make us laugh—a world where there is nothing more pressing to do than to 'glide over the face of the waters, discussing everything and settling nothing', is not the world of pure fantasy; it is close enough to be a parody of our world and to make our own follies and the solemnities of our institutions look a little silly.

The satirist does not, like the psychologist, labour under the oppression of omniscience. He has leisure to play with his mind freely, ironically. His sympathies are not deeply engaged. His sense of humour is not submerged.

But the prime distinction lies in the changed attitude towards reality. In the psychologists the huge burden of facts is based upon a firm foundation of dinner, luncheon, bed, and breakfast. It is with surprise, yet with relief and a start of pleasure, that we accept Peacock's version of the world, which ignores so much, simplifies so much, gives the old globe a spin and shows another face of it on the other side. It is unnecessary to be quite so painstaking, it seems. And, after all, is not this quite as real, as true as the other? And perhaps all this pother about 'reality' is overdone. The great gain is perhaps that our relation with things is more distant. We reap the benefit of a more poetic point of view. A line like the charming 'At Godstow, they gathered hazel on the grave of Rosamond' could be written only by a writer who was at a certain distance from his people, so that there need be no explanations. For certainly with Trollope's people explanations would have been necessary; we should have wanted to know what they had been doing, gathering hazel, and where they had gone for dinner afterwards and how the carriage had met them. 'They', however, being Chainmail, Skionar, and the rest, are at liberty to gather hazel on the grave of Rosamond if they like; as they are free to sing a song if it so pleases them or to debate the march of mind.

The romantic took the same liberty but for another purpose. In the satirist we get not a sense of wildness and the soul's adventures, but that mind is free and therefore sees through and dispenses with much that is taken seriously by writers of another calibre.

There are, of course, limitations, reminders, even in the midst of our pleasure, of boundaries that we must not pass. We cannot imagine in the first place that the writer of such exquisite sentences can cover many reams of paper; they cost too much to make. Then again a writer who gives us so keen a sense of his own personality by the shape of his phrase is limited. We are always being brought into touch, not with Peacock himself, as with Trollope himself (for there is no giving away of his own secrets; he does not conjure up the very shape of himself and the sound of his laughter as Trollope does), but all the time our thought is taking the colour of his thought, we are insensibly thinking in his measure. If we write, we try to write in his manner, and this brings us into far greater intimacy with him than with writers like Trollope again or Scott, who wrap their thought up quite adequately in a duffle grey blanket which wears well and suits everything. This may in the end, of course, lead to some restriction. Style may carry with it, especially in prose, so much personality that it keeps us within the range of that personality. Peacock pervades his book.

In order that we may consider this more fully let us turn from Peacock to Sterne, a much greater writer, yet sufficiently in the family of Peacock to let us carry on the same train of thought uninterruptedly.

At once we are aware that we are in the presence of a much subtler mind, a mind of far greater reach and intensity. Peacock's sentences, firmly shaped and beautifully polished as they are, cannot stretch as these can. Here our sense of elasticity is increased so much that we scarcely know where we are. We lose our sense of direction. We go backwards instead of forwards. A simple statement starts a digression; we circle; we soar; we turn round; and at last back we come again to Uncle Toby who has been sitting meanwhile in his black plush breeches with his pipe in his hand. Proust, it may be said, was as tortuous, but his indirectness was due to his immense powers of analysis and to the fact that directly he had made a simple statement he perceived and must make us perceive all that it implied. Sterne is not an analyst of other people's sensations. Those remain simple, eccentric, erratic. It is his own mind that fascinates him, its oddities and its whims, its fancies and its sensibilities; and it is his own mind that colours the book and gives it walls and shape. Yet it is obvious that his claim is just when he says that however widely he may digress, to my Aunt Dinah and the coachman and then 'some millions of miles into the very heart of the planetary system', when he is by way of telling about Uncle Toby's character, still 'the drawing of my Uncle Toby's character went on gently all the time—not the great contours of it—that was impossible—but some familiar strokes and faint designations of it . . . so that you are much better acquainted with my Uncle Toby now than you were before'. It is true, for we are always alighting as we skim and circle to deposit some little grain of observation upon the figure of Uncle Toby sitting there with his pipe in his hand. There is thus built up intermittently, irregularly, an extraordinary portrait of a character—a character shown most often in a passive state, sitting still, through the quick glancing eyes of an erratic observer, who never lets his character speak more than a few words or take more than a few steps in his proper person, but is forever circling round and playing with the lapels of his coat and peering up into his face and teasing him affectionately, whimsically, as if he were the attendant sprite in charge of some unconscious mortal. Two such opposites were made to show each other off and draw each other out. One relishes the simplicity, the modesty, of Uncle Toby all the more for comparing them with the witty, indecent, disagreeable, yet highly sympathetic, character of the author.

All through *Tristram Shandy* we are aware of this blend and contrast. Laurence Sterne is the most important character in the book. It is true that at the critical moment the author obliterates himself and gives his characters that little extra push which frees them from his tutelage so that they are something more than the whims and fancies of a brilliant brain. But since character is largely made up of surroundings and circumstances, these people whose surroundings are so queer, who are often silent themselves but always so whimsically talked about, are a race apart among the people of fiction. There is nothing like them elsewhere, for in no other book are the characters so closely dependent on the author. In no other book are the writer and reader so involved together. So, finally, we get a book in which all the usual conventions are consumed and yet no ruin or catastrophe comes to pass; the whole subsists complete by itself, like a house which is miraculously habitable without the help of walls, staircases, or partitions. We live in the humours, contortions, and oddities of the spirit, not in the slow unrolling of the long length of life. And the reflection comes, as we sun ourselves on one of these high pinnacles, can we not escape even further, so that we are not conscious of any author at all? Can we not find poetry in some novel or other? For Sterne by the beauty of his style has let us pass beyond the range of personality into a world which is not altogether the world of fiction. It is above.

The Poets

Certain phrases have brought about this change in us. They have raised us out of the atmosphere of fiction; they have made us pause to wonder. For instance:

> I will not argue the matter; Time wastes too fast: every letter I trace tells me with what rapidity Life follows my pen; the days and hours of it more precious,—my dear Jenny—than the rubies about thy neck, are flying over our heads like light clouds of a windy day, never to return more; everything presses on,—whilst thou art twisting that lock;—see! it grows grey; and every time I kiss thy hand to bid adieu, and every absence which follows it, are preludes to that eternal separation which we are shortly to make.

Phrases like this bring, by the curious rhythm of their phrasing, by a touch on the visual sense, an alteration in the movement of the mind which makes it pause and widen its gaze and slightly change its attention. We are looking out at life in general.

But though Sterne with his extraordinary elasticity could use this effect, too, without incongruity, that is only possible because his genius is rich enough to let him sacrifice some of the qualities that are native to the character of the novel without our feeling it. It is obvious that there is no massing together of the experiences of many lives and many minds as in *War and Peace*; and, too, that there is something of the essayist, something of the soliloquist in the quips and quirks of this brilliant mind. He is sometimes sentimental, as if after so great a display of singularity he must assert his interest in the normal lives and affections of his people. Tears are necessary; tears are pumped up. Be that as it may, exquisite and individual as his poetry is, there is another poetry which is more natural to the novel, because it uses the material which the novelist provides. It is the poetry of situation rather than of language, the poetry which we perceive when Catherine in *Wuthering Heights* pulls the feathers from the pillow; when Natasha in *War and Peace* looks out of the window at the stars. And it is significant that we recall this poetry, not as we recall it in verse, by the words, but by the scene. The prose remains casual and quiet enough so that to quote it is to do little or nothing to explain its effect. Often we have to go farther back and read a chapter or more before we can come by the impression of beauty or intensity that possessed us.

Yet it is not to be denied that two of the novelists who are most frequently poetical—Meredith and Hardy—are as novelists imperfect. Both *The Ordeal of Richard Feverel* and *Far from the Madding Crowd* are books of great inequality. In both we feel a lack of control, an incoherence such as we never feel in *War and Peace* or in *A la Recherche du Temps perdu* or in *Pride and Prejudice*. Both Hardy and Meredith are too fully charged, it would seem, with a sense of poetry and have too limited or too imperfect a sympathy with human beings to express it adequately through that channel. Hence, as we so often find in Hardy, the impersonal element— Fate, the Gods, whatever name we choose to call it—dominates the people. They appear wooden, melodramatic, unreal. They cannot express the poetry with which the writer himself is charged through their own lips, for their psychology is inadequate, and thus the expression is left to the writer, who assumes a character apart from his people and cannot return to them with perfect ease when the time comes.

Again, in Meredith the writer's sense of the poetry of youth, of love, of nature is heard like a song to which the characters listen passively without moving a muscle; and then, when the song is done, on they move again with a jerk. This would seem to prove that a profound poetic sense is a dangerous gift for the novelist; for in Hardy and Meredith poetry seems to mean something impersonal, generalized, hostile to the idiosyncrasy of character, so that the two suffer if brought into touch. It may be that the perfect novelist expresses a different sort of poetry, or has the power of expressing it in a manner which is not harmful to the other qualities of the novel. If we recall the passages that have seemed to us, in retrospect at any rate, to be poetical in fiction we remember them as part of the novel. When Natasha in *War and Peace* looks out of the window at the stars, Tolstoy produces a feeling of deep and intense poetry without disruption or that disquieting sense of song being sung to people who listen. He does this because his poetic sense finds expression in the poetry of the situation or because his characters express it in their own words, which are often of the simplest. We have been living in them and knowing them, so that, when Natasha leans on the window sill and thinks of her life to come, our feelings of the poetry of the moment do not lie in what she says so much as in our sense of her who is saying it.

Wuthering Heights again is steeped in poetry. But here there is a difference, for one can hardly say that the profound poetry of the scene where Catherine pulls the feathers from the pillow has anything to do with our knowledge of her or adds to our understanding or our feeling about her future. Rather it deepens and controls the wild, stormy atmosphere of the whole book. By a master stroke of vision, rarer in prose than in poetry, people and scenery and atmosphere are all in keeping. And, what is still rarer and more impressive, through that atmosphere we seem to catch sight of larger men and women, of other symbols and significances. Yet the characters of Heathcliff and Catherine are perfectly natural; they contain all the poetry that Emily Brontë herself feels without effort. We never feel that this is a poetic moment, apart from the rest, or that here Emily Brontë is speaking to us through her characters. Her emotion has not overflowed and risen up independently, in some comment or attitude of her own. She is using her characters to express her conception, so that her people are active agents in the book's life, adding to its impetus and not impeding it. The same thing happens, more explicitly but with less concentration, in *Moby Dick*. In both books we get a vision of presence outside the human beings, of a meaning that they stand for, without ceasing to be themselves. But it is notable that both Emily Brontë and Herman Melville ignore the greater part of those spoils of the modern spirit which Proust grasps so tenaciously and transforms so triumphantly. Both the earlier writers simplify their characters till only the great contour, the clefts and ridges of the face, are visible. Both seem to have been content with the novel as their form and with prose as their instrument provided that they could remove the scene far from towns, simplify the actors and allow nature at her wildest to take part in the scene. Thus we can say that there is poetry in novels both where the poetry is expressed not so much by the particular character in a particular situation, like Natasha in the window, but rather by the whole mood and temper of the book, like the mood and temper of *Wuthering Heights* or *Moby Dick* to which the characters of Catherine or Heathcliff or Captain Ahab give expression.

In *A la Recherche du Temps perdu*, however, there is as much poetry as in any of these books; but it is poetry of a different kind. The analysis of emotion is carried further by Proust than by any other novelist; and the poetry comes, not in the situation, which is too fretted and voluminous for such an effect, but in those frequent passages of elaborate metaphor, which spring out of the rock of thought like fountains of sweet water and serve as translations from one language into another. It is as though there were two faces to every situation; one full in the light so that it can be described as accurately and examined as minutely as possible; the other half in shadow so that it can be described only in a moment of faith and vision by the use of metaphor. The longer the novelist pores over the analysis, the more he becomes conscious of something that forever escapes. And it is this double vision that makes the work of Proust to us in our generation so spherical, so comprehensive. Thus, while Emily Brontë and Herman Melville turn the novel away from shore out to sea, Proust on the other hand rivets his eyes on men.

And here we may pause, not, certainly, that there are no more books to read or no more changes of mood to satisfy, but for a reason which springs from the youth and vigour of the art itself. We can imagine so many different sorts of novels, we are conscious of so many relations and susceptibilities the novelist has not expressed that we break off in the middle with Emily Brontë or with Tolstoy without any pretence that the phases of fiction are complete or that our desires as a reader have received full satisfaction. On the contrary, reading excites them; they well up and make us inarticulately aware of a dozen different novels that wait just below the horizon unwritten. Hence the futility at present of any theory of 'the future of fiction'. The next ten years will certainly upset it; the next century will blow it to the winds. We have only to remember the comparative youth of the novel, that it is, roughly speaking, about the age of English poetry in the time of Shakespeare, to realize the folly of any summary, or theory of the future of the art. Moreover, prose itself is still in its infancy, and capable, no doubt, of infinite change and development.

But our rapid journey from book to book has left us with some notes made by the way and these we may sort out, not so much to seek a conclusion as to express the brooding, the meditative mood which follows the activity of reading. So then, in the first place, even though the time at our disposal has been short, we have travelled, in reading these few books, a great distance emotionally. We have plodded soberly along the high road talking plain sense and meeting many interesting adventures; turning romantic, we have lived in castles and been hunted on moors and fought gallantly and died; then tired of this, we have come into touch with humanity again, at first romantically prodigiously, enjoying the society of giants and dwarfs, the huge and the deformed, and then again tiring of this extravagance, have reduced them, by means of Jane Austen's microscope, to perfectly proportioned and normal men and women and the chaotic world to English parsonage, shrubberies, and lawns.

But a shadow next falls upon that bright prospect, distorting the lovely harmony of its proportions. The shadow of our own minds has fallen upon it and gradually we have drawn within, and gone exploring with Henry James endless filaments of feeling and relationship in which men and women are enmeshed, and so we have been led on with Dostoevsky to descend miles and miles into the deep and yeasty surges of the soul.

At last Proust brings the light of an immensely civilized and saturated intelligence to bear upon this chaos and reveals the infinite range and complexity of human sensibility. But in following him we lose the sense of outline, and to recover it seek out the satirists and the fantastics, who stand aloof and hold the world at a distance and eliminate and reduce so that we have the satisfaction of seeing round things after being immersed in them. And the satirists and the fantastics, like Peacock and Sterne, because of their detachment, write often as poets write, for the sake of the beauty of the sentence and not for the sake of its use, and so stimulate us to wish for poetry in the novel. Poetry, it would seem, requires a different ordering of the scene; human beings are needed, but needed in their relation to love, or death, or nature rather than to each other. For this reason their psychology is simplified, as it is both in Meredith and Hardy, and instead of feeling the intricacy of life, we feel its passion, its tragedy. In *Wuthering Heights* and in *Moby Dick* this simplification, far from being empty, has greatness, and we feel that something beyond, which is not human yet does not destroy their humanity or the actions. So, briefly, we may sum up our impressions. Brief and fragmentary as they are, we have gained some sense of the vastness of fiction and the width of its range.

As we look back it seems that the novelist can do anything.

There is room in a novel for story-telling, for comedy, for tragedy, for criticism and information and philosophy and poetry. Something of its appeal lies in the width of its scope and the satisfaction it offers to so many different moods, desires, and instincts on the part of the reader. But however the novelist may vary his scene and alter the relations of one thing to another—and as we look back we see the whole world in perpetual transformation—one element remains constant in all novels, and that is the human element; they are about people, they excite in us the feelings that people excite in us in real life. The novel is the only form of art which seeks to make us believe that it is giving a full and truthful record of the life of a real person. And in order to give that full record of life, not the climax and the crisis but the growth and development of feelings, which is the novelist's aim, he copies the order of the day, observes the sequence of ordinary things even if such fidelity entails chapters of description and hours of research. Thus we glide into the novel with far less effort and less break with our surroundings than into any other form of imaginative literature. We seem to be continuing to live, only in another house or country perhaps. Our most habitual and natural sympathies are roused with the first words; we feel them expand and contract, in liking or disliking, hope or fear on every page. We watch the character and behaviour of Becky Sharp or Richard Feverel and instinctively come to an opinion about them as about real people, tacitly accepting this or that impression, judging each motive, and forming the opinion that they are charming but insincere, good or dull, secretive but interesting, as we make up our minds about the characters of the people we meet.

This engaging lack of artifice and the strength of the emotion that he is able to excite are great advantages to the novelist, but they are also great dangers. For it is inevitable that the reader who is invited to live in novels as in life should go on feeling as he feels in life. Novel and life are laid side by side. We want happiness for the character we like, punishment for those we dislike. We have secret sympathies for those who seem to resemble us. It is difficult to admit that the book may have merit if it outrages our sympathies, or describes a life which seems unreal to us. Again we are acutely aware of the novelist's character and speculate upon his life and adventures. These personal standards extend

99

in every direction, for every sort of prejudice, every sort of vanity, can be snubbed or soothed by the novelist. Indeed the enormous growth of the psychological novel in our time has been prompted largely by the mistaken belief, which the reader has imposed upon the novelist, that truth is always good; even when it is the truth of the psychoanalyst and not the truth of imagination.

Such vanities and emotions on the part of the reader are perpetually forcing the novelist to gratify them. And the result, though it may give the novel a short life of extreme vigour, is, as we know even while we are enjoying the tears and laughs and excitement of that life, fatal to its endurance. For the accuracy of representation, the looseness and simplicity of its method, its denial of artifice and convention, its immense power to imitate the surface reality—all the qualities that make a novel the most popular form of literature—also make it, even as we read it, turn stale and perish on our hands. Already some of the 'great novels' of the past, like *Robert Elsmere* or *Uncle Tom's Cabin,* are perished except in patches because they were originally bolstered up with so much that had virtue and vividness only for those who lived at the moment that the books were written. Directly manners change, or the contemporary idiom alters, page after page, chapter after chapter, become obsolete and lifeless.

But the novelist is aware of this too and, while he uses the power of exciting human sympathy which belongs to him, he also attempts to control it. Indeed the first sign that we are reading a writer of merit is that we feel this control at work on us. The barrier between us and the book is raised higher. We do not slip so instinctively and so easily into a world that we know already. We feel that we are being compelled to accept an order and to arrange the elements of the novel—man, nature, God—in certain relations at the novelist's bidding. In looking back at the few novels that we have glanced at here we can see how astonishingly we lend ourselves to first one vision and then to another which is its opposite. We obliterate a whole universe at the command of Defoe; we see every blade of grass and snail shell at the command of Proust. From the first page we feel our minds trained upon a point which becomes more and more perceptible as the book proceeds and the writer brings his conception out of darkness. At last the whole is exposed to view. And then, when the book is finished, we seem to see (it is strange how visual the impression is) something girding it about like the firm road of Defoe's storytelling; or we see it shaped and symmetrical with dome and column complete, like *Pride and Prejudice* and *Emma*. A power which is not the power of accuracy or of humour or of pathos is also used by the great novelists to shape their work. As the pages are turned, something is built up which is not the story itself. And this power, if it accentuates and concentrates and gives the fluidity of the novel endurance and strength, so that no novel can survive even a few years without it, is also a danger. For the most characteristic qualities of the novel —that it registers the slow growth and development of feeling, that it follows many lives and traces their unions and fortunes over a long stretch of time—are the very qualities that are most incompatible with design and order. It is the gift of style, arrangement, construction, to put us at a distance from the special life and to obliterate its features; while it is the gift of the novel to bring us into close touch with life. The two powers fight if they are brought into combination. The most complete novelist must be the novelist who can balance the two powers so that the one enhances the other.

This would seem to prove that the novel is by its nature doomed to compromise, wedded to mediocrity. Its province, one may conclude, is to deal with the commoner but weaker emotions; to express the bulk and not the essence of life. But any such verdict must be based upon the supposition that 'the novel' has a certain character which is now fixed and cannot be altered, that 'life' has a certain limit which can be defined. And it is precisely this conclusion that the novels we have been reading tend to upset.

The process of discovery goes on perpetually. Always more of life is being reclaimed and recognized. Therefore, to fix the character of the novel, which is the youngest and most vigorous of the arts, at this moment would be like fixing the character of poetry in the eighteenth century and saying that because Gray's *Elegy* was 'poetry' *Don Juan* was impossible. An art practised by hosts of people, sheltering diverse minds, is also bound to be simmering, volatile, unstable. And for some reason not here to be examined, fiction is the most hospitable of hosts; fiction today draws to itself writers who would even yesterday have been poets, dramatists, pamphleteers, historians. Thus 'the novel', as we still call it with such parsimony of language, is clearly splitting apart into books which have nothing in common but this one inadequate title. Already the novelists·are so far apart that they scarcely communicate, and to one novelist the work of another is quite genuinely unintelligible or quite genuinely negligible.

The most significant proof of this fertility, however, is provided by our sense of feeling something that has not yet been said; of some desire still unsatisfied. A very general, a very elementary, view of this desire would seem to show that it points in two directions. Life—it is a commonplace—is growing more complex. Our self-consciousness is becoming far more alert and better trained. We are aware of relations and subtleties which have not yet been explored. Of this school Proust is the pioneer, and undoubtedly there are still to be born writers who will carry the analysis of Henry James still further, who will reveal and relate finer threads of feeling, stranger and more obscure imaginations.

But also we desire synthesis. The novel, it is agreed, can follow life; it can amass details. But can it also select? Can it symbolize? Can it give us an epitome as well as an inventory? It was some such function as this that poetry discharged in the past. But, whether for the moment or for some longer time, poetry with her rhythms, her poetic diction, her strong flavour of tradition, is too far from us today to do for us what she did for our parents. Prose perhaps is the instrument best fitted to the complexity and difficulty of modern life. And prose—we have to repeat it—is still so youthful that we scarcely know what powers it may not hold concealed within it. Thus it is possible that the novel in time to come may differ as widely from the novel of Tolstoy and Jane Austen as the poetry of Browning and Byron differs from the poetry of Lydgate and Spenser. In time to come—but time to come lies far beyond our province.

Modern Fiction

IN making any survey, even the freest and loosest, of modern fiction, it is difficult not to take it for granted that the modern practice of the art is somehow an improvement upon the old. With their simple tools and primitive materials, it might be said, Fielding did well and Jane Austen even better, but compare their opportunities with ours! Their masterpieces certainly have a strange air of simplicity. And yet the analogy between literature and the process, to choose an example, of making motor cars scarcely holds good beyond the first glance. It is doubtful whether in the course of the centuries, though we have learnt much about making machines, we have learnt anything about making literature. We do not come to write better; all that we can be said to do is to keep moving, now a little in this direction, now in that, but with a circular tendency should the whole course of the track be viewed from a sufficiently lofty pinnacle. It need scarcely be said that we make no claim to stand, even momentarily, upon that vantage-ground. On the flat, in the crowd, half blind with dust, we look back with envy to those happier warriors, whose battle is won and whose achievements wear so serene an air of accomplishment that we can scarcely refrain from whispering that the fight was not so fierce for them as for us. It is for the historian of literature to decide; for him to say if we are now beginning or ending or standing in the middle of a great period of prose fiction, for down in the plain little is visible. We only know that certain gratitudes and hostilities inspire us; that certain paths seem to lead to fertile land, others to the dust and the desert; and of this perhaps it may be worth while to attempt some account.

Our quarrel, then, is not with the classics, and if we speak of quarrelling with Mr. Wells, Mr. Bennett, and Mr. Galsworthy, it is partly that by the mere fact of their existence in the flesh their work has a living, breathing, everyday imperfection which bids us take what liberties with it we choose. But it is also true that, while we thank them for a thousand gifts, we reserve our unconditional gratitude for Mr. Hardy, for Mr. Conrad, and in much lesser degree for the Mr. Hudson of *The Purple Land, Green Mansions,* and *Far Away and Long Ago.* Mr. Wells, Mr. Bennett, and Mr. Galsworthy have excited so many hopes and disappointed them so persistently that our gratitude largely takes the form of thanking them for having shown us what they might have done but have not done; what we certainly could not do, but as certainly, perhaps, do not wish to do. No single phrase will sum up the charge or grievance which we have to bring against a mass of work so large in its volume and embodying so many qualities, both admirable and the reverse. If we tried to formulate our meaning in one word we should say that these three writers are materialists. It is because they are concerned not with the spirit but with the body that they have disappointed us, and left us with the feeling that the sooner English fiction turns its back upon them, as politely as may be, and marches, if only into the desert, the better for its soul. Naturally, no single word reaches the centre of three separate targets. In the case of Mr. Wells it falls notably wide of the mark. And yet even with him it indicates to our thinking the fatal alloy in his genius, the great clod of clay that has got itself mixed up with the purity of his inspiration. But Mr. Bennett is perhaps the worst culprit of the three, inasmuch as he is by far the best workman. He can make a book so well constructed and solid in its craftsmanship that it is difficult for the most exacting of critics to see through what chink or crevice decay can creep in. There is not so much as a draught between the frames of the windows, or a crack in the boards. And yet—if life should refuse to live there? That is a risk which the creator of *The Old Wives' Tale,* George Cannon, Edwin Clayhanger, and hosts of other figures, may well claim to have surmounted. His characters live abundantly, even unexpectedly, but it remains to ask how do they live, and what do they live for? More and more they seem to us, deserting even the well-built villa in the Five Towns, to spend their time in some softly padded first-class railway carriage, pressing bells and buttons innumerable; and the destiny to which they travel so luxuriously becomes more and more unquestionably an eternity of bliss spent in the very best hotel in Brighton. It can scarcely be said of Mr. Wells that he is a materialist in the sense that he takes too much delight in the solidity of his fabric. His mind is too generous in its sympathies to allow him to spend much time in making things shipshape and substantial. He is a materialist from sheer goodness of heart, taking upon his shoulders the work that ought to have been discharged by Government officials, and in the plethora of his ideas and facts scarcely having leisure to realize, or forgetting to think important, the crudity and coarseness of his human beings. Yet what more damaging criticism can there be both of his earth and of his Heaven than that they are to be inhabited here and hereafter by his Joans and his Peters? Does not the inferiority of their natures tarnish whatever institutions and ideals may be provided for them by the generosity of their creator? Nor, profoundly though we respect the integrity and humanity of Mr. Galsworthy, shall we find what we seek in his pages.

If we fasten, then, one label on all these books, on which is one word, materialists, we mean by it that they write of unimportant things; that they spend immense skill and immense industry making the trivial and the transitory appear the true and the enduring.

We have to admit that we are exacting, and, further, that we find it difficult to justify our discontent by explaining what it is that we exact. We frame our question differently at different times. But it reappears most persistently as we drop the finished novel on the crest of a sigh—Is it worth while? What is the point of it all? Can it be that, owing to one of those little deviations which the human spirit seems to make from time to time, Mr. Bennett has come down with his magnificent apparatus for catching life just an inch or two on the wrong side? Life escapes; and perhaps without life nothing else is worth while. It is a confession of vagueness to have to make use of such a figure as this, but we scarcely better the matter by speaking, as critics are prone to do, of reality. Admitting the vagueness which afflicts all criticism of novels, let us hazard the opinion that for us at this moment the form of fiction most in vogue more often misses than secures the thing we seek. Whether we call it life or spirit, truth or reality, this, the essential thing, has moved off, or on, and refuses to be contained any longer in such ill-fitting vestments as we provide. Nevertheless, we go on perseveringly, conscientiously, constructing our two and thirty chapters after a design which more and more ceases to resemble the vision in our minds. So much of the enormous labour of proving the solidity, the likeness to life, of the story is not merely labour thrown away but labour misplaced to the extent of obscuring and blotting out the light of the conception. The writer seems constrained, not by his own free will but by some powerful and unscrupulous tyrant who has him in thrall, to provide a plot, to provide comedy, tragedy, love interest, and an air of probability embalming the whole so impeccable that if all his figures were to come to life they would find themselves dressed down to the last button of their coats in the fashion of the hour. The tyrant is obeyed; the novel is done to a turn. But sometimes, more and more often as time goes by, we suspect a momentary doubt, a spasm of rebellion, as the pages fill themselves in the customary way. Is life like this? Must novels be like this?

Look within and life, it seems, is very far from being 'like this'. Examine for a moment an ordinary mind on an ordinary day. The mind receives a myriad impressions—trivial, fantastic, evanescent, or engraved with the sharpness of steel. From all sides they come, an incessant shower of innumerable atoms; and as they fall, as they shape themselves into the life of Monday or Tuesday, the accent falls differently from of old; the moment of importance came not here but there; so that, if a writer were a free man and not a slave, if he could write what he chose, not what he must, if he could base his work upon his own feeling and not upon convention, there would be no plot, no comedy, no tragedy, no love interest or catastrophe in the accepted style, and perhaps not a single button sewn on as the Bond Street tailors would have it. Life is not a series of gig-lamps symmetrically arranged; life is a luminous halo, a semi-transparent envelope surrounding us from the beginning of consciousness to the end. Is it not the task of the novelist to convey this varying, this unknown and uncircumscribed spirit, whatever aberration or complexity it may display, with as little mixture of the alien and external as possible? We are not pleading merely for courage and sincerity; we are suggesting that the proper stuff of fiction is a little other than custom would have us believe it.

It is, at any rate, in some such fashion as this that we seek to define the quality which distinguishes the work of several young writers, among whom Mr. James Joyce is the most notable, from that of their predecessors. They attempt to come closer to life, and to preserve more sincerely and exactly what interests and moves them, even if to do so they must discard most of the conventions which are commonly observed by the novelist. Let us record the atoms as they fall upon the mind in the order in which they fall, let us trace the pattern, however disconnected and incoherent in appearance, which each sight or incident scores upon the consciousness. Let us not take it for granted that life exists more fully in what is commonly thought big than in what is commonly thought small. Anyone who has read *A Portrait of the Artist as a Young Man* or, what promises to be a far more interesting work, *Ulysses*, now appearing[1] in the *Little Review*, will have hazarded some theory of this nature as to Mr. Joyce's intention. On our part, with such a fragment before us, it is hazarded rather than affirmed; but whatever the intention of the whole, there can be no question but that it is of the utmost sincerity and that the result, difficult or unpleasant as we may judge it, is undeniably important. In contrast with those whom we have called materialists, Mr. Joyce is spiritual; he is concerned at all costs to reveal the flickerings of that innermost flame which flashes its messages through the brain, and in order to preserve it he disregards with complete courage whatever seems to him adventitious, whether it be probability, or coherence, or any other of these signposts which for generations have served to support the imagination of a reader when called upon to imagine what he can neither touch nor see. The scene in the cemetery, for instance, with its brilliancy, its sordidity, its incoherence, its sudden lightning flashes of significance, does undoubtedly come so close to the quick of the mind that, on a first reading at any rate, it is difficult not to acclaim a masterpiece. If we want life itself, here surely we have it. Indeed, we find ourselves fumbling rather awkwardly if we try to say what else we wish, and for what reason a work of such originality yet fails to compare, for we must take high examples, with *Youth* or *The Mayor of Casterbridge*. It fails because of the comparative poverty of the writer's mind, we might say simply and have done with it. But it is possible to press a little further and wonder whether we may not refer our sense of being in a bright yet

---

[1] Written April 1919

narrow room, confined and shut in, rather than enlarged and set free, to some limitation imposed by the method as well as by the mind. Is it the method that inhibits the creative power? Is it due to the method that we feel neither jovial nor magnanimous, but centred in a self which, in spite of its tremor of susceptibility, never embraces or creates what is outside itself and beyond? Does the emphasis laid, perhaps didactically, upon indecency contribute to the effect of something angular and isolated? Or is it merely that in any effort of such originality it is much easier, for contemporaries especially, to feel what it lacks than to name what it gives? In any case it is a mistake to stand outside examining 'methods'. Any method is right, every method is right, that expresses what we wish to express, if we are writers; that brings us closer to the novelist's intention if we are readers. This method has the merit of bringing us closer to what we were prepared to call life itself; did not the reading of *Ulysses* suggest how much of life is excluded or ignored, and did it not come with a shock to open *Tristram Shandy* or even *Pendennis* and be by them convinced that there are not only other aspects of life, but more important ones into the bargain.

However this may be, the problem before the novelist at present, as we suppose it to have been in the past, is to contrive means of being free to set down what he chooses. He has to have the courage to say that what interests him is no longer 'this' but 'that': out of 'that' alone must he construct his work. For the moderns 'that', the point of interest, lies very likely in the dark places of psychology. At once, therefore, the accent falls a little differently; the emphasis is upon something hitherto ignored; at once a different outline of form becomes necessary, difficult for us to grasp, incomprehensible to our predecessors. No one but a modern, no one perhaps but a Russian, would have felt the interest of the situation which Tchekov has made into the short story which he calls 'Gusev'. Some Russian soldiers lie ill on board a ship which is taking them back to Russia. We are given a few scraps of their talk and some of their thoughts; then one of them dies and is carried away; the talk goes on among the others for a time, until Gusev himself dies, and looking 'like a carrot or a radish' is thrown overboard. The emphasis is laid upon such unexpected places that at first it seems as if there were no emphasis at all; and then, as the eyes accustom themselves to twilight and discern the shapes of things in a room we see how complete the story is, how profound, and how truly in obedience to his vision Tchekov has chosen this, that, and the other, and placed them together to compose something new. But it is impossible to say 'this is comic', or 'that is tragic', nor are we certain, since short stories, we have been taught, should be brief and conclusive, whether this, which is vague and inconclusive, should be called a short story at all.

The most elementary remarks upon modern English fiction can hardly avoid some mention of the Russian influence, and if the Russians are mentioned one runs the risk of feeling that to write of any fiction save theirs is waste of time. If we want understanding of the soul and heart where else shall we find it of comparable profundity? If we are sick of our own materialism the least considerable of their novelists has by right of birth a natural reverence for the human spirit. 'Learn to make yourself akin to people. . . . But let this sympathy be not with the mind—for it is easy with the mind—but with the heart, with love towards them.' In every great Russian writer we seem to discern the features of a saint, if sympathy for the sufferings of others, love towards them, endeavour to reach some goal worthy of the most exacting demands of the spirit constitute saintliness. It is the saint in them which confounds us with a feeling of our own irreligious triviality, and turns so many of our famous novels to tinsel and trickery. The conclusions of the Russian mind, thus comprehensive and compassionate, are inevitably, perhaps, of the utmost sadness. More accurately indeed we might speak of the inconclusiveness of the Russian mind. It is the sense that there is no answer, that if honestly examined life presents question after question which must be left to sound on and on after the story is over in hopeless interrogation that fills us with a deep, and finally it may be with a resentful, despair. They are right perhaps; unquestionably they see further than we do and without our gross impediments of vision. But perhaps we see something that escapes them, or why should this voice of protest mix itself with our gloom? The voice of protest is the voice of another and an ancient civilization which seems to have bred in us the instinct to enjoy and fight rather than to suffer and understand. English fiction from Sterne to

Meredith bears witness to our natural delight in humour and comedy, in the beauty of earth, in the activities of the intellect, and in the splendour of the body. But any deductions that we may draw from the comparison of two fictions so immeasurably far apart are futile save indeed as they flood us with a view of the infinite possibilities of the art and remind us that there is no limit to the horizon, and that nothing—no 'method', no experiment, even of the wildest—is forbidden, but only falsity and pretence. 'The proper stuff of fiction' does not exist; everything is the proper stuff of fiction, every feeling, every thought; every quality of brain and spirit is drawn upon; no perception comes amiss. And if we can imagine the art of fiction come alive and standing in our midst, she would undoubtedly bid us break her and bully her, as well as honour and love her, for so her youth is renewed and her sovereignty assured.

American Fiction[1]

EXCURSIONS into the literature of a foreign country much resemble our travels abroad. Sights that are taken for granted by the inhabitants seem to us astonishing; however well we seemed to know the language at home, it sounds differently on the lips of those who have spoken it from birth; and above all, in our desire to get at the heart of the country we seek out whatever it may be that is most unlike what we are used to, and, declaring this to be the very essence of the French or American genius, proceed to lavish upon it a credulous devotion, to build up upon it a structure of theory which may well amuse, annoy, or even momentarily enlighten those who are French or American by birth.

The English tourist in American literature wants above all things something different from what he has at home. For this reason the one American writer whom the English wholeheartedly admire is Walt Whitman. There, you will hear them say, is the real American undisguised. In the whole of English literature there is no figure which resembles his—among all our poetry none in the least comparable to *Leaves of Grass*. This very unlikeness becomes a merit, and leads us, as we steep ourselves in the refreshing unfamiliarity, to become less and less able to appreciate Emerson, Lowell, Hawthorne, who have had their counterparts among us and drew their culture from our books. The obsession, whether well or ill founded, fair or unfair in its results, persists at the present moment. To dismiss such distinguished names as those of Henry James, Mr. Hergesheimer, and Mrs. Wharton would be impossible; but their praises are qualified with the reservation—they are not Americans; they do not give us anything that we have not got already.

Thus having qualified the tourist's attitude, in its crudity and onesidedness, let us begin our excursion into modern American fiction by asking what are the sights we ought to see. Here our bewilderment begins; for the names of so many authors, the titles

---

[1] Written in 1925

of so many books, rise at once to the lips. Mr. Dreiser, Mr. Cabell, Miss Canfield, Mr. Sherwood Anderson, Miss Hurst, Mr. Sinclair Lewis, Miss Willa Cather, Mr. Ring Lardner—all have done work which, if time allowed, we should do well to examine carefully, and, if we must concentrate upon two or three at most, it is because, travellers and tourists as we are, it seems best to sketch a theory of the tendency of American fiction from the inspection of a few important books rather than to examine each writer separately by himself. Of all American novelists the most discussed and read in England at the present moment are probably Mr. Sherwood Anderson and Mr. Sinclair Lewis. And among all their fiction we find one volume, *A Story Teller's Story*, which, being fact rather than fiction, may serve as interpreter, may help us to guess the nature of American writers' problems before we see them tussled with or solved. Peering over Mr. Sherwood Anderson's shoulder, we may get a preliminary view of the world as it looks to the novelist before it is disguised and arranged for the reception of his characters. Indeed, if we look over Mr. Anderson's shoulder, America appears a very strange place. What is it that we see here? A vast continent, scattered here and there with brand new villages which nature has not absorbed into herself with ivy and moss, summer and winter, as in England, but man has built recently, hastily, economically, so that the village is like the suburb of a town. The slow English wagons are turned into Ford cars; the primrose banks have become heaps of old tins; the barns sheds of corrugated iron. It is cheap, it is new, it is ugly, it is made of odds and ends, hurriedly flung together, loosely tied in temporary cohesion—that is the burden of Mr. Anderson's complaint. And, he proceeds to ask, how can the imagination of an artist take root here, where the soil is stony and the imagination stubs itself upon the rocks? There is one solution and one only—by being resolutely and defiantly American. Explicitly and implicitly that is the conclusion he reaches; that is the note which turns the discord to harmony. Mr. Anderson is for ever repeating over and over like a patient hypnotising himself, 'I am the American man'. The words rise in his mind with the persistency of a submerged but fundamental desire. Yes, he is the American man; it is a terrible misfortune; it is an enormous opportunity; but for good or for bad, he is the American man. 'Behold in me the American man striving to become an artist, to become conscious of himself, filled with wonder concerning himself and others, trying to have a good time and not fake a good time. I am not English, Italian, Jew, German, Frenchman, Russian. What am I?' Yes, we may be excused for repeating, what is he? One thing is certain—whatever the American man may be, he is not English; whatever he may become, he will not become an Englishman.

For that is the first step in the process of being American—to be not English. The first step in the education of an American writer is to dismiss the whole army of English words which have marched so long under the command of dead English generals. He must tame and compel to his service the 'little American words'; he must forget all that he learnt in the school of Fielding and Thackeray; he must learn to write as he talks to men in Chicago barrooms, to men in the factories of Indiana. That is the first step; but the next step is far more difficult. For having decided what he is not, he must proceed to discover what he is. This is the beginning of a stage of acute self-consciousness which manifests itself in writers otherwise poles asunder. Nothing, indeed, surprises the English tourist more than the prevalence of this self-consciousness and the bitterness, for the most part against England, with which it is accompanied. One is reminded constantly of the attitude of another race, till lately subject and still galled by the memory of its chains. Women writers have to meet many of the same problems that beset Americans. They too are conscious of their own peculiarities as a sex; apt to suspect insolence, quick to avenge grievances, eager to shape an art of their own. In both cases all kinds of consciousness—consciousness of self, of race, of sex, of civilization—which have nothing to do with art, have got between them and the paper, with results that are, on the surface at least, unfortunate. It is easy enough to see that Mr. Anderson, for example, would be a much more perfect artist if he could forget that he is an American; he would write better prose if he could use all words impartially, new or old, English or American, classical or slang.

Nevertheless as we turn from his autobiography to his fiction we are forced to own (as some women writers also make us own) that to come fresh to the world, to turn a new angle to the light, is so great an achievement that for its sake we can pardon the bitterness, the self-consciousness, the angularity which inevitably go with it. In *The Triumph of the Egg* there is some rearrangement of the old elements of art which makes us rub our eyes. The feeling recalls that with which we read Chekhov for the first time. There are no familiar handles to lay hold of in *The Triumph of the Egg*. The stories baffle our efforts, slip through our fingers and leave us feeling, not that it is Mr. Anderson who has failed us, but that we as readers have muffled our work and must go back, like chastened school-children, and spell the lesson over again in the attempt to lay hold of the meaning.

Mr. Anderson has bored into that deeper and warmer layer of human nature which it would be frivolous to ticket new or old, American or European. In his determination to be 'true to the essence of things' he has fumbled his way into something genuine, persistent, of universal significance, in proof of which he has done what, after all, very few writers succeed in doing—he has made a world of his own. It is a world in which the senses flourish; it is dominated by instincts rather than by ideas; racehorses make the hearts of little boys beat high; cornfields flow around the cheap towns like golden seas, illimitable and profound; everywhere boys and girls are dreaming of voyages and adventures, and this world of sensuality and instinctive desire is clothed in a warm cloudy atmosphere, wrapped about in a soft caressing envelope, which always seems a little too loose to fit the shape. Pointing to the formlessness of Mr. Anderson's work, the vagueness of his language, his tendency to land his stories softly in a bog, the English tourist would say that all this confirms him in his theory of what is to be expected of an American writer of insight and sincerity. The softness, the shellessness of Mr. Anderson are inevitable since he has scooped out from the heart of America matter which has never been confined in a shell before. He is too much enamoured of this precious stuff to squeeze it into any of those old and intricate poems which the art and industry of Europe have secreted. Rather he will leave what he has found exposed, defenceless, naked to scorn and laughter.

But if this theory holds good of the work of American novelists, how then are we to account for the novels of Mr. Sinclair Lewis? Does it not explode at the first touch of *Babbitt* and *Main Street* and *Our Mr. Wrenn* like a soap bubble dashed against the edge of a hard mahogany wardrobe? For it is precisely by its hardness, its efficiency, its compactness that Mr. Lewis's work excels. Yet he also is an American; he also has devoted book after book to the description and elucidation of America. Far from being shelless, however, his books, one is inclined to say, are all shell; the only doubt is whether he has left any room for the snail. At any rate *Babbitt* completely refutes the theory that an American writer, writing about America, must necessarily lack the finish, the technique, the power to model and control his material which one might suppose to be the bequest of an old civilization to its artists. In all these respects, *Babbitt* is the equal of any novel written in English in the present century. The tourist therefore must make his choice between two alternatives. Either there is no profound difference between English and American writers, and their experience is so similar that it can be housed in the same form; or Mr. Lewis has modelled himself so closely upon the English— H. G. Wells is a very obvious master—that he has sacrificed his American characteristics in the process. But the art of reading would be simpler and less adventurous than it is if writers could be parcelled out in strips of green and blue. Study of Mr. Lewis more and more convinces us that the surface appearance of downright decision is deceptive; the outer composure hardly holds together the warring elements within; the colours have run.

For though *Babbitt* would appear as solid and authentic a portrait of the American business man as can well be painted, certain doubts run across us and shake our conviction. But, we may ask, where all is so masterly, self-assured, and confident, what foothold can there be for doubt to lodge upon? To begin with we doubt Mr. Lewis himself: we doubt, that is to say, that he is nearly as sure of himself or of his subject as he would have us believe. For he, too, though in a way very different from Mr. Anderson's way, is writing with one eye on Europe, a division of attention which the reader is quick to feel and resent. He too has the American self-consciousness, though it is masterfully suppressed and allowed only to utter itself once or twice in a sharp cry of bitterness ('Babbitt was as much amused by the antiquated provincialism as any proper Englishman by any American'). But the uneasiness is there. He has not identified himself with America; rather he has constituted himself the guide and interpreter between the Americans and the English, and, as he conducts his party of Europeans over the typical American city (of which he is a native) and shows them the typical American citizen (to whom he is related) he is equally divided between shame at what he has to show and anger at the Europeans for laughing at it. Zenith is a despicable place, but the English are even more despicable for despising it.

In such an atmosphere intimacy is impossible. All that a writer of Mr. Lewis's powers can do is to be unflinchingly accurate and more and more on his guard against giving himself away. Accordingly, never was so complete a model of a city made before. We turn on the taps and the water runs; we press a button and cigars are lit and beds warmed. But this glorification of machinery, this lust for 'toothpastes, socks, tires, cameras, instantaneous hot water bottles . . . at first the signs, then the substitutes for joy and passion and wisdom' is only a device for putting off the evil day which Mr. Lewis sees looming ahead. However he may dread what people will think of him, he must give himself away. Babbitt must be proved to possess some share in truth and beauty, some character, some emotion of his own, or Babbitt will be nothing but an improved device for running motor cars, a convenient surface for the display of mechanical ingenuity. To make us care for Babbitt—that was his problem. With this end in view Mr. Lewis shamefacedly assures us that Babbitt has his dreams. Stout though he is, this elderly business man dreams of a fairy child waiting at a gate. 'Her dear and tranquil hand caressed his cheek. He was gallant and wise and well-beloved; warm ivory were her arms; and beyond perilous moors the brave sea glittered.' But that is not a dream; that is simply the protest of a man who has never dreamed in his life, but is determined to prove that dreaming is as easy as shelling peas. What are dreams made of— the most expensive dreams? Seas, fairies, moors? Well, he will have a little of each, and if that is not a dream, he seems to demand, jumping out of bed in a fury, what then is it? With sex relations and family affection he is much more at ease. Indeed it would be impossible to deny that if we put our ears to his shell, the foremost citizen in Zenith can be heard moving cumbrously but unmistakably within. One has moments of affection for him, moments of sympathy and even of desire that some miracle may happen, the rock be cleft asunder, and the living creature, with his capacity for fun, suffering, and happiness, be set at liberty. But no; his movements are too sluggish; Babbitt will never escape; he will die in his prison, bequeathing only the chance of escape to his son.

In some such way as this, then, the English tourist makes his theory embrace both Mr. Anderson and Mr. Sinclair Lewis. Both suffer as novelists from being American; Mr. Anderson, because he must protest his pride; Mr. Lewis, because he must conceal his bitterness. Mr. Anderson's way is the less injurious to him as an artist, and his imagination is the more vigorous of the two. He has gained more than he has lost by being the spokesman of a new country, the worker in fresh clay. Mr. Lewis it would seem was meant by nature to take his place with Mr. Wells and Mr. Bennett, and had he been born in England would undoubtedly have proved himself the equal of these two famous men. Denied, however, the richness of an old civilization—the swarm of ideas upon which the art of Mr. Wells has battened, the solidity of custom which has nourished the art of Mr. Bennett—he has been forced to criticize rather than to explore, and the object of his criticism—the civilization of Zenith—was unfortunately too meagre to sustain him. Yet a little reflection, and a comparison between Mr. Anderson and Mr. Lewis, put a different colour on our conclusion. Look at Americans as an American, see Mrs. Opal Emerson Mudge as she is herself, not as a type and symbol of America displayed for the amusement of the condescending Britisher, and then, we dimly suspect, Mrs. Mudge is no type, no scarecrow, no abstraction. Mrs. Mudge is—but it is not for an English writer to say what. He can only peep and peer between the chinks of the barrier and hazard the opinion that Mrs. Mudge and the Americans generally are, somehow, human beings into the bargain.

That suspicion suddenly becomes a certainty as we read the first pages of Mr. Ring Lardner's *You Know Me, Al,* and the change is bewildering. Hitherto we have been kept at arm's length, reminded constantly of our superiority, of our inferiority, of the fact, anyhow, that we are alien blood and bone. But Mr. Lardner is not merely unaware that we differ; he is unaware that we exist. When a crack player is in the middle of an exciting game of baseball he does not stop to wonder whether the audience likes the colour of his hair. All his mind is on the game. So Mr. Lardner does not waste a moment when he writes in thinking whether he is using American slang or Shakespeare's English; whether he is remembering Fielding or forgetting Fielding; whether he is proud of being American or ashamed of not being Japanese; all his mind is on the story. Hence all our minds are on the story. Hence, incidentally, he writes the best prose that has come our way. Hence we feel at last freely admitted to the society of our fellows.

That this should be true of *You Know Me, Al*, a story about baseball, a game which is not played in England, a story written often in a language which is not English, gives us pause. To what does he owe his success? Besides his unconsciousness and the additional power which he is thus free to devote to his art, Mr. Lardner has talents of a remarkable order. With extraordinary ease and aptitude, with the quickest strokes, the surest touch, the sharpest insight, he lets Jack Keefe the baseball player cut out his own outline, fill in his own depths, until the figure of the foolish, boastful, innocent athlete lives before us. As he babbles out his mind on paper there rise up friends, sweethearts, the scenery, town, and country—all surround him and make him up in his completeness. We gaze into the depths of a society which goes its ways intent on its own concerns. There, perhaps, is one of the elements of Mr. Lardner's success. He is not merely himself intent on his own game, but his characters are equally intent on theirs. It is no coincidence that the best of Mr. Lardner's stories are about games, for one may guess that Mr. Lardner's interest in games has solved one of the most difficult problems of the American writer; it has given him a clue, a centre, a meeting place for the divers activities of people whom a vast continent isolates, whom no tradition controls. Games give him what society gives his English brother. Whatever the precise reason, Mr. Lardner at any rate provides something unique in its kind, something indigenous to the soil, which the traveller may carry off as a trophy to prove to the incredulous that he has actually been to America and found it a foreign land. But the time has come when the tourist must reckon up his expenses and experiences, and attempt to cast up his account of the tour as a whole.

At the outset let us admit that our impressions are highly mixed and the opinions we have come to, if anything, less definite, less assured than those with which we started. For when we consider the mixed origin of the literature we are trying to understand, its youth, its age, and all those currents which are blowing across the stream of its natural development, we may well exclaim that French is simpler, English is simpler, all modern literatures are simpler to sum up and understand than this new American literature. A discord lies at the root of it; the natural bent of the American is twisted at the start. For the more sensitive he is, the more he must read English literature; the more he reads English literature, the more alive he must become to the puzzle and perplexity of this great art which uses the language on his own lips to express an experience which is not his and to mirror a civilization which he has never known. The choice has to be made— whether to yield or to rebel. The more sensitive, or at least the more sophisticated, the Henry Jameses, the Hergesheimers, the Edith Whartons, decide in favour of England and pay the penalty by exaggerating the English culture, the traditional English good manners, and stressing too heavily or in the wrong places those social differences which, though the first to strike the foreigner, are by no means the most profound. What their work gains in refinement it loses in that perpetual distortion of values, that obsession with surface distinctions—the age of old houses, the glamour of great names—which makes it necessary to remember that Henry James was a foreigner if we are not to call him a snob.

On the other hand, the simpler and cruder writers, like Walt Whitman, Mr. Anderson, Mr. Masters—decide in favour of America, but truculently, self-consciously, protestingly, 'showing off', as the nurses would say, their newness, their independence, their individuality. Both influences are unfortunate and serve to obscure and delay the development of the real American literature itself. But, some critics would interpose, are we not making mountains out of molehills, conjuring up distinctions where none exist? The 'real American literature' in the time of Hawthorne, Emerson, and Lowell was much of a piece with contemporary English literature, and the present movement towards a national literature is confined to a few enthusiasts and extremists who will grow older and wiser and see the folly of their ways.

But the tourist can no longer accept this comfortable doctrine, flattering though it be to his pride of birth. Obviously there are American writers who do not care a straw for English opinion or for English culture, and write very vigorously none the less—witness Mr. Lardner; there are Americans who have all the accomplishments of culture without a trace of its excess—witness Miss Willa Cather; there are Americans whose aim it is to write a book off their own bat and no one else's—witness Miss Fannie Hurst. But the shortest tour, the most superficial inspection, must impress him with what is of far greater importance—the fact that where the land itself is so different, and the society so different, the literature must needs differ, and differ more and more widely as time goes by, from those of other countries.

American literature will be influenced, no doubt, like all others, and the English influence may well predominate. But clearly the English tradition is already unable to cope with this vast land, these prairies, these cornfields, these lonely little groups of men and women scattered at immense distances from each other, these vast industrial cities with their skyscrapers and their night signs and their perfect organization of machinery. It cannot extract their meaning and interpret their beauty. How could it be otherwise? The English tradition is formed upon a little country; its centre is an old house with many rooms each crammed with objects and crowded with people who know each other intimately, whose manners, thoughts, and speech are ruled all the time, if unconsciously, by the spirit of the past. But in America there is baseball instead of society; instead of the old landscape which has moved men to emotion for endless summers and springs, a new land, its tin cans, its prairies, its cornfields flung disorderly about like a mosaic of incongruous pieces waiting order at the artist's hands; while the people are equally diversified into fragments of many nationalities.

To describe, to unify, to make order out of all these severed parts, a new art is needed and the control of a new tradition. That both are in process of birth the language itself gives us proof. For the Americans are doing what the Elizabethans did—they are coining new words. They are instinctively making the language adapt itself to their needs. In England, save for the impetus given by the war, the word-coining power has lapsed; our writers vary the metres of their poetry, remodel the rhythms of prose, but one may search English fiction in vain for a single new word. It is significant that when we want to freshen our speech we borrow from America—poppycock, rambunctious, flipflop, booster, good-mixer—all the expressive ugly vigorous slang which creeps into use among us first in talk, later in writing, comes from across the Atlantic. Nor does it need much foresight to predict that when words are being made, a literature will be made out of them. Already we hear the first jars and dissonances, the strangled difficult music of the prelude. As we shut our books and look out again upon the English fields a strident note rings in our ears. We hear the first lovemaking and the first laughter of the child who was exposed by its parents three hundred years ago upon a rocky shore and survived solely by its own exertions and is a little sore and proud and diffident and self-assertive in consequence and is now on the threshold of man's estate.

On Re-reading Novels

SO there are to be new editions of Jane Austen and the Brontës and George Meredith. Left in trains, forgotten in lodging-houses, thumbed and tattered to destruction, the old ones have served their day, and for the new-comers in their new houses there are to be new editions and new readings and new friends. It speaks very well for the Georgians. It is still more to the credit of the Victorians. In spite of the mischief-makers, the grand-children, it seems, get along very nicely with the grandparents; and the sight of their concord points inevitably to the later breach between the generations, a breach more complete than the other, and perhaps more momentous. The failure of the Edwardians, comparative yet disastrous—that is a question which waits to be discussed. How the year 1860 was a year of empty cradles; how the reign of Edward the Seventh was barren of poet, novelist, or critic; how it followed that the Georgians read Russian novels in translations; how they benefited and suffered; how different a story we might have told today had there been living heroes to worship and destroy—all this we find significant in view of the new editions of the old books. The Georgians, it seems, are in the odd predicament of turning for solace and guidance not to their parents who are alive, but to their grandparents who are dead. And so, as likely as not, we shall be faced one of these days by a young man reading Meredith for the first time. But before, inspired by his example, we risk the dangerous experiment of reading *Harry Richmond* for a second time, let us consider a few of the questions which the prospect of reading a long Victorian novel at once arouses in us.

First, there is the boredom of it. The national habit of reading has been formed by the drama, and the drama has always recognized the fact that human beings cannot sit for more than five hours at a stretch in front of a stage. Read *Harry Richmond* for five hours at a stretch and we shall only have broken off a fragment. Days may pass before we can add to it; meanwhile the plan is lost; the book pours to waste; we blame ourselves; we abuse the author; nothing is more exasperating and dispiriting. That is the first obstacle to be overcome. Next, we cannot doubt that we are by temperament and tradition poetic. There still lingers among us the belief that poetry is the senior branch of the service. If we have an hour to spend, we feel that we lay it out to better advantage with Keats than with Macaulay. Novels, however, besides being so long and so badly written, are all about the old, familiar things; what we do, week in, week out, between break-fast and bedtime; they are about life, and one has life enough on one's hands already without living it all over again in prose.

That is another obstacle. Yet these stock complaints which we begin to hear and, perhaps, to utter (as we get on in life) lose nothing of their acrimony if with the same breath we have to admit that we owe more to Tolstoy, Flaubert, and Hardy than we can measure; that if we wish to recall our happier hours, they would be those Conrad has given us and Henry James; and that to have seen a young man bolting Meredith whole recalls the pleasure of so many first readings that we are even ready to venture a second. The question is whether, if we venture ourselves a second time with *Vanity Fair*, the Copperfields, the Richmonds, we shall be able to find some other form of pleasure to take the place of that careless rapture which floated us along so tri-umphantly in the first instance. The pleasure we shall now look for will lie not so obviously on the surface; and we shall find ourselves hard pressed to make out what is the lasting quality, if such there be, which justifies these long books about modern life in prose.

Some months ago Mr. Percy Lubbock applied himself to answer some of these questions in *The Craft of Fiction*, a book which is likely to have much influence upon readers and may perhaps eventually reach the critics and the writers. The subject is vast and the book short; but it will be our fault, not Mr. Lubbock's, if we talk as vaguely about novels in the future as we have done in the past. For example, do we say that we cannot read *Harry Richmond* twice? We are led by Mr. Lubbock to suspect that it was our first reading that was to blame. A strong but vague emotion, two or three characters, half a dozen scattered scenes—if that is all that *Harry Richmond* recalls to us, the fault lies perhaps not with Meredith, but with ourselves. Did we read the book as he meant it to be read, or did we not reduce it to chaos through our own incompetency? Novels, above all other books, we are reminded, bristle with temptations. We identify ourselves with this person or with that. We fasten upon the character or the scene which is congenial. We swing our imaginations capriciously from spot to spot. We compare the world of fiction with the real world and judge it by the same standards. Undoubtedly we do all this and easily find excuses for so doing. 'But meanwhile the book, the thing he made, lies imprisoned in the volume, and our glimpse of it was too fleeting, it seems, to leave us with a lasting knowledge of its form.' That is the point. There is something lasting that we can know, something solid that we can lay hands on. There is, Mr. Lubbock argues, such a thing as the book itself. To perceive this we should read at arm's length from the distractions we have named. We must receive impressions but we must relate them to each other as the author intended. And it is when we have shaped our impressions as the author intended that we are then in a position to perceive the form itself, and it is this which endures, however mood or fashion may change. In Mr. Lubbock's own words:

> But with the book in this condition of a defined shape, firm of outline, its form shows for what it is indeed—not an attribute, one of many and possibly not the most important, but the book itself, as the form of the statue is the statue itself.

Now, as Mr. Lubbock laments, the criticism of fiction is in its infancy, and its language, though not all of one syllable, is baby language. This word 'form', of course, comes from the visual arts, and for our part we wish that he could have seen his way to do without it. It is confusing. The form of the novel differs from the dramatic form—that is true; we can, if we choose, say that we see the difference in our mind's eyes. But can we see that the form of *The Egoist* differs from the form of *Vanity Fair*? We do not raise the question in order to stickle for accuracy where most words are provisional, many metaphorical, and some on trial for the first time. The question is not one of words only. It goes deeper than that, into the very process of reading itself. Here we have Mr. Lubbock telling us that the book itself is equivalent to its form, and seeking with admirable subtlety and lucidity to trace out those methods by which novelists build up the final and enduring structure of their books. The very patness with which the image comes to the pen makes us suspect that it fits a little loosely. And in these circumstances it is best to shake oneself free from images and start afresh with a definite subject to work upon. Let us read a story and set down our impressions as we go along, and so perhaps discover what it is that bothers us in Mr. Lubbock's use of the word 'form'. For this purpose there is no more appropriate author than Flaubert; and, not to strain our space, let us choose a short story, *Un Cœur Simple*, for example, for, as it happens, it is one that we have practically forgotten.

The title gives us our bearings, and the first words direct our attention to Madame Aubain's faithful servant Félicité. And now the impressions begin to arrive. Madame's character; the look of her house; Félicité's appearance; her love affair with Théodore; Madame's children; her visitors; the angry bull. We accept them, but we do not use them. We lay them aside in reserve. Our attention flickers this way and that, from one to another. Still the impressions accumulate, and still, almost ignoring their individual quality, we read on, noting the pity, the irony, hastily observing certain relations and contrasts, but stressing nothing; always awaiting the final signal. Suddenly we have it. The mistress and the maid are turning over the dead child's clothes. 'Et des papillons s'envolèrent de l'armoire.' The mistress kisses the servant for the first time. 'Félicité lui en fut reconnaissante comme d'un bienfait, et désormais la chérit avec un dévouement bestial et une vénération religieuse.' A sudden intensity of phrase, something which for good reasons or for bad we feel to be emphatic, startles us into a flash of understanding. We see now why the story was written. Later in the same way we are roused by a sentence with a very different intention: 'Et Félicité priait en regardant l'image, mais de temps à autre se tournait un peu vers l'oiseau.' Again we have the same conviction that we know why the story was written. And then it is finished. All the observations which we have put aside now come out and range themselves according to the directions we have received. Some are relevant; others we can find no place for. On a second reading we are able to use our observations from the start, and they are much more precise; but they are still controlled by these moments of understanding.

Therefore the 'book itself' is not form which you see, but emotion which you feel, and the more intense the writer's feeling the more exact without slip or chink its expression in words. And whenever Mr. Lubbock talks of form it is as if something were interposed between us and the book as we know it. We feel the presence of an alien substance which requires to be visualized imposing itself upon emotions which we feel naturally, and name simply, and range in final order by feeling their right relations to each other. Thus we have reached our conception of *Un Cœur Simple* by working from the emotion outwards, and, the reading over, there is nothing to be seen; there is everything to be felt. And only when the emotion is feeble and the workmanship excellent can we separate what is felt from the expression and remark, for example, what excellence of form *Esther Waters* possesses in comparison with *Jane Eyre*. But consider the *Princesse de Clèves*. There is vision and there is expression. The two blend so perfectly that when Mr. Lubbock asks us to test the form with our eyes we see nothing at all. But we feel with singular satisfaction, and since all our feelings are in keeping, they form a whole which remains in our minds as the book itself. The point is worth labouring, not simply to substitute one word for another, but to insist, among all this talk of methods, that both in writing and in reading it is the emotion that must come first.

Still, we have only made a beginning and a very dangerous one at that. To snatch an emotion and luxuriate in it and tire of it and throw it away is as dissipating in literature as in life. Yet if we wring this pleasure from Flaubert, the most austere of writers, there is no limit to be put upon the intoxicating effects of Meredith and Dickens and Dostoevsky and Scott and Charlotte Brontë. Or rather there is a limit, and we have found it over and over again in the extremes of satiety and disillusionment. If we are to read them again we must somehow discriminate. Emotion is our material; but what value do we put on the emotion? How many different kinds of emotion are there not in one short story, of how many qualities, and composed of how many different elements? And therefore to get our emotion directly and for ourselves is only the first step. We must go on to test it and riddle it with questions. If nothing survives, well and good; toss it into the waste-paper basket and have done with it. If something survives, place it for ever among the treasures of the universe. Is there not something beyond emotion, something which though it is inspired by emotion, tranquillizes it, orders it, composes it?—that which Mr. Lubbock calls form, which, for simplicity's sake, we will call art? Can we not discover even in the vortex and whirlpool of Victorian fiction some constraint which the most ebullient of novelists forced himself to lay on his material, to reduce it to symmetry? Of a playwright it would scarcely be necessary to ask so simple-minded a question. The most casual visitor to the theatre must instantly perceive how straitly even the crudest drama is shepherded by conventions; and can bring to mind subtler instances of dramatic technique which have been in force and have obtained recognition these many hundred years. In *Macbeth*, for instance, critic after critic points out the effect of change from tragedy to comedy in the scene of the porter; and in the *Antigone* of Sophocles we are bidden to remark how the messenger rearranges the story so as make the discovery of the death of Antigone succeed, instead of preceding, the funeral.

The drama, however, is hundreds of years in advance of the novel. We must have known that a novelist, before he can persuade us that his world is real and his people alive, before he can begin to move us by the sight of their joys and sufferings, must solve certain questions and acquire certain skill. But so far we have swallowed our fiction with our eyes shut. We have not named and therefore presumably not recognized the simplest of devices by which every novel has to come into being. We have not taken the pains to watch our story-teller as he decides which method he will use; we have not applauded his choice, deplored his lack of judgment, or followed with delight and interest his use of some dangerous new device which, for all we know, may do his job to perfection or blow the whole book to smithereens.

In excuse of our slovenliness it must be admitted, not only that the methods are unnamed, but that no writer has so many at his disposal as a novelist. He can put himself at any point of view; he can to some extent combine several different views. He can appear in person, like Thackeray; or disappear (never perhaps completely), like Flaubert. He can state the facts, like Defoe, or give the thought without the fact, like Henry James. He can sweep the widest horizons, like Tolstoy, or seize upon one old apple-woman and her basket, like Tolstoy again. Where there is every freedom there is every licence; and the novel, open-armed, free to all comers, claims more victims than the other forms of literature all put together. But let us look at the victors. We are tempted, indeed, to look at them a great deal more closely than space allows. For they too look different if you watch them at work. There is Thackeray always taking measures to avoid a scene, and Dickens (save in *David Copperfield*) invariably seeking one. There is Tolstoy dashing into the midst of his story without staying to lay foundations, and Balzac laying foundations so deep that the story itself seems never to begin. But we must check the desire to see where Mr. Lubbock's criticism would lead us in reading particular books. The general view is more striking and a general view is to be had.

Let us look, not at each story separately, but at the method of telling stories as a whole, and its development from generation to generation. Let us look at it in Richardson's hands, and watch it changing and developing as Thackeray applies it, and Dickens and Tolstoy and Meredith and Flaubert and the rest. Then let us see how in the end Henry James, endowed not with greater genius but with greater knowledge and craftsmanship, surmounts in *The Ambassadors* problems which baffled Richardson in *Clarissa*. The view is difficult; the light is bad. At every angle someone rises to protest that novels are the outburst of spontaneous inspiration, and that Henry James lost as much by his devotion to art as he gained. We will not silence that protest, for it is the voice of an immediate joy in reading without which second readings would be impossible, for there would be no first. And yet the conclusion seems to us undeniable, Henry James achieved what Richardson attempted. 'The only real *scholar* in the art' beats the amateurs. The late-comer improves upon the pioneers. More is implied than we can even attempt to state.

For from that vantage ground the art of fiction can be seen, not clearly indeed, but in a new proportion. We may speak of infancy, of youth, and of maturity. We may say that Scott is childish and Flaubert by comparison a grown man. We may go on to say that the vigour and splendour of youth almost outweigh the more deliberate virtues of maturity. And then we may pause upon the significance of 'almost', and wonder whether, perhaps, it has not some bearing upon our reluctance to read the Victorians twice. The gigantic, sprawling books still seem to reverberate the yawns and lamentations of their makers. To build a castle, sketch a profile, fire off a poem, reform a workhouse, or pull down a prison were occupations more congenial to the writers, or more befitting their manhood, than to sit chained at a desk scribbling novels for a simple-minded public. The genius of Victorian fiction seems to be making its magnificent best of an essentially bad job. But it is never possible to say of Henry James that he is making the best of a bad job. In all the long stretch of *The Wings of the Dove* and *The Ambassadors* there is not the hint of a yawn, not a sign of condescension. The novel is his job. It is the appropriate form for what he has to say. It wins a beauty from that fact—a fine and noble beauty which it has never worn before. And now at last it has worked itself free and made itself distinct from its companions. It will not burden itself with other people's relics. It will choose to say whatever it says best. Flaubert will take for his subject an old maid and a stuffed parrot. Henry James will find all he needs round a tea-table in a drawing-room. The nightingales and roses are banished—or at least the nightingale sounds strange against the traffic, and the roses in the light of the arc lamps are not quite so red. There are new combinations of old material, and the novel, when it is used for the sake of its qualities and not for the sake of its defects, enforces fresh aspects of the perennial story.

Mr. Lubbock prudently carries his survey no further than the novels of Henry James. But already the years have mounted up. We may expect the novel to change and develop as it is explored by the most vigorous minds of a very complex age. What have we not, indeed, to expect from M. Proust alone? But if he will listen to Mr. Lubbock, the common reader will refuse to sit any longer open-mouthed in passive expectation. That is to encourage the charlatan to shock us and the conjuror to play us tricks.

From all this some conclusions seem to emerge. First, that when we speak of form we mean that certain emotions have been placed in the right relations to each other; then that the novelist is able to dispose these emotions and make them tell by methods which he inherits, bends to his purpose, models anew, or even invents for himself. Further, that the reader can detect these devices, and by so doing will deepen his understanding of the book, while, for the rest, it may be expected that novels will lose their chaos and become more and more shapely as the novelist explores and perfects his technique. Finally, perhaps, a charge is laid upon the indolence and credulity of the reader. Let him press hard upon the novelist's heels; be quick to follow, quick to understand, and so bring to bear upon him, even in his study, with reams of paper at his disposal and publishers eager to accept the bloated productions of his solitude, the chastening and salutary pressure which a dramatist has to reckon with, from actors, the spectators, and the audience trained for generations in the art of going to the play.

Life and the Novelist[1]

THE novelist—it is his distinction and his danger—is terribly exposed to life. Other artists, partially at least, withdraw; they shut themselves up for weeks alone with a dish of apples and a paint-box, or a roll of music paper and a piano. When they emerge it is to forget and distract themselves. But the novelist never forgets and is seldom distracted. He fills his glass and lights his cigarette, he enjoys presumably all the pleasures of talk and table, but always with a sense that he is being stimulated and played upon by the subject-matter of his art. Taste, sound, movement, a few words here, a gesture there, a man coming in, a woman going out, even the motor that passes in the street or the beggar who shuffles along the pavement, and all the reds and blues and lights and shades of the scene claim his attention and rouse his curiosity. He can no more cease to receive impressions than a fish in mid-ocean can cease to let the water rush through his gills.

But if this sensibility is one of the conditions of the novelist's life, it is obvious that all writers whose books survive have known how to master it and make it serve their purposes. They have finished the wine and paid the bill and gone off, alone, into some solitary room where, with toil and pause, in agony (like Flaubert), with struggle and rush, tumultuously (like Dostoevsky) they have mastered their perceptions, hardened them, and changed them into the fabrics of their art.

So drastic is the process of selection that in its final state we can often find no trace of the actual scene upon which the chapter was based. For in that solitary room, whose door the critics are for ever trying to unlock, processes of the strangest kind are gone through. Life is subjected to a thousand disciplines and exercises. It is curbed; it is killed. It is mixed with this, stiffened with that, brought into contrast with something else; so that when we get our scene at a café a year later the surface signs by which we remembered it have disappeared. There emerges from the mist something stark, something formidable and enduring, the bone

[1] *New York Herald Tribune*, November 7, 1926

and substance upon which our rush of indiscriminating emotion was founded.

Of these two processes, the first—to receive impressions—is undoubtedly the easier, the simpler, and the pleasanter. And it is quite possible, provided one is gifted with a sufficiently receptive temperament and a vocabulary rich enough to meet its demands, to make a book out of this preliminary emotion alone. Three-quarters of the novels that appear today are concocted of experience to which no discipline, except the mild curb of grammar and the occasional rigours of chapter divisions, has been applied. Is Miss Stern's *A Deputy Was King* another example of this class of writing, has she taken her material away with her into solitude, or is it neither one nor the other, but an incongruous mixture of soft and hard, transient and enduring?

A Deputy Was King continues the story of the Rakonitz family which was begun some years ago in *The Matriarch*. It is a welcome reappearance, for the Rakonitz family is a gifted and cosmopolitan family with the admirable quality, so rare now in English fiction, of belonging to no particular sect. No parish boundary contains them. They overflow the continent. They are to be found in Italy and Austria, in Paris and Bohemia. If they lodge temporarily in some London studio they are not condemning themselves thereby to wear forever the livery of Chelsea, or Bloomsbury, or Kensington. Abundantly nourished on a diet of rich meats and rare wines, expensively but exquisitely clothed, enviably though inexplicably flush of ready money, no restraint of class or convention lies upon them, if we except the year 1921; it is essential that they should be up to date. They dance, they marry, they live with this man or with that; they bask in the Italian sun; they swarm in and out of each other's houses and studios, gossiping, quarrelling, making it up again. For, after all, besides the constraint of fashion, they lie, consciously or unconsciously, under the bond of family. They have that Jewish tenacity of affection which common hardship has bred in an outcast race. Hence, in spite of their surface gregariousness, they are fundamentally loyal to each other underneath. Toni and Val and Loraine may quarrel and tear each other asunder publicly, but in private the Rakonitz women are indissolubly united. The present instalment of the family history, which, though it introduces the Goddards and relates the marriage of Toni and Giles Goddard, is really the history of a family, and not of an episode, pauses, for the time presumably, in an Italian villa provided with seventeen bedrooms, so that uncles, aunts, cousins can all come to lodge there. For Toni Goddard, with all her fashion and modernity, would rather shelter uncles and aunts than entertain emperors, and a second cousin whom she has not seen since she was a child is a prize above rubies.

From such materials surely a good novel might be made—that is what one catches oneself saying, before a hundred pages are finished. And this voice, which is not altogether our own, but the voice of that dissentient spirit which may split off and take a line of its own as we read, should be cross-examined instantly, lest its hints should spoil the pleasure of the whole. What, then, does it mean by insinuating this doubtful, grudging sentiment in the midst of our general well-being? Hitherto nothing has interfered with our enjoyment. Short of being a Rakonitz oneself, of actually taking part in one of those 'diamonded evenings', dancing, drinking, flirting with the snow upon the roof and the gramophone braying out 'It's moonlight in Kalua', short of seeing Betty and Colin 'slightly grotesque advancing . . . in full panoply; velvet spread like a huge inverted cup round Betty's feet, as she minced over the pure, sparkling strip of snow, the absurd tangle of plumes on Colin's helmet'—short of taking hold of all this glitter and fantasy with one's own fingers and thumbs, what is better than Miss Stern's report of it?

The grudging voice will concede that it is all very brilliant; will admit that a hundred pages have flashed by like a hedge seen from an express train; but will reiterate that for all that something is wrong. A man can elope with a woman without our noticing it. That is a proof that there are no values. There is no shape for these apparitions. Scene melts into scene; person into person. People rise out of a fog of talk, and sink back into talk again. They are soft and shapeless with words. There is no grasping them.

The charge has substance in it, because it is true, when we consider it, that Giles Goddard can run off with Loraine, and it is to us as if somebody had got up and gone out of the room—a matter of no importance. We have been letting ourselves bask in appearances. All this representation of the movement of life has sapped our imaginative power. We have sat receptive and watched, with our eyes rather than with our minds, as we do at the cinema, what passes on the screen in front of us. When we want to use what we have learnt about one of the characters to urge them through some crisis we realize that we have no steam up; no energy at our disposal. How they dressed, what they ate, the slang they used—we know all that; but not what they are. For what we know about these people has been given us (with one exception) by following the methods of life. The characters are built up by observing the incoherence, the fresh natural sequences of a person who, wishing to tell the story of a friend's life in talk, breaks off a thousand times to bring in something fresh, to add something forgotten, so that in the end, though one may feel that one has been in the presence of life, the particular life in question remains vague. This hand-to-mouth method, this ladling out of sentences which have the dripping brilliance of words that live upon real lips, is admirable for one purpose, disastrous for another. All is fluent and graphic; but no character or situation emerges cleanly. Bits of extraneous matter are left sticking to the edges. For all their brilliancy the scenes are clouded; the crises are blurred. A passage of description will make both the merit and the defect of the method clear. Miss Stern wants us to realize the beauty of a Chinese coat.

> Gazing at it, you might think you had never seen embroidery before, for it was the very climax of all that was brilliant and exotic. The flower-petals were worked in a flaming pattern round the broad bands of kingfisher blue embroidery; and again round each oval plaque that was woven of a silvery heron with a long green beak, and behind his outstretched wings a rainbow. All among the silver arabesques, butterflies were delicately poised, golden butterflies and black butterflies, and butterflies that were gold and black. The closer you looked the more there was to see; intricate markings on the butterfly wings, purple and grass-green and apricot . . .

As if we had not enough to see already, she goes on to add how there were tiny stamens springing from every flower, and circles ringing the eye of each separate stork, until the Chinese coat wobbles before our eyes and merges in one brilliant blur.

The same method applied to people has the same result. Quality is added to quality, fact to fact, until we cease to discriminate and our interest is suffocated under a plethora of words. For it is true of every object—coat or human being—that the more one looks the more there is to see. The writer's task is to take one thing and let it stand for twenty: a task of danger and difficulty; but only so is the reader relieved of the swarm and confusion of life and branded effectively with the particular aspect which the writer wishes him to see. That Miss Stern has other tools at her disposal, and could use them if she liked, is hinted now and again, and is revealed for a moment in the brief chapter describing the death of the matriarch, Anastasia Rakonitz. Here suddenly the flow of words seems to darken and thicken. We are aware of something beneath the surface, something left unsaid for us to find out for ourselves and think over. The two pages in which we are told how the old woman died asking for goose-liver sausage and a tortoiseshell comb, short though they are, hold, to my thinking, twice the substance of any other thirty pages in the book.

These remarks bring me back to the question with which I started: the relation of the novelist to life and what it should be. That he is terribly exposed to life A Deputy Was King proves once more. He can sit and watch life and make his book out of the very foam and effervescence of his emotions; or he can put his glass down, retire to his room and subject his trophy to those mysterious processes by which life becomes, like the Chinese coat, able to stand by itself—a sort of impersonal miracle. But in either case he is faced by a problem which does not afflict the workers in any other arts to the same extent. Stridently, clamorously, life is forever pleading that she is the proper end of fiction and that the more he sees of her and catches of her the better his book will be. She does not add, however, that she is grossly impure; and that the side she flaunts uppermost is often, for the novelist, of no value whatever. Appearance and movement are the lures she trails to entice him after her, as if these were her essence, and by catching them he gained his goal. So believing, he rushes feverishly in her wake, ascertains what fox-trot is being played at the Embassy, what skirt is being worn in Bond Street, worms and winds his way into the last flings of topical slang, and imitates to perfection the last toss of colloquial jargon. He becomes terrified more than anything of falling behind the times: his chief concern is that the thing described shall be fresh from the shell with the down on its head.

This kind of work requires great dexterity and nimbleness, and gratifies a real desire. To know the outside of one's age, its dresses and its dances and its catchwords, has an interest and even a value which the spiritual adventures of a curate, or the aspirations of a high-minded schoolmistress, solemn as they are, for the most part lack. It might well be claimed, too, that to deal with the crowded dance of modern life so as to produce the illusion of reality needs far higher literary skill than to write a serious essay upon the poetry of John Donne or the novels of M. Proust. The novelist, then, who is a slave to life and concocts his books out of the froth of the moment is doing something difficult, something which pleases, something which, if you have a mind that way, may even instruct. But his work passes as the year 1921 passes, as fox-trots pass, and in three years' time looks as dowdy and dull as any other fashion which has served its turn and gone its way.

On the other hand, to retire to one's study in fear of life is equally fatal. It is true that plausible imitations of Addison, say, can be manufactured in the quiet there, but they are as brittle as plaster and as insipid. To survive, each sentence must have, at its heart, a little spark of fire, and this, whatever the risk, the novelist must pluck with his own hands from the blaze. His state then is a precarious one. He must expose himself to life; he must risk the danger of being led away and tricked by her deceitfulness; he must seize her treasure from her and let her trash run to waste. But at a certain moment he must leave the company and withdraw, alone, to that mysterious room where his body is hardened and fashioned into permanence by processes which, if they elude the critic, hold for him so profound a fascination.

The Anatomy of Fiction[1]

SOMETIMES at country fairs you may have seen a professor on a platform exhorting the peasants to come up and buy his wonder-working pills. Whatever their disease, whether of body or mind, he has a name for it and a cure; and if they hang back in doubt he whips out a diagram and points with a stick at different parts of the human anatomy, and gabbles so quickly such long Latin words that first one shyly stumbles forward and then another, and takes his bolus and carries it away and unwraps it secretly and swallows it in hope. 'The young aspirant to the art of fiction who knows himself to be an incipient realist', Mr. Hamilton vociferates from his platform,[2] and the incipient realists advance and receive—for the professor is generous—five pills together with nine suggestions for home treatment. In other words they are given five 'review questions' to answer, and are advised to read nine books or parts of books. '1. Define the difference between realism and romance. 2. What are the advantages and disadvantages of the realistic method? 3. What are the advantages and disadvantages of the romantic method?'—that is the kind of thing they work out at home, and with such success that a 'revised and enlarged edition' of the book has been issued on the tenth anniversary of the first publication. In America, evidently, Mr. Hamilton is considered a very good professor, and has no doubt a bundle of testimonials to the miraculous nature of his cures. But let us consider: Mr. Hamilton is not a professor; we are not credulous ploughboys; and fiction is not a disease.

In England we have been in the habit of saying that fiction is an art. We are not taught to write novels; dissuasion is our most usual incentive; and though perhaps the critics have 'deduced and formulated the general principles of the art of fiction', they have done their work as a good housemaid does hers; they have tidied up after the party is over. Criticism seldom or never applies to the problems of the present moment. On the other hand, any

[1] *The Athenaeum*, May 16, 1919
[2] *Materials and Methods of Fiction*, by Clayton Hamilton. With an Introduction by Brander Matthews

good novelist, whether he be dead or alive, has something to say about them, though it is said very indirectly, differently to different people, and differently at different stages of the same person's development. Thus, if anything is essential, it is essential to do your reading with your own eyes. But, to tell the truth, Mr. Hamilton has sickened us of the didactic style. Nothing appears to be essential save perhaps an elementary knowledge of the A.B.C., and it is pleasant to remember that Henry James, when he took to dictation, dispensed even with that. Still, if you have a natural taste for books it is probable that after reading *Emma*, to take an instance, some reflections upon the art of Jane Austen may occur to you—how exquisitely one incident relieves another; how definitely, by not saying something, she says it; how surprising, therefore, her expressive phrases when they come. Between the sentences, apart from the story, a little shape of some kind builds itself up. But learning from books is a capricious business at best, and the teaching so vague and changeable that in the end, far from calling books either 'romantic' or 'realistic', you will be more inclined to think them, as you think people, very mixed, very distinct, very unlike one another. But this would never do for Mr. Hamilton. According to him every work of art can be taken to pieces, and those pieces can be named and numbered, divided and subdivided, and given their order of precedence, like the internal organs of a frog. Thus we learn how to put them together again—that is, according to Mr. Hamilton, we learn how to write. There is the complication, the major knot, and the explication; the inductive and the deductive methods; the kinetic and the static; the direct and the indirect with subdivisions of the same; connotation, annotation, personal equation, and denotation; logical sequence and chronological succession—all parts of the frog and all capable of further dissection. Take the case of 'emphasis' alone. There are eleven kinds of emphasis. Emphasis by terminal position, by initial position, by pause, by direct proportion, by inverse proportion, by iteration, by antithesis, by surprise, by suspense—are you tired already? But consider the Americans. They have written one story eleven times over, with a different kind of emphasis in each. Indeed, Mr. Hamilton's book teaches us a great deal about the Americans.

Still, as Mr. Hamilton uneasily perceives now and then, you

may dissect your frog, but you cannot make it hop; there is, unfortunately, such a thing as life. Directions for imparting life to fiction are given, such as to 'train yourself rigorously never to be bored', and to cultivate 'a lively curiosity and a ready sympathy'. But it is evident that Mr. Hamilton does not like life, and, with such a tidy museum as his, who can blame him? He has found life very troublesome, and, if you come to consider it, rather unnecessary; for, after all, there are books. But Mr. Hamilton's views on life are so illuminating that they must be given in his own words:

Perhaps in the actual world we should never bother to converse with illiterate provincial people; and yet we do not feel it a waste of time and energy to meet them in the pages of *Middlemarch*. For my own part, I have always, in actual life, avoided meeting the sort of people that appear in Thackeray's *Vanity Fair*; and yet I find it not only interesting but profitable to associate with them through the entire extent of a rather lengthy novel.

'Illiterate provincial people'—'interesting but profitable'— 'waste of time and energy'—now after much wandering and painful toil we are on the right track at last. For long it seemed that nothing could reward the American people for having written eleven themes upon the eleven kinds of emphasis. But now we perceive dimly that there is something to be gained by the daily flagellation of the exhausted brain. It is not a title; it has nothing to do with pleasure or with literature; but it appears that Mr. Hamilton and his industrious band see far off upon the horizon a circle of superior enlightenment to which, if only they can keep on reading long enough, they may attain. Every book demolished is a milestone passed. Books in foreign languages count twice over. And a book like this is of the nature of a dissertation to be sent up to the supreme examiner, who may be, for anything we know, the ghost of Matthew Arnold. Will Mr. Hamilton be admitted? Can they have the heart to reject anyone so ardent, so dusty, so worthy, so out of breath? Alas! look at his quotations; consider his comments upon them:

'The murmuring of innumerable bees.' . . . The word

innumerable, which denotes to the intellect merely 'incapable of being numbered,' is, in this connection, made to suggest to the senses the murmuring of bees.

The credulous ploughboy could have told him more than that. It is not necessary to quote what he says about 'magic casements' and the 'iniquity of oblivion'. Is there not, upon page 208, a definition of style?

No; Mr. Hamilton will never be admitted; he and his disciples must toil for ever in the desert sand, and the circle of illumination will, we fear, grow fainter and farther upon their horizon. It is curious to find, after writing the above sentence, how little one is ashamed of being, where literature is concerned, an unmitigated snob.

Women and Fiction[1]

THE title of this article can be read in two ways; it may allude to women and the fiction that they write, or to women and the fiction that is written about them. The ambiguity is intentional, for in dealing with women as writers, as much elasticity as possible is desirable; it is necessary to leave oneself room to deal with other things besides their work, so much has that work been influenced by conditions that have nothing whatever to do with art.

The most superficial inquiry into women's writing instantly raises a host of questions. Why, we ask at once, was there no continuous writing done by women before the eighteenth century? Why did they then write almost as habitually as men, and in the course of that writing produce, one after another, some of the classics of English fiction? And why did their art then, and why to some extent does their art still, take the form of fiction?

A little thought will show us that we are asking questions to which we shall get, as answer, only further fiction. The answer lies at present locked in old diaries, stuffed away in old drawers, half obliterated in the memories of the aged. It is to be found in the lives of the obscure—in those almost unlit corridors of history where the figures of generations of women are so dimly, so fitfully perceived. For very little is known about women. The history of England is the history of the male line, not of the female. Of our fathers we know always some fact, some distinction. They were soldiers or they were sailors; they filled that office or they made that law. But of our mothers, our grandmothers, our great-grandmothers, what remains? Nothing but a tradition. One was beautiful; one was red-haired; one was kissed by a Queen. We know nothing of them except their names and the dates of their marriages and the number of children they bore.

Thus, if we wish to know why at any particular time women did this or that, why they wrote nothing, why on the other hand they wrote masterpieces, it is extremely difficult to tell. Anyone

[1] *The Forum*, March 1929

who should seek among those old papers, who should turn history wrong side out and so construct a faithful picture of the daily life of the ordinary woman in Shakespeare's time, in Milton's time, in Johnson's time, would not only write a book of astonishing interest, but would furnish the critic with a weapon which he now lacks. The extraordinary woman depends on the ordinary woman. It is only when we know what were the conditions of the average woman's life—the number of her children, whether she had money of her own, if she had a room to herself, whether she had help in bringing up her family, if she had servants, whether part of the housework was her task—it is only when we can measure the way of life and the experience of life made possible to the ordinary woman that we can account for the success or failure of the extraordinary woman as a writer.

Strange spaces of silence seem to separate one period of activity from another. There was Sappho and a little group of women all writing poetry on a Greek island six hundred years before the birth of Christ. They fall silent. Then about the year 1000 we find a certain court lady, the Lady Murasaki, writing a very long and beautiful novel in Japan. But in England in the sixteenth century, when the dramatists and poets were most active, the women were dumb. Elizabethan literature is exclusively masculine. Then, at the end of the eighteenth century and in the beginning of the nineteenth, we find women again writing—this time in England —with extraordinary frequency and success.

Law and custom were of course largely responsible for these strange intermissions of silence and speech. When a woman was liable, as she was in the fifteenth century, to be beaten and flung about the room if she did not marry the man of her parents' choice, the spiritual atmosphere was not favourable to the production of works of art. When she was married without her own consent to a man who thereupon became her lord and master, 'so far at least as law and custom could make him', as she was in the time of the Stuarts, it is likely she had little time for writing, and less encouragement. The immense effect of environment and suggestion upon the mind, we in our psychoanalytical age are beginning to realize. Again, with memoirs and letters to help us, we are beginning to understand how abnormal is the effort needed to produce a work of art, and what shelter and what support the mind of the artist requires. Of those facts the lives and letters of men like Keats and Carlyle and Flaubert assure us.

Thus it is clear that the extraordinary outburst of fiction in the beginning of the nineteenth century in England was heralded by innumerable slight changes in law and customs and manners. And women of the nineteenth century had some leisure; they had some education. It was no longer the exception for women of the middle and upper classes to choose their own husbands. And it is significant that of the four great women novelists—Jane Austen, Emily Brontë, Charlotte Brontë, and George Eliot—not one had a child, and two were unmarried.

Yet, though it is clear that the ban upon writing had been removed, there was still, it would seem, considerable pressure upon women to write novels. No four women can have been more unlike in genius and character than these four. Jane Austen can have had nothing in common with George Eliot; George Eliot was the direct opposite of Emily Brontë. Yet all were trained for the same profession; all, when they wrote, wrote novels.

Fiction was, as fiction still is, the easiest thing for a woman to write. Nor is it difficult to find the reason. A novel is the least concentrated form of art. A novel can be taken up or put down more easily than a play or a poem. George Eliot left her work to nurse her father. Charlotte Brontë put down her pen to pick the eyes out of the potatoes. And living as she did in the common sitting-room, surrounded by people, a woman was trained to use her mind in observation and upon the analysis of character. She was trained to be a novelist and not to be a poet.

Even in the nineteenth century, a woman lived almost solely in her home and her emotions. And those nineteenth-century novels, remarkable as they were, were profoundly influenced by the fact that the women who wrote them were excluded by their sex from certain kinds of experience. That experience has a great influence upon fiction is indisputable. The best part of Conrad's novels, for instance, would be destroyed if it had been impossible for him to be a sailor. Take away all that Tolstoy knew of war as a soldier, of life and society as a rich young man whose education admitted him to all sorts of experience, and *War and Peace* would be incredibly impoverished.

Yet *Pride and Prejudice, Wuthering Heights, Villette,* and *Middle-*

march were written by women from whom was forcibly withheld all experience save that which could be met with in a middle-class drawing-room. No first-hand experience of war or seafaring or politics or business was possible for them. Even their emotional life was strictly regulated by law and custom. When George Eliot ventured to live with Mr. Lewes without being his wife, public opinion was scandalized. Under its pressure she withdrew into a suburban seclusion which, inevitably, had the worst possible effects upon her work. She wrote that unless people asked of their own accord to come and see her, she never invited them. At the same time, on the other side of Europe, Tolstoy was living a free life as a soldier, with men and women of all classes, for which nobody censured him and from which his novels drew much of their astonishing breadth and vigour.

But the novels of women were not affected only by the necessarily narrow range of the writer's experience. They showed, at least in the nineteenth century, another characteristic which may be traced to the writer's sex. In *Middlemarch* and in *Jane Eyre* we are conscious not merely of the writer's character, as we are conscious of the character of Charles Dickens, but we are conscious of a woman's presence—of someone resenting the treatment of her sex and pleading for its rights. This brings into women's writing an element which is entirely absent from a man's, unless, indeed, he happens to be a working man, a negro, or one who for some other reason is conscious of disability. It introduces a distortion and is frequently the cause of weakness. The desire to plead some personal cause or to make a character the mouthpiece of some personal discontent or grievance always has a distressing effect, as if the spot at which the reader's attention is directed were suddenly twofold instead of single.

The genius of Jane Austen and Emily Brontë is never more convincing than in their power to ignore such claims and solicitations and to hold on their way unperturbed by scorn or censure. But it needed a very serene or a very powerful mind to resist the temptation to anger. The ridicule, the censure, the assurance of inferiority in one form or another which were lavished upon women who practised an art, provoked such reactions naturally enough. One sees the effect in Charlotte Brontë's indignation, in George Eliot's resignation. Again and again one finds it in the work of the lesser women writers—in their choice of a subject, in their unnatural self-assertiveness, in their unnatural docility. Moreover, insincerity leaks in almost unconsciously. They adopt a view in deference to authority. The vision becomes too masculine or it becomes too feminine; it loses its perfect integrity and, with that, its most essential quality as a work of art.

The great change that has crept into women's writing is, it would seem, a change of attitude. The woman writer is no longer bitter. She is no longer angry. She is no longer pleading and protesting as she writes. We are approaching, if we have not yet reached, the time when her writing will have little or no foreign influence to disturb it. She will be able to concentrate upon her vision without distraction from outside. The aloofness that was once within the reach of genius and originality is only now coming within the reach of ordinary women. Therefore the average novel by a woman is far more genuine and far more interesting today than it was a hundred or even fifty years ago.

But it is still true that before a woman can write exactly as she wishes to write, she has many difficulties to face. To begin with, there is the technical difficulty—so simple, apparently; in reality, so baffling—that the very form of the sentence does not fit her. It is a sentence made by men; it is too loose, too heavy, too pompous for a woman's use. Yet in a novel, which covers so wide a stretch of ground, an ordinary and usual type of sentence has to be found to carry the reader on easily and naturally from one end of the book to the other. And this a woman must make for herself, altering and adapting the current sentence until she writes one that takes the natural shape of her thought without crushing or distorting it.

But that, after all, is only a means to an end, and the end is still to be reached only when a woman has the courage to surmount opposition and the determination to be true to herself. For a novel, after all, is a statement about a thousand different objects—human, natural, divine; it is an attempt to relate them to each other. In every novel of merit these different elements are held in place by the force of the writer's vision. But they have another order also, which is the order imposed upon them by convention. And as men are the arbiters of that convention, as they have established an order of values in life, so too, since fiction is largely based on life, these values prevail there also to a very great extent.

It is probable, however, that both in life and in art the values of a woman are not the values of a man. Thus, when a woman comes to write a novel, she will find that she is perpetually wishing to alter the established values—to make serious what appears insignificant to a man, and trivial what is to him important. And for that, of course, she will be criticized; for the critic of the opposite sex will be genuinely puzzled and surprised by an attempt to alter the current scale of values, and will see in it not merely a difference of view, but a view that is weak, or trivial, or sentimental, because it differs from his own.

But here, too, women are coming to be more independent of opinion. They are beginning to respect their own sense of values. And for this reason the subject matter of their novels begins to show certain changes. They are less interested, it would seem, in themselves; on the other hand, they are more interested in other women. In the early nineteenth century, women's novels were largely autobiographical. One of the motives that led them to write was the desire to expose their own suffering, to plead their own cause. Now that this desire is no longer so urgent, women are beginning to explore their own sex, to write of women as women have never been written of before; for of course, until very lately, women in literature were the creation of men.

Here again there are difficulties to overcome, for, if one may generalize, not only do women submit less readily to observation than men, but their lives are far less tested and examined by the ordinary processes of life. Often nothing tangible remains of a woman's day. The food that has been cooked is eaten; the children that have been nursed have gone out into the world. Where does the accent fall? What is the salient point for the novelist to seize upon? It is difficult to say. Her life has an anonymous character which is baffling and puzzling in the extreme. For the first time, this dark country is beginning to be explored in fiction; and at the same moment a woman has also to record the changes in women's minds and habits which the opening of the professions has introduced. She has to observe how their lives are ceasing to run underground; she has to discover what new colours and shadows are showing in them now that they are exposed to the outer world.

If, then, one should try to sum up the character of women's

fiction at the present moment, one would say that it is courageous; it is sincere; it keeps closely to what women feel. It is not bitter. It does not insist upon its femininity. But at the same time, a woman's book is not written as a man would write it. These qualities are much commoner than they were, and they give even to second- and third-rate work the value of truth and the interest of sincerity.

But in addition to these good qualities, there are two that call for a word more of discussion. The change which has turned the English woman from a nondescript influence, fluctuating and vague, to a voter, a wage-earner, a responsible citizen, has given her both in her life and in her art a turn toward the impersonal. Her relations now are not only emotional; they are intellectual, they are political. The old system which condemned her to squint askance at things through the eyes or through the interests of husband or brother, has given place to the direct and practical interests of one who must act for herself, and not merely influence the acts of others. Hence her attention is being directed away from the personal centre which engaged it exclusively in the past to the impersonal, and her novels naturally become more critical of society, and less analytical of individual lives.

We may expect that the office of gadfly to the state, which has been so far a male prerogative, will now be discharged by women also. Their novels will deal with social evils and remedies. Their men and women will not be observed wholly in relation to each other emotionally, but as they cohere and clash in groups and classes and races. That is one change of some importance. But there is another more interesting to those who prefer the butterfly to the gadfly—that is to say, the artist to the reformer. The greater impersonality of women's lives will encourage the poetic spirit, and it is in poetry that women's fiction is still weakest. It will lead them to be less absorbed in facts and no longer content to record with astonishing acuteness the minute details which fall under their own observation. They will look beyond the personal and political relationships to the wider questions which the poet tries to solve—of our destiny and the meaning of life.

The basis of the poetic attitude is of course largely founded upon material things. It depends upon leisure, and a little money, and the chance which money and leisure give to observe impersonally and dispassionately. With money and leisure at their service, women will naturally occupy themselves more than has hitherto been possible with the craft of letters. They will make a fuller and a more subtle use of the instrument of writing. Their technique will become bolder and richer.

In the past, the virtue of women's writing often lay in its divine spontaneity, like that of the blackbird's song or the thrush's. It was untaught; it was from the heart. But it was also, and much more often, chattering and garrulous—mere talk spilt over paper and left to dry in pools and blots. In future, granted time and books and a little space in the house for herself, literature will become for women, as for men, an art to be studied. Women's gift will be trained and strengthened. The novel will cease to be the dumping-ground for the personal emotions. It will become, more than at present, a work of art like any other, and its resources and its limitations will be explored.

From this it is a short step to the practice of the sophisticated arts, hitherto so little practised by women—to the writing of essays and criticism, of history and biography. And that, too, if we are considering the novel, will be of advantage; for besides improving the quality of the novel itself, it will draw off the aliens who have been attracted to fiction by its accessibility while their hearts lay elsewhere. Thus will the novel be rid of those excrescences of history and fact which, in our time, have made it so shapeless.

So, if we may prophesy, women in time to come will write fewer novels, but better novels; and not novels only, but poetry and criticism and history. But in this, to be sure, one is looking ahead to that golden, that perhaps fabulous, age when women will have what has so long been denied them—leisure, and money, and a room to themselves.

The Patron and the Crocus

YOUNG men and women beginning to write are generally given the plausible but utterly impracticable advice to write what they have to write as shortly as possible, as clearly as possible, and without other thought in their minds except to say exactly what is in them. Nobody ever adds on these occasions the one thing needful: 'And be sure you choose your patron wisely', though that is the gist of the whole matter. For a book is always written for somebody to read, and, since the patron is not merely the paymaster, but also in a very subtle and insidious way the instigator and inspirer of what is written, it is of the utmost importance that he should be a desirable man.

But who, then, is the desirable man—the patron who will cajole the best out of the writer's brain and bring to birth the most varied and vigorous progeny of which he is capable? Different ages have answered the question differently. The Elizabethans, to speak roughly, chose the aristocracy to write for and the playhouse public. The eighteenth-century patron was a combination of coffee-house wit and Grub Street bookseller. In the nineteenth century the great writers wrote for the half-crown magazines and the leisured classes. And looking back and applauding the splendid results of these different alliances, it all seems enviably simple, and plain as a pikestaff compared with our own predicament— for whom should we write? For the present supply of patrons is of unexampled and bewildering variety. There is the daily Press, the weekly Press, the monthly Press; the English public and the American public; the best-seller public and the worst-seller public; the high-brow public and the red-blood public; all now organized self-conscious entities capable through their various mouthpieces of making their needs known and their approval or displeasure felt. Thus the writer who has been moved by the sight of the first crocus in Kensington Gardens has, before he sets pen to paper, to choose from a crowd of competitors the particular patron who suits him best. It is futile to say, 'Dismiss them all; think only of your crocus', because writing is a method of communication; and the crocus is an imperfect crocus until it has been shared. The first man or the last may write for himself alone, but he is an exception and an unenviable one at that, and the gulls are welcome to his works if the gulls can read them.

Granted, then, that every writer has some public or other at the end of his pen, the high-minded will say that it should be a submissive public, accepting obediently whatever he likes to give it. Plausible as the theory sounds, great risks are attached to it. For in that case the writer remains conscious of his public, yet is superior to it—an uncomfortable and unfortunate combination, as the works of Samuel Butler, George Meredith, and Henry James may be taken to prove. Each despised the public; each desired a public; each failed to attain a public; and each wreaked his failure upon the public by a succession, gradually increasing in intensity, of angularities, obscurities, and affectations which no writer whose patron was his equal and friend would have thought it necessary to inflict. Their crocuses, in consequence, are tortured plants, beautiful and bright, but with something wry-necked about them, malformed, shrivelled on the one side, overblown on the other. A touch of the sun would have done them a world of good. Shall we then rush to the opposite extreme and accept (if in fancy alone) the flattering proposals which the editors of the *Times* and the *Daily News* may be supposed to make us—'Twenty pounds down for your crocus in precisely fifteen hundred words, which shall blossom upon every breakfast table from John o' Groats to the Land's End before nine o'clock to-morrow morning with the writer's name attached'?

But will one crocus be enough, and must it not be a very brilliant yellow to shine so far, to cost so much, and to have one's name attached to it? The Press is undoubtedly a great multiplier of crocuses. But if we look at some of these plants, we shall find that they are only very distantly related to the original little yellow or purple flower which pokes up through the grass in Kensington Gardens early in March every year. The newspaper crocus is an amazing but still a very different plant. It fills precisely the space allotted to it. It radiates a golden glow. It is genial, affable, warm-hearted. It is beautifully finished, too, for let nobody think that the art of 'our dramatic critic' of the *Times* or of Mr. Lynd of the *Daily News* is an easy one. It is no despicable feat to start a million brains running at nine o'clock in the morning, to give two million eyes something bright and brisk and amusing to look at. But the night comes and these flowers fade. So little bits of glass lose their lustre if you take them out of the sea; great prima donnas howl like hyenas if you shut them up in telephone boxes; and the most brilliant of articles when removed from its element is dust and sand and the husks of straw. Journalism embalmed in a book is unreadable.

The patron we want, then, is one who will help us to preserve our flowers from decay. But as his qualities change from age to age, and it needs considerable integrity and conviction not to be dazzled by the pretensions or bamboozled by the persuasions of the competing crowd, this business of patron-finding is one of the tests and trials of authorship. To know whom to write for is to know how to write. Some of the modern patron's qualities are, however, fairly plain. The writer will require at this moment, it is obvious, a patron with the book-reading habit rather than the play-going habit. Nowadays, too, he must be instructed in the literature of other times and races. But there are other qualities which our special weaknesses and tendencies demand in him. There is the question of indecency, for instance, which plagues us and puzzles us much more than it did the Elizabethans. The twentieth-century patron must be immune from shock. He must distinguish infallibly between the little clod of manure which sticks to the crocus of necessity, and that which is plastered to it out of bravado. He must be a judge, too, of those social influences which inevitably play so large a part in modern literature, and able to say which matures and fortifies, which inhibits and makes sterile. Further, there is emotion for him to pronounce on, and in no department can he do more useful work than in bracing a writer against sentimentality on the one hand and a craven fear of expressing his feeling on the other. It is worse, he will say, and perhaps more common, to be afraid of feeling than to feel too much. He will add, perhaps, something about language, and point out how many words Shakespeare used and how much grammar Shakespeare violated, while we, though we keep our fingers so demurely to the black notes on the piano, have not appreciably improved upon *Antony and Cleopatra*. And if you can forget your sex altogether, he will say, so much the better; a writer has none. But all this is by the way—elementary and disputable. The patron's prime quality is something different, only to be expressed perhaps by the use of that convenient word which cloaks so much —atmosphere. It is necessary that the patron should shed and envelop the crocus in an atmosphere which makes it appear a plant of the very highest importance, so that to misrepresent it is the one outrage not to be forgiven this side of the grave. He must make us feel that a single crocus, if it be a real crocus, is enough for him; that he does not want to be lectured, elevated, instructed, or improved; that he is sorry that he bullied Carlyle into vociferation, Tennyson into idyllics, and Ruskin into insanity; that he is now ready to efface himself or assert himself as his writers require; that he is bound to them by a more than maternal tie; that they are twins indeed, one dying if the other dies, one flourishing if the other flourishes; that the fate of literature depends upon their happy alliance—all of which proves, as we began by saying, that the choice of a patron is of the highest importance. But how to choose rightly? How to write well? Those are the questions.

How It Strikes a Contemporary

IN the first place a contemporary can scarcely fail to be struck by the fact that two critics at the same table at the same moment will pronounce completely different opinions about the same book. Here, on the right, it is declared a masterpiece of English prose; on the left, simultaneously, a mere mass of wastepaper which, if the fire could survive it, should be thrown upon the flames. Yet both critics are in agreement about Milton and about Keats. They display an exquisite sensibility and have undoubtedly a genuine enthusiasm. It is only when they discuss the work of contemporary writers that they inevitably come to blows. The book in question, which is at once a lasting contribution to English literature and a mere farrago of pretentious mediocrity, was published about two months ago. That is the explanation; that is why they differ.

The explanation is a strange one. It is equally disconcerting to the reader who wishes to take his bearings in the chaos of contemporary literature and to the writer who has a natural desire to know whether his own work, produced with infinite pains and in almost utter darkness, is likely to burn for ever among the fixed luminaries of English letters or, on the contrary, to put out the fire. But if we identify ourselves with the reader and explore his dilemma first, our bewilderment is short-lived enough. The same thing has happened so often before. We have heard the doctors disagreeing about the new and agreeing about the old twice a year on the average, in spring and autumn, ever since Robert Elsmere, or was it Stephen Phillips, somehow pervaded the atmosphere, and there was the same disagreement among grown-up people about these books too. It would be much more marvellous, and indeed much more upsetting, if, for a wonder, both gentlemen agreed, pronounced Blank's book an undoubted masterpiece, and thus faced us with the necessity of deciding whether we should back their judgment to the extent of ten and sixpence. Both are critics of reputation; the opinions tumbled out so spontaneously here will be starched and stiffened into columns of sober prose which will uphold the dignity of letters in England and America.

It must be some innate cynicism, then, some ungenerous distrust of contemporary genius, which determines us automatically as the talk goes on that, were they to agree—which they show no signs of doing—half a guinea is altogether too large a sum to squander upon contemporary enthusiasms, and the case will be met quite adequately by a card to the library. Still the question remains, and let us put it boldly to the critics themselves. Is there no guidance nowadays for a reader who yields to none in reverence for the dead, but is tormented by the suspicion that reverence for the dead is vitally connected with understanding of the living? After a rapid survey both critics are agreed that there is unfortunately no such person. For what is their own judgment worth where new books are concerned? Certainly not ten and sixpence. And from the stores of their experience they proceed to bring forth terrible examples of past blunders; crimes of criticism which, if they had been committed against the dead and not against the living, would have lost them their jobs and imperilled their reputations. The only advice they can offer is to respect one's own instincts, to follow them fearlessly and, rather than submit them to the control of any critic or reviewer alive, to check them by reading and reading again the masterpieces of the past.

Thanking them humbly, we cannot help reflecting that it was not always so. Once upon a time, we must believe, there was a rule, a discipline, which controlled the great republic of readers in a way which is now unknown. That is not to say that the great critic—the Dryden, the Johnson, the Coleridge, the Arnold—was an impeccable judge of contemporary work, whose verdicts stamped the book indelibly and saved the reader the trouble of reckoning the value for himself. The mistakes of these great men about their own contemporaries are too notorious to be worth recording. But the mere fact of their existence had a centralizing influence. That alone, it is not fantastic to suppose, would have controlled the disagreements of the dinner-table and given to random chatter about some book just out an authority now entirely to seek. The diverse schools would have debated as hotly as ever, but at the back of every reader's mind would have been the consciousness that there was at least one man who kept the main principles of literature closely in view: who, if you had taken to him some eccentricity of the moment, would have brought it into touch with permanence and tethered it by his own authority in the contrary blasts of praise and blame.[1] But when it comes to the making of a critic, nature must be generous and society ripe. The scattered dinner-tables of the modern world, the chase and eddy of the various currents which compose the society of our time, could only be dominated by a giant of fabulous dimensions. And where is even the very tall man whom we have the right to expect? Reviewers we have but no critic; a million competent and incorruptible policemen but no judge. Men of taste and learning and ability are for ever lecturing the young and celebrating the dead. But the too frequent result of their able and industrious pens is a desiccation of the living tissues of literature into a network of little bones. Nowhere shall we find the downright vigour of a Dryden, or Keats with his fine and natural bearing, his profound insight and sanity, or Flaubert and the tremendous power of his fanaticism, or Coleridge, above all, brewing in his head the whole of poetry and letting issue now and then one of those profound general statements which are caught up by the mind when hot with the friction of reading as if they were of the soul of the book itself.

And to all this, too, the critics generously agree. A great critic, they say, is the rarest of beings. But should one miraculously appear, how should we maintain him, on what should we feed him? Great critics, if they are not themselves great poets, are bred from the profusion of the age. There is some great man to be vindicated, some school to be founded or destroyed. But our age is meagre to the verge of destitution. There is no name which dominates the rest. There is no master in whose workshop the young are proud to serve apprenticeship. Mr. Hardy has long since withdrawn from the arena, and there is something exotic

[1] How violent these are two quotations will show. 'It [*Told by an Idiot*] should be read as the *Tempest* should be read, and as *Gulliver's Travels* should be read, for if Miss Macaulay's poetic gift happens to be less sublime than those of the author of the *Tempest*, and if her irony happens to be less tremendous than that of the author of *Gulliver's Travels*, her justice and wisdom are no less noble than theirs.' — *The Daily News*

The next day we read: 'For the rest one can only say that if Mr. Eliot had been pleased to write in demotic English *The Waste Land* might not have been, as it just is to all but anthropologists, and literati, so much waste-paper.' — *The Manchester Guardian*

about the genius of Mr. Conrad which makes him not so much an influence as an idol, honoured and admired, but aloof and apart. As for the rest, though they are many and vigorous and in the full flood of creative activity, there is none whose influence can seriously affect his contemporaries, or penetrate beyond our day to that not very distant future which it pleases us to call immortality. If we make a century our test, and ask how much of the work produced in these days in England will be in existence then, we shall have to answer not merely that we cannot agree upon the same book, but that we are more than doubtful whether such a book there is. It is an age of fragments. A few stanzas, a few pages, a chapter here and there, the beginning of this novel, the end of that, are equal to the best of any age or author. But can we go to posterity with a sheaf of loose pages, or ask the readers of those days, with the whole of literature before them, to sift our enormous rubbish heaps for our tiny pearls? Such are the questions which the critics might lawfully put to their companions at table, the novelists and poets.

At first the weight of pessimism seems sufficient to bear down all opposition. Yes, it is a lean age, we repeat, with much to justify its poverty; but, frankly, if we pit one century against another the comparison seems overwhelmingly against us. *Waverley, The Excursion, Kubla Khan, Don Juan, Hazlitt's Essays, Pride and Prejudice, Hyperion,* and *Prometheus Unbound* were all published between 1800 and 1821. Our century has not lacked industry; but if we ask for masterpieces it appears on the face of it that the pessimists are right. It seems as if an age of genius must be succeeded by an age of endeavour; riot and extravagance by cleanliness and hard work. All honour, of course, to those who have sacrificed their immortality to set the house in order. But if we ask for masterpieces, where are we to look? A little poetry, we may feel sure, will survive; a few poems by Mr. Yeats, by Mr. Davies, by Mr. De la Mare. Mr. Lawrence, of course, has moments of greatness, but hours of something very different. Mr. Beerbohm, in his way, is perfect, but it is not a big way. Passages in *Far Away and Long Ago* will undoubtedly go to posterity entire. *Ulysses* was a memorable catastrophe—immense in daring, terrific in disaster. And so, picking and choosing, we select now this, now that, hold it up for display, hear it defended or derided, and finally have to meet the objection that even so we are only agreeing with the critics that it is an age incapable of sustained effort, littered with fragments, and not seriously to be compared with the age that went before.

But it is just when opinions universally prevail and we have added lip service to their authority that we become sometimes most keenly conscious that we do not believe a word that we are saying. It is a barren and exhausted age, we repeat; we must look back with envy to the past. Meanwhile it is one of the first fine days of spring. Life is not altogether lacking in colour. The telephone, which interrupts the most serious conversations and cuts short the most weighty observations, has a romance of its own. And the random talk of people who have no chance of immortality and thus can speak their minds out has a setting, often, of lights, streets, houses, human beings, beautiful or grotesque, which will weave itself into the moment for ever. But this is life; the talk is about literature. We must try to disentangle the two, and justify the rash revolt of optimism against the superior plausibility, the finer distinction, of pessimism.

Our optimism, then, is largely instinctive. It springs from the fine day and the wine and the talk; it springs from the fact that when life throws up such treasures daily, daily suggests more than the most voluble can express; much though we admire the dead, we prefer life as it is. There is something about the present which we would not exchange, though we were offered a choice of all past ages to live in. And modern literature, with all its imperfections, has the same hold on us and the same fascination. It is like a relation whom we snub and scarify daily, but, after all, cannot do without. It has the same endearing quality of being that which we are, that which we have made, that in which we live, instead of being something, however august, alien to ourselves and beheld from the outside. Nor has any generation more need than ours to cherish its contemporaries. We are sharply cut off from our predecessors. A shift in the scale—the sudden slip of masses held in position for ages—has shaken the fabric from top to bottom, alienated us from the past and made us perhaps too vividly conscious of the present. Every day we find ourselves doing, saying, or thinking things that would have been impossible to our fathers. And we feel the differences which have not been noted far more keenly than the resemblances which have been very perfectly expressed. New books lure us to read them partly in the hope that they will reflect this rearrangement of our attitude—these scenes, thoughts, and apparently fortuitous groupings of incongruous things which impinge upon us with so keen a sense of novelty—and, as literature does, give it back into our keeping, whole and comprehended. Here indeed there is every reason for optimism. No age can have been more rich than ours in writers determined to give expression to the differences which separate them from the past and not to the resemblances which connect them with it. It would be invidious to mention names, but the most casual reader dipping into poetry, into fiction, into biography can hardly fail to be impressed by the courage, the sincerity, in a word, by the widespread originality of our time. But our exhilaration is strangely curtailed. Book after book leaves us with the same sense of promise unachieved, of intellectual poverty, of brilliance which has been snatched from life but not transmuted into literature. Much of what is best in contemporary work has the appearance of being noted under pressure, taken down in a bleak shorthand which preserves with astonishing brilliance the movements and expressions of the figures as they pass across the screen. But the flash is soon over, and there remains with us a profound dissatisfaction. The irritation is as acute as the pleasure was intense.

After all, then, we are back at the beginning, vacillating from extreme to extreme, at one moment enthusiastic, at the next pessimistic, unable to come to any conclusion about our contemporaries. We have asked the critics to help us, but they have deprecated the task. Now, then, is the time to accept their advice and correct these extremes by consulting the masterpieces of the past. We feel ourselves indeed driven to them, impelled not by calm judgment but by some imperious need to anchor our instability upon their security. But, honestly, the shock of the comparison between past and present is at first disconcerting. Undoubtedly there is a dullness in great books. There is an unabashed tranquillity in page after page of Wordsworth and Scott and Miss Austen which is sedative to the verge of somnolence. Opportunities occur and they neglect them. Shades and subtleties accumulate and they ignore them. They seem deliberately to refuse to gratify those senses which are stimulated so briskly by the moderns; the senses of sight, of sound, of touch—above all, the sense of the human being, his depth and the variety of his perceptions, his complexity, his confusion, his self, in short. There is little of all this in the works of Wordsworth and Scott and Jane Austen. From what, then, arises that sense of security which gradually, delightfully, and completely overcomes us? It is the power of their belief —their conviction, that imposes itself upon us. In Wordsworth, the philosophic poet, this is obvious enough. But it is equally true of the careless Scott, who scribbled masterpieces to build castles before breakfast, and of the modest maiden lady who wrote furtively and quietly simply to give pleasure. In both there is the same natural conviction that life is of a certain quality. They have their judgment of conduct. They know the relations of human beings towards each other and towards the universe. Neither of them probably has a word to say about the matter outright, but everything depends on it. Only believe, we find ourselves saying, and all the rest will come of itself. Only believe, to take a very simple instance which the recent publication of *The Watsons* brings to mind, that a nice girl will instinctively try to soothe the feelings of a boy who has been snubbed at a dance, and then, if you believe it implicitly and unquestioningly, you will not only make people a hundred years later feel the same thing, but you will make them feel it as literature. For certainty of that kind is the condition which makes it possible to write. To believe that your impressions hold good for others is to be released from the cramp and confinement of personality. It is to be free, as Scott was free, to explore with a vigour which still holds us spellbound the whole world of adventure and romance. It is also the first step in that mysterious process in which Jane Austen was so great an adept. The little grain of experience once selected, believed in, and set outside herself, could be put precisely in its place, and she was then free to make it, by a process which never yields its secrets to the analyst, into that complete statement which is literature.

So then our contemporaries afflict us because they have ceased to believe. The most sincere of them will only tell us what it is that happens to himself. They cannot make a world, because they are not free of other human beings. They cannot tell stories because they do not believe that stories are true. They cannot generalize. They depend on their senses and emotions, whose testimony is trustworthy, rather than on their intellects, whose message is obscure. And they have perforce to deny themselves the use of some of the most powerful and some of the most exquisite of the weapons of their craft. With the whole wealth of the English language at the back of them, they timidly pass about from hand to hand and book to book only the meanest copper coins. Set down at a fresh angle of the eternal prospect they can only whip out their notebooks and record with agonized intensity the flying gleams, which light on what? and the transitory splendours, which may, perhaps, compose nothing whatever. But here the critics interpose, and with some show of justice.

If this description holds good, they say, and is not, as it may well be, entirely dependent upon our position at the table and certain purely personal relationships to mustard pots and flower vases, then the risks of judging contemporary work are greater than ever before. There is every excuse for them if they are wide of the mark; and no doubt it would be better to retreat, as Matthew Arnold advised, from the burning ground of the present to the safe tranquillity of the past. 'We enter on burning ground', wrote Matthew Arnold, 'as we approach the poetry of times so near to us, poetry like that of Byron, Shelley, and Wordsworth, of which the estimates are so often not only personal, but personal with passion', and this, they remind us, was written in the year 1880. Beware, they say, of putting under the microscope one inch of a ribbon which runs many miles; things sort themselves out if you wait; moderation, and a study of the classics are to be recommended. Moreover, life is short; the Byron centenary is at hand; and the burning question of the moment is, did he, or did he not, marry his sister? To sum up, then—if indeed any conclusion is possible when everybody is talking at once and it is time to be going—it seems that it would be wise for the writers of the present to renounce the hope of creating masterpieces. Their poems, plays, biographies, novels are not books but notebooks, and Time, like a good schoolmaster, will take them in his hands, point to their blots and scrawls and erasions, and tear them across; but he will not throw them into the waste-paper basket. He will keep them because other students will find them very useful. It is from the notebooks of the present that the masterpieces of the future are made. Literature, as the critics were saying just now, has lasted long, has undergone many changes, and it is only a short sight and a parochial mind that will exaggerate the importance of these squalls, however they may agitate the little boats now tossing out at sea. The storm and the drenching are on the surface; continuity and calm are in the depths.

As for the critics whose task it is to pass judgment upon the books of the moment, whose work, let us admit, is difficult, dangerous, and often distasteful, let us ask them to be generous of encouragement, but sparing of those wreaths and coronets which are so apt to get awry, and fade, and make the wearers, in six months' time, look a little ridiculous. Let them take a wider, a less personal view of modern literature, and look indeed upon the writers as if they were engaged upon some vast building, which being built by common effort, the separate workmen may well remain anonymous. Let them slam the door upon the cosy company where sugar is cheap and butter plentiful, give over, for a time at least, the discussion of that fascinating topic—whether Byron married his sister—and, withdrawing, perhaps a hand's-breadth from the table where we sit chattering, say something interesting about literature itself. Let us buttonhole them as they leave, and recall to their memory that gaunt aristocrat, Lady Hester Stanhope, who kept a milk-white horse in her stable in readiness for the Messiah and was for ever scanning the mountain-tops, impatiently but with confidence, for signs of his approach, and ask them to follow her example; scan the horizon; see the past in relation to the future; and so prepare the way for masterpieces to come.

The Leaning Tower[1]

A WRITER is a person who sits at a desk and keeps his eye fixed, as intently as he can, upon a certain object—that figure of speech may help to keep us steady on our path if we look at it for a moment. He is an artist who sits with a sheet of paper in front of him trying to copy what he sees. What is his object—his model? Nothing so simple as a painter's model; it is not a bowl of flowers, a naked figure, or a dish of apples and onions. Even the simplest story deals with more than one person, with more than one time. Characters begin young; they grow old; they move from scene to scene, from place to place. A writer has to keep his eye upon a model that moves, that changes, upon an object that is not one object but innumerable objects. Two words alone cover all that a writer looks at—they are, human life.

Let us look at the writer next. What do we see—only a person who sits with a pen in his hand in front of a sheet of paper? That tells us little or nothing. And we know very little. Considering how much we talk about writers, how much they talk about themselves, it is odd how little we know about them. Why are they so common sometimes; then so rare? Why do they sometimes write nothing but masterpieces, then nothing but trash? And why should a family, like the Shelleys, like the Keatses, like the Brontës, suddenly burst into flame and bring to birth Shelley, Keats, and the Brontës? What are the conditions that bring about that explosion? There is no answer—naturally. Since we have not yet discovered the germ of influenza, how should we yet have discovered the germ of genius? We know even less about the mind than about the body. We have less evidence. It is less than two hundred years since people took an interest in themselves; Boswell was almost the first writer who thought that a man's life was worth writing a book about. Until we have more facts, more biographies, more autobiographies, we cannot know much about ordinary people, let alone about extraordinary people. Thus at present we have only theories about writers—a great many

[1] A paper read to the Workers' Educational Association, Brighton, May 1940

theories, but they all differ. The politician says that a writer is the product of the society in which he lives, as a screw is the product of a screw machine; the artist, that a writer is a heavenly apparition that slides across the sky, grazes the earth, and vanishes. To the psychologists a writer is an oyster; feed him on gritty facts, irritate him with ugliness, and by way of compensation, as they call it, he will produce a pearl. The genealogists say that certain stocks, certain families, breed writers as fig trees breed figs— Dryden, Swift, and Pope they tell us were all cousins. This proves that we are in the dark about writers; anybody can make a theory; the germ of a theory is almost always the wish to prove what the theorist wishes to believe.

Theories then are dangerous things. All the same we must risk making one this afternoon since we are going to discuss modern tendencies. Directly we speak of tendencies or movements we commit ourselves to the belief that there is some force, influence, outer pressure which is strong enough to stamp itself upon a whole group of different writers so that all their writing has a certain common likeness. We must then have a theory as to what this influence is. But let us always remember—influences are infinitely numerous; writers are infinitely sensitive; each writer has a different sensibility. That is why literature is always changing, like the weather, like the clouds in the sky. Read a page of Scott; then of Henry James; try to work out the influences that have transformed the one page into the other. It is beyond our skill. We can only hope therefore to single out the most obvious influences that have formed writers into groups. Yet there are groups. Books descend from books as families descend from families. Some descend from Jane Austen; others from Dickens. They resemble their parents, as human children resemble their parents; yet they differ as children differ, and revolt as children revolt. Perhaps it will be easier to understand living writers as we take a quick look at some of their forebears. We have not time to go far back—certainly we have not time to look closely. But let us glance at English writers as they were a hundred years ago—that may help us to see what we ourselves look like.

In 1815 England was at war, as England is now. And it is natural to ask, how did their war—the Napoleonic war—affect them? Was that one of the influences that formed them into groups? The answer is a very strange one. The Napoleonic wars did not affect the great majority of those writers at all. The proof of that is to be found in the work of two great novelists—Jane Austen and Walter Scott. Each lived through the Napoleonic wars; each wrote through them. But, though novelists live very close to the life of their time, neither of them in all their novels mentioned the Napoleonic wars. This shows that their model, their vision of human life, was not disturbed or agitated or changed by war. Nor were they themselves. It is easy to see why that was so. Wars were then remote; wars were carried on by soldiers and sailors, not by private people. The rumour of battles took a long time to reach England. It was only when the mail coaches clattered along the country roads hung with laurels that the people in villages like Brighton knew that a victory had been won and lit their candles and stuck them in their windows. Compare that with our state to-day. To-day we hear the gunfire in the Channel. We turn on the wireless; we hear an airman telling us how this very afternoon he shot down a raider; his machine caught fire; he plunged into the sea; the light turned green and then black; he rose to the top and was rescued by a trawler. Scott never saw the sailors drowning at Trafalgar; Jane Austen never heard the cannon roar at Waterloo. Neither of them heard Napoleon's voice as we hear Hitler's voice as we sit at home of an evening.

That immunity from war lasted all through the nineteenth century. England, of course, was often at war—there was the Crimean War; the Indian Mutiny; all the little Indian frontier wars, and at the end of the century the Boer War. Keats, Shelley, Byron, Dickens, Thackeray, Carlyle, Ruskin, the Brontës, George Eliot, Trollope, the Brownings—all lived through all those wars. But did they ever mention them? Only Thackeray, I think; in *Vanity Fair* he described the Battle of Waterloo long after it was fought; but only as an illustration, as a scene. It did not change his characters' lives; it merely killed one of his heroes. Of the poets, only Byron and Shelley felt the influence of the nineteenth-century wars profoundly.

War then we can say, speaking roughly, did not affect either the writer or his vision of human life in the nineteenth century. But peace—let us consider the influence of peace. Were the nineteenth-century writers affected by the settled, the peaceful and prosperous state of England? Let us collect a few facts before we launch out into the dangers and delights of theory. We know for a fact, from their lives, that the nineteenth-century writers were all of them fairly well-to-do middle-class people. Most had been educated either at Oxford or at Cambridge. Some were civil servants like Trollope and Matthew Arnold. Others, like Ruskin, were professors. It is a fact that their work brought them considerable fortunes. There is visible proof of that in the houses they built. Look at Abbotsford, bought out of the proceeds of Scott's novels; or at Farringford, built by Tennyson from his poetry. Look at Dickens's great house in Marylebone; and at his great house at Gadshill. All these are houses needing many butlers, maids, gardeners, grooms to keep the tables spread, the cans carried, and the gardens neat and fruitful. Not only did they leave behind them large houses; they left too an immense body of literature—poems, plays, novels, essays, histories, criticism. It was a very prolific, creative, rich century—the nineteenth century. Now let us ask—is there any connexion between that material prosperity and that intellectual creativeness? Did one lead to the other? How difficult it is to say—for we know so little about writers, and what conditions help them, what hinder them. It is only a guess, and a rough guess; yet I think that there is a connexion. 'I think'—perhaps it would be nearer the truth to say 'I see'. Thinking should be based on facts; and here we have intuitions rather than facts—the lights and shades that come after books are read, the general shifting surface of a large expanse of print. What I see, glancing over that shifting surface, is the picture I have already shown you; the writer seated in front of human life in the nineteenth century; and, looking at it through their eyes, I see that life divided up, herded together, into many different classes. There is the aristocracy; the landed gentry; the professional class; the commercial class; the working class; and there, in one dark blot, is that great class which is called simply and comprehensively 'The Poor'. To the nineteenth-century writer human life must have looked like a landscape cut up into separate fields. In each field was gathered a different group of people. Each to some extent had its own traditions; its own manners; its own speech; its own dress; its own occupation. But owing to that peace, to that prosperity, each group was tethered, stationary—a herd grazing within its own hedges. And the nineteenth-century writer did not seek to change those divisions; he accepted them. He accepted them so completely that he became unconscious of them. Does that serve to explain why it is that the nineteenth-century writers are able to create so many characters who are not types but individuals? Is it because he did not see the hedges that divide classes; he saw only the human beings that live within those hedges? Is that why he could get beneath the surface and create many-sided characters— Pecksniff, Becky Sharp, Mr. Woodhouse—who change with the years, as the living change? To us now the hedges are visible. We can see now that each of those writers only dealt with a very small section of human life—all Thackeray's characters are upper middle-class people; all Dickens's characters come from the lower middle class. We can see that now; but the writer himself seems unconscious that he is only dealing with one type; with the type formed by the class into which the writer was born himself, with which he is most familiar. And that unconsciousness was an immense advantage to him.

Unconsciousness, which means presumably that the under-mind works at top speed while the upper-mind drowses, is a state we all know. We all have experience of the work done by unconsciousness in our own daily lives. You have had a crowded day, let us suppose, sightseeing in London. Could you say what you had seen and done when you came back? Was it not all a blur, a confusion? But after what seemed a rest, a chance to turn aside and look at something different, the sights and sounds and sayings that had been of most interest to you swam to the surface, apparently of their own accord; and remained in memory; what was unimportant sank into forgetfulness. So it is with the writer. After a hard day's work, trudging round, seeing all he can, feeling all he can, taking in the book of his mind innumerable notes, the writer becomes—if he can—unconscious. In fact, his under-mind works at top speed while his upper-mind drowses. Then, after a pause the veil lifts; and there is the thing—the thing he wants to write about—simplified, composed. Do we strain Wordsworth's famous saying about emotion recollected in tranquillity when we infer that by tranquillity he meant that the writer needs to become unconscious before he can create?

If we want to risk a theory, then, we can say that peace and prosperity were influences that gave the nineteenth-century writers a family likeness. They had leisure; they had security; life was not going to change; they themselves were not going to change. They could look; and look away. They could forget; and then— in their books—remember. Those then are some of the conditions that brought about a certain family likeness, in spite of the great individual differences, among the nineteenth-century writers. The nineteenth century ended; but the same conditions went on. They lasted, roughly speaking, till the year 1914. Even in 1914 we can still see the writer sitting as he sat all through the nineteenth century looking at human life; and that human life is still divided into classes; he still looks most intently at the class from which he himself springs; the classes are still so settled that he has almost forgotten that there are classes; and he is still so secure himself that he is almost unconscious of his own position and of its security. He believes that he is looking at the whole of life; and will always so look at it. That is not altogether a fancy picture. Many of those writers are still alive. Sometimes they describe their own position as young men, beginning to write, just before August 1914. How did you learn your art? one can ask them. At College they say— by reading; by listening; by talking. What did they talk about? Here is Mr. Desmond MacCarthy's answer, as he gave it, a week or two ago, in the *Sunday Times*. He was at Cambridge just before the war began and he says: 'We were not very much interested in politics. Abstract speculation was much more absorbing; philosophy was more interesting to us than public causes. . . . What we chiefly discussed were those "goods" which were ends in themselves . . . the search for truth, aesthetic emotions, and personal relations.' In addition they read an immense amount; Latin and Greek, and of course French and English. They wrote too—but they were in no hurry to publish. They travelled;—some of them went far afield—to India, to the South Seas. But for the most part they rambled happily in the long summer holidays through England, through France, through Italy. And now and then they published books—books like Rupert Brooke's poems; novels like E. M. Forster's *Room with a View*; essays like G. K. Chesterton's essays, and reviews. It seemed to them that they were to go on living like that, and writing like that, for ever and ever. Then suddenly, like a chasm in a smooth road, the war came.

But before we go on with the story of what happened after 1914, let us look more closely for a moment, not at the writer himself, nor at his model; but at his chair. A chair is a very important part of a writer's outfit. It is the chair that gives him his attitude towards his model; that decides what he sees of human life; that profoundly affects his power of telling us what he sees. By his chair we mean his upbringing, his education. It is a fact, not a theory, that all writers from Chaucer to the present day, with so few exceptions that one hand can count them, have sat upon the same kind of chair—a raised chair. They have all come from the middle class; they have had good, at least expensive, educations. They have all been raised above the mass of people upon a tower of stucco—that is their middle-class birth; and of gold—that is their expensive education. That was true of all the nineteenth-century writers, save Dickens; it was true of all the 1914 writers, save D. H. Lawrence. Let us run through what are called 'representative names': G. K. Chesterton; T. S. Eliot; Belloc; Lytton Strachey; Somerset Maugham; Hugh Walpole; Wilfred Owen; Rupert Brooke; J. E. Flecker; E. M. Forster; Aldous Huxley; G. M. Trevelyan; O. and S. Sitwell; Middleton Murry. Those are some of them; and all, with the exception of D. H. Lawrence, came of the middle class, and were educated at public schools and universities. There is another fact, equally indisputable: the books that they wrote were among the best books written between 1910 and 1925. Now let us ask, is there any connexion between those facts? Is there a connexion between the excellence of their work and the fact that they came of families rich enough to send them to public schools and universities?

Must we not decide, greatly though those writers differ, and shallow as we admit our knowledge of influences to be, that there must be a connexion between their education and their work? It cannot be a mere chance that this minute class of educated people has produced so much that is good as writing; and that the vast mass of people without education has produced so little that is good. It is a fact, however. Take away all that the working class has given to English literature and that literature would scarcely suffer; take away all that the educated class has given, and English literature would scarcely exist. Education must then play a very important part in a writer's work.

That seems so obvious that it is astonishing how little stress has been laid upon the writer's education. It is perhaps because a writer's education is so much less definite than other educations. Reading, listening, talking, travel, leisure—many different things it seems are mixed together. Life and books must be shaken and taken in the right proportions. A boy brought up alone in a library turns into a bookworm; brought up alone in the fields he turns into an earthworm. To breed the kind of butterfly a writer is you must let him sun himself for three or four years at Oxford or Cambridge—so it seems. However it is done, it is there that it is done—there that he is taught his art. And he has to be taught his art. Again, is that strange? Nobody thinks it strange if you say that a painter has to be taught his art; or a musician; or an architect. Equally a writer has to be taught. For the art of writing is at least as difficult as the other arts. And though, perhaps because the education is indefinite, people ignore this education; if you look closely you will see that almost every writer who has practised his art successfully had been taught it. He had been taught it by about eleven years of education—at private schools, public schools, and universities. He sits upon a tower raised above the rest of us; a tower built first on his parents' station, then on his parents' gold. It is a tower of the utmost importance; it decides his angle of vision; it affects his power of communication.

All through the nineteenth century, down to August 1914, that tower was a steady tower. The writer was scarcely conscious either of his high station or of his limited vision. Many of them had sympathy, great sympathy, with other classes; they wished to help the working class to enjoy the advantages of the tower class; but they did not wish to destroy the tower, or to descend from it—rather to make it accessible to all. Nor had the model, human life, changed essentially since Trollope looked at it, since Hardy looked at it: and Henry James, in 1914, was still looking at it. Further, the tower itself held firm beneath the writer during all the most impressionable years, when he was learning his art, and receiving all those complex influences and instructions that are summed up by the word education. These were conditions that influenced their work profoundly. For when the crash came in 1914 all those young men, who were to be the representative writers of their time, had their past, their education, safe behind them, safe within them. They had known security; they had the memory of a peaceful boyhood, the knowledge of a settled civilization. Even though the war cut into their lives, and ended some of them, they wrote, and still write, as if the tower were firm beneath them. In one word, they are aristocrats; the unconscious inheritors of a great tradition. Put a page of their writing under the magnifying-glass and you will see, far away in the distance, the Greeks, the Romans; coming nearer, the Elizabethans; coming nearer still, Dryden, Swift, Voltaire, Jane Austen, Dickens, Henry James. Each, however much he differs individually from the others, is a man of education; a man who has learnt his art.

From that group let us pass to the next—to the group which began to write about 1925 and, it may be, came to an end as a group in 1939. If you read current literary journalism you will be able to rattle off a string of names—Day Lewis, Auden, Spender, Isherwood, Louis MacNeice and so on. They adhere much more closely than the names of their predecessors. But at first sight there seems little difference, in station, in education. Mr. Auden in a poem written to Mr. Isherwood says: Behind us we have stucco suburbs and expensive educations. They are tower dwellers like their predecessors, the sons of well-to-do parents, who could afford to send them to public schools and universities. But what a difference in the tower itself, in what they saw from the tower! When they looked at human life what did they see? Everywhere change; everywhere revolution. In Germany, in Russia, in Italy, in Spain, all the old hedges were being rooted up; all the old towers were being thrown to the ground. Other hedges were being planted; other towers were being raised. There was communism in one country; in another fascism. The whole of civilization, of society, was changing. There was, it is true, neither war nor revolution in England itself. All those writers had time to write many books before 1939. But even in England towers that were built of gold and stucco were no longer steady towers. They were leaning towers. The books were written under the influence of change, under the threat of war. That perhaps is why the names adhere so closely; there was one influence that affected them all and made them, more than their predecessors, into groups. And that influence, let us remember, may well have excluded from that string of names the poets whom posterity will value most highly, either because they could not fall into step, as leaders or as followers, or because the influence was adverse to poetry, and until that influence relaxed, they could not write. But the tendency that makes it possible for us to group the names of these writers together, and gives their work a common likeness, was the tendency of the tower they sat on—the tower of middle-class birth and expensive education —to lean.

Let us imagine, to bring this home to us, that we are actually upon a leaning tower and note our sensations. Let us see whether they correspond to the tendencies we observe in those poems, plays, and novels. Directly we feel that a tower leans we become acutely conscious that we are upon a tower. All those writers too are acutely tower conscious; conscious of their middle-class birth; of their expensive educations. Then when we come to the top of the tower how strange the view looks—not altogether upside down, but slanting, sidelong. That too is characteristic of the leaning-tower writers; they do not look any class straight in the face; they look either up, or down, or sidelong. There is no class so settled that they can explore it unconsciously. That perhaps is why they create no characters. Then what do we feel next, raised in imagination on top of the tower? First discomfort; next self-pity for that discomfort; which pity soon turns to anger—to anger against the builder, against society, for making us uncomfortable. Those too seem to be tendencies of the leaning-tower writers. Discomfort; pity for themselves; anger against society. And yet—here is another tendency—how can you altogether abuse a society that is giving you, after all, a very fine view and some sort of security? You cannot abuse that society whole-heartedly while you continue to profit by that society. And so very naturally you abuse society in the person of some retired admiral or spinster or armament manufacturer; and by abusing them hope to escape whipping yourself. The bleat of the scapegoat sounds loud in their work, and the whimper of the schoolboy crying 'Please, Sir, it was the other fellow, not me'. Anger; pity; scapegoat beating; excuse finding— these are all very natural tendencies; if we were in their position we should tend to do the same. But we are not in their position; we have not had eleven years of expensive education. We have only been climbing an imaginary tower. We can cease to imagine. We can come down.

But they cannot. They cannot throw away their education; they cannot throw away their upbringing. Eleven years at school and college have been stamped upon them indelibly. And then, to their credit but to their confusion, the leaning tower not only leant in the thirties, but it leant more and more to the left. Do you remember what Mr. MacCarthy said about his own group at the university in 1914? 'We were not very much interested in politics ... philosophy was more interesting to us than public causes'? That shows that his tower leant neither to the right nor to the left. But in 1930 it was impossible—if you were young, sensitive, imaginative—not to be interested in politics; not to find public causes of much more pressing interest than philosophy. In 1930 young men at college were forced to be aware of what was happening in Russia; in Germany; in Italy; in Spain. They could not go on discussing aesthetic emotions and personal relations. They could not confine their reading to the poets; they had to read the politicians. They read Marx. They became communists; they became anti-fascists. The tower they realized was founded upon injustice and tyranny; it was wrong for a small class to possess an education that other people paid for; wrong to stand upon the gold that a bourgeois father had made from his bourgeois profession. It was wrong; yet how could they make it right? Their education could not be thrown away; as for their capital—did Dickens, did Tolstoy ever throw away their capital? Did D. H. Lawrence, a miner's son, continue to live like a miner? No; for it is death for a writer to throw away his capital; to be forced to earn his living in a mine or a factory. And thus, trapped by their education, pinned down by their capital, they remained on top of their leaning tower, and their state of mind as we see it reflected in their poems and plays and novels is full of discord and bitterness, full of confusion and of compromise.

These tendencies are better illustrated by quotation than by analysis. There is a poem by one of those writers, Louis MacNeice, called *Autumn Journal*. It is dated March 1939. It is feeble as poetry, but interesting as autobiography. He begins of course with a snipe at the scapegoat—the bourgeois, middle-class family from which he sprang. The retired admirals, the retired generals, and the spinster lady have breakfasted off bacon and eggs served on a silver dish, he tells us. He sketches that family as if it were already a little remote and more than a little ridiculous. But they could afford to send him to Marlborough and then to Merton, Oxford. This is what he learnt at Oxford:

> *We learned that a gentleman never misplaces his accents,*
> *That nobody knows how to speak, much less how to write*
> *English who has not hob-nobbed with the great-grandparents of English.*

Besides that he learnt at Oxford Latin and Greek; and philosophy, logic, and metaphysics:

> *Oxford* [he says] *crowded the mantelpiece with gods—*
> *Scaliger, Heinsius, Dindorf, Bentley, Wilamowitz.*

It was at Oxford that the tower began to lean. He felt that he was living under a system—

> *That gives the few at fancy prices their fancy lives*
> *While ninety-nine in the hundred who never attend the banquet*
> *Must wash the grease of ages off the knives.*

But at the same time, an Oxford education had made him fastidious:

> *It is so hard to imagine*
> *A world where the many would have their chance without*
> *A fall in the standard of intellectual living*
> *And nothing left that the highbrow cares about.*

At Oxford he got his honours degree; and that degree—in humane letters—put him in the way of a 'cushy job'—seven hundred a year, to be precise, and several rooms of his own.

> *If it were not for Lit. Hum. I might be climbing*
> *A ladder with a hod,*
> *And seven hundred a year*
> *Will pay the rent and the gas and the phone and the grocer—*

And yet, again, doubts break in; the 'cushy job' of teaching more Latin and Greek to more undergraduates does not satisfy him—

> . . . the so-called humane studies
> May lead to cushy jobs
> But leave the men who land them spiritually bankrupt,
> Intellectual snobs.

And what is worse, that education and that 'cushy job' cut one off, he complains, from the common life of one's kind.

> All that I would like to be is human, having a share
> In a civilized, articulate and well-adjusted
> Community where the mind is given its due
> But the body is not distrusted.

Therefore in order to bring about that well-adjusted community he must turn from literature to politics, remembering, he says,

> Remembering that those who by their habit
> Hate politics, can no longer keep their private
> Values unless they open the public gate
> To a better political system.

So, in one way or another, he takes part in politics, and finally he ends:

> What is it we want really?
> For what end and how?
> If it is something feasible, obtainable,
> Let us dream it now,
> And pray for a possible land
> Not of sleep-walkers, not of angry puppets,
> But where both heart and brain can understand
> The movements of our fellows,
> Where life is a choice of instruments and none
> Is debarred his natural music . . .
> Where the individual, no longer squandered
> In self-assertion, works with the rest . . .

Those quotations give a fair description of the influences that have told upon the leaning-tower group. Others could easily be discovered. The influence of the films explains the lack of transitions in their work and the violently opposed contrasts. The influence of poets like Mr. Yeats and Mr. Eliot explains the obscurity. They took over from the elder poets a technique which, after many years of experiment, those poets used skilfully, and used it clumsily and often inappropriately. But we have time only to point to the most obvious influences; and these can be summed up as Leaning Tower Influences. If you think of them, that is, as people trapped on a leaning tower from which they cannot descend, much that is puzzling in their work is easier to understand. It explains the violence of their attack upon bourgeois society and also its half-heartedness. They are profiting by a society which they abuse. They are flogging a dead or dying horse because a living horse, if flogged, would kick them off its back. It explains the destructiveness of their work; and also its emptiness. They can destroy bourgeois society, in part at least; but what have they put in its place? How can a writer who has no first-hand experience of a towerless, of a classless society create that society? Yet as Mr. MacNeice bears witness, they feel compelled to preach, if not by their living, at least by their writing, the creation of a society in which everyone is equal and everyone is free. It explains the pedagogic, the didactic, the loud-speaker strain that dominates their poetry. They must teach; they must preach. Everything is a duty—even love. Listen to Mr. Day Lewis ingeminating love. 'Mr. Spender', he says, 'speaking from the living unit of himself and his friends appeals for the contraction of the social group to a size at which human contact may again be established and demands the destruction of all impediments to love. Listen.' And we listen to this:

> *We have come at last to a country*
> *Where light, like shine from snow, strikes all faces.*
> *Here you may wonder*
> *How it was that works, money, interest, building could ever*
> *Hide the palpable and obvious love of man for man.*

We listen to oratory, not poetry. It is necessary, in order to feel the emotion of those lines, that other people should be listening too. We are in a group, in a class-room as we listen.

Listen now to Wordsworth:

> *Lover had he known in huts where poor men dwell,*
> *His daily teachers had been woods and rills,*
> *The silence that is in the starry sky,*
> *The sleep that is among the lonely hills.*

We listen to that when we are alone. We remember that in solitude. Is that the difference between politician's poetry and poet's poetry? We listen to the one in company; to the other when we are alone? But the poet in the thirties was forced to be a politician. That explains why the artist in the thirties was forced to be a scapegoat. If politics were 'real', the ivory tower was an escape from 'reality'. That explains the curious, bastard language in which so much of this leaning-tower prose and poetry is written. It is not the rich speech of the aristocrat: it is not the racy speech of the peasant. It is betwixt and between. The poet is a dweller in two worlds, one dying, the other struggling to be born. And so we come to what is perhaps the most marked tendency of leaning-tower literature—the desire to be whole; to be human. 'All that I would like to be is human'—that cry rings through their books—the longing to be closer to their kind, to write the common speech of their kind, to share the emotions of their kind, no longer to be isolated and exalted in solitary state upon their tower, but to be down on the ground with the mass of human kind.

These then, briefly and from a certain angle, are some of the tendencies of the modern writer who is seated upon a leaning tower. No other generation has been exposed to them. It may be that none has had such an appallingly difficult task. Who can wonder if they have been incapable of giving us great poems, great plays, great novels? They had nothing settled to look at; nothing peaceful to remember; nothing certain to come. During all the most impressionable years of their lives they were stung into consciousness—into self-consciousness, into class-consciousness, into the consciousness of things changing, of things falling, of death perhaps about to come. There was no tranquillity in which they could recollect. The inner mind was paralysed because the surface mind was always hard at work.

Yet if they have lacked the creative power of the poet and the novelist, the power—does it come from a fusion of the two minds, the upper and the under?—that creates characters that live, poems that we all remember, they have had a power which, if literature continues, may prove to be of great value in the future. They have been great egotists. That too was forced upon them by their circumstances. When everything is rocking round one, the only person who remains comparatively stable is oneself. When all faces are changing and obscured, the only face one can see clearly is one's own. So they wrote about themselves—in their plays, in their poems, in their novels. No other ten years can have produced so much autobiography as the ten years between 1930 and 1940. No one, whatever his class or his obscurity, seems to have reached the age of thirty without writing his autobiography. But the leaning-tower writers wrote about themselves honestly, therefore creatively. They told the unpleasant truths, not only the flattering truths. That is why their autobiography is so much better than their fiction or their poetry. Consider how difficult it is to tell the truth about oneself—the unpleasant truth; to admit that one is petty, vain, mean, frustrated, tortured, unfaithful, and unsuccessful. The nineteenth-century writers never told that kind of truth, and that is why so much of the nineteenth-century writing is worthless; why, for all their genius, Dickens and Thackeray seem so often to write about dolls and puppets, not about full-grown men and women; why they are forced to evade the main themes and make do with diversions instead. If you do not tell the truth about yourself you cannot tell it about other people. As the nineteenth century wore on, the writers knew that they were crippling themselves, diminishing their material, falsifying their object. 'We are condemned', Stevenson wrote, 'to avoid half the life that passes us by. What books Dickens could have written had he been permitted! Think of Thackeray as unfettered as Flaubert or Balzac! What books I might have written myself? But they give us a little box of toys and say to us "You mustn't play with any-thing but these"!' Stevenson blamed society—bourgeois society was his scapegoat too. Why did he not blame himself? Why did he consent to go on playing with his little box of toys?

The leaning-tower writer has had the courage, at any rate, to throw that little box of toys out of the window. He has had the courage to tell the truth, the unpleasant truth, about himself.

That is the first step towards telling the truth about other people. By analysing themselves honestly, with help from Dr. Freud, these writers have done a great deal to free us from nineteenth-century suppressions. The writers of the next generation may inherit from them a whole state of mind, a mind no longer crippled, evasive, divided. They may inherit that unconsciousness which, as we guessed—it is only a guess—at the beginning of this paper, is necessary if writers are to get beneath the surface, and to write something that people remember when they are alone. For that great gift of unconsciousness the next generation will have to thank the creative and honest egotism of the leaning-tower group.

The next generation—there will be a next generation, in spite of this war and whatever it brings. Have we time then for a rapid glance, for a hurried guess at the next generation? The next generation will be, when peace comes, a post-war generation too. Must it too be a leaning-tower generation—an oblique, sidelong, squinting, self-conscious generation with a foot in two worlds? Or will there be no more towers and no more classes and shall we stand, without hedges between us, on the common ground?

There are two reasons which lead us to think, perhaps to hope, that the world after the war will be a world without classes or towers. Every politician who has made a speech since September 1939 has ended with a peroration in which he has said that we are not fighting this war for conquest; but to bring about a new order in Europe. In that order, they tell us, we are all to have equal opportunities, equal chances of developing whatever gifts we may possess. That is one reason why, if they mean what they say, and can effect it, classes and towers will disappear. The other reason is given by the income tax. The income tax is already doing in its own way what the politicians are hoping to do in theirs. The income tax is saying to middle-class parents: You cannot afford to send your sons to public schools any longer; you must send them to the elementary schools. One of these parents wrote to the *New Statesman* a week or two ago. Her little boy, who was to have gone to Winchester, had been taken away from his elementary school and sent to the village school. 'He has never been happier in his life', she wrote. 'The question of class does not arise; he is merely interested to find how many different kinds of people there are in the world. . . .' And she is only paying twopence-halfpenny a week for that happiness and instruction instead of 35 guineas a term and extras. If the pressure of the income tax continues, classes will disappear. There will be no more upper classes; middle classes; lower classes. All classes will be merged in one class. How will that change affect the writer who sits at his desk looking at human life? It will not be divided by hedges any more. Very likely that will be the end of the novel, as we know it. Literature, as we know it, is always ending, and beginning again. Remove the hedges from Jane Austen's world, from Trollope's world, and how much of their comedy and tragedy would remain? We shall regret our Jane Austens and our Trollopes; they gave us comedy, tragedy, and beauty. But much of that old-class literature was very petty; very false; very dull. Much is already unreadable. The novel of a classless and towerless world should be a better novel than the old novel. The novelist will have more interesting people to describe —people who have had a chance to develop their humour, their gifts, their tastes; real people, not people cramped and squashed into featureless masses by hedges. The poet's gain is less obvious; for he has been less under the dominion of hedges. But he should gain words; when we have pooled all the different dialects, the clipped and cabined vocabulary which is all that he uses now should be enriched. Further, there might then be a common belief which he could accept, and thus shift from his shoulders the burden of didacticism, of propaganda. These then are a few reasons, hastily snatched, why we can look forward hopefully to a stronger, a more varied literature in the classless and towerless society of the future.

But it is in the future; and there is a deep gulf to be bridged between the dying world and the world that is struggling to be born. For there are still two worlds, two separate worlds. 'I want', said the mother who wrote to the paper the other day about her boy, 'the best of both worlds for my son.' She wanted, that is, the village school, where he learnt to mix with the living; and the other school—Winchester it was—where he mixed with the dead. 'Is he to continue', she asked, 'under the system of free national education, or shall he go on—or should I say back—to the old public-school system which really is so very, very private?' She wanted the new world and the old world to unite, the world of the present and the world of the past.

But there is still a gulf between them, a dangerous gulf, in which, possibly, literature may crash and come to grief. It is easy to see that gulf; it is easy to lay the blame for it upon England. England has crammed a small aristocratic class with Latin and Greek and logic and metaphysics and mathematics until they cry out like the young men on the leaning tower, 'All that I would like to be is human'. She has left the other class, the immense class to which almost all of us must belong, to pick up what we can in village schools; in factories; in workshops; behind counters; and at home. When one thinks of that criminal injustice one is tempted to say England deserves to have no literature. She deserves to have nothing but detective stories, patriotic songs, and leading articles for generals, admirals, and business-men to read themselves to sleep with when they are tired of winning battles and making money. But let us not be unfair; let us avoid if we can joining the embittered and futile tribe of scapegoat-hunters. For some years now England has been making an effort—at last—to bridge the gulf between the two worlds. Here is one proof of that effort—this book. This book was not bought; it was not hired. It was borrowed from a public library. England lent it to a common reader, saying, 'It is time that even you, whom I have shut out from all my universities for centuries, should learn to read your mother tongue. I will help you.' If England is going to help us, we must help her. But how? Look at what is written in the book she has lent us. 'Readers are requested to point out any defects that they may observe to the local librarian.' That is England's way of saying: 'If I lend you books, I expect you to make yourselves critics'.

We can help England very greatly to bridge the gulf between the two worlds if we borrow the books she lends us and if we read them critically. We have got to teach ourselves to understand literature. Money is no longer going to do our thinking for us. Wealth will no longer decide who shall be taught and who not. In future it is we who shall decide whom to send to public schools and universities; how they shall be taught; and whether what they write justifies their exemption from other work. In order to do that we must teach ourselves to distinguish—which is the book that is going to pay dividends of pleasure for ever; which is the book that will pay not a penny in two years' time? Try it for yourselves on new books as they come out; decide which are the lasting, which are the perishing. That is very difficult. Also we must become critics because in future we are not going to leave writing to be done for us by a small class of well-to-do young men who have only a pinch, a thimbleful of experience to give us. We are going to add our own experience, to make our own contribution. That is even more difficult. For that too we need to be critics. A writer, more than any other artist, needs to be a critic because words are so common, so familiar, that he must sieve them and sift them if they are to become enduring. Write daily; write freely; but let us always compare what we have written with what the great writers have written. It is humiliating, but it is essential. If we are going to preserve and to create, that is the only way. And we are going to do both. We need not wait till the end of the war. We can begin now. We can begin, practically and prosaically, by borrowing books from public libraries; by reading omnivorously, simultaneously, poems, plays, novels, histories, biographies, the old and the new. We must sample before we can select. It never does to be a nice feeder; each of us has an appetite that must find for itself the food that nourishes it. Nor let us shy away from the kings because we are commoners. That is a fatal crime in the eyes of Aeschylus, Shakespeare, Virgil, and Dante, who, if they could speak—and after all they can—would say, 'Don't leave me to the wigged and gowned. Read me, read me for yourselves.' They do not mind if we get our accents wrong, or have to read with a crib in front of us. Of course—are we not commoners, outsiders?—we shall trample many flowers and bruise much ancient grass. But let us bear in mind a piece of advice that an eminent Victorian who was also an eminent pedestrian once gave to walkers: 'Whenever you see a board up with "Trespassers will be prosecuted", trespass at once'.

Let us trespass at once. Literature is no one's private ground; literature is common ground. It is not cut up into nations; there are no wars there. Let us trespass freely and fearlessly and find our own way for ourselves. It is thus that English literature will survive this war and cross the gulf—if commoners and outsiders like ourselves make that country our own country, if we teach ourselves how to read and to write, how to preserve, and how to create.

A Letter to a Young Poet[1]

My Dear John,

Did you ever meet, or was he before your day, that old gentleman—I forget his name—who used to enliven conversation, especially at breakfast when the post came in, by saying that the art of letter-writing is dead? The penny post, the old gentleman used to say, has killed the art of letter-writing. Nobody, he continued, examining an envelope through his eye-glasses, has the time even to cross their t's. We rush, he went on, spreading his toast with marmalade, to the telephone. We commit our half-formed thoughts in ungrammatical phrases to the postcard. Gray is dead, he continued; Horace Walpole is dead; Madame de Sévigné—she is dead too, I suppose he was about to add, but a fit of choking cut him short, and he had to leave the room before he had time to condemn all the arts, as his pleasure was, to the cemetery. But when the post came in this morning and I opened your letter stuffed with little blue sheets written all over in a cramped but not illegible hand—I regret to say, however, that several t's were uncrossed and the grammar of one sentence seems to me dubious—I replied after all these years to the elderly necrophilist—Nonsense. The art of letter-writing has only just come into existence. It is the child of the penny post. And there is some truth in that remark, I think. Naturally when a letter cost half a crown to send, it had to prove itself a document of some importance; it was read aloud; it was tied up with green silk; after a certain number of years it was published for the infinite delectation of posterity. But your letter, on the contrary, will have to be burnt. It only cost three-halfpence to send. Therefore you could afford to be intimate, irreticent, indiscreet in the extreme. What you tell me about poor dear C. and his adventure on the Channel boat is deadly private; your ribald jests at the expense of M. would certainly ruin your friendship if they got about; I doubt, too, that posterity, unless it is much quicker in the wit than I expect, could follow the line of your thoughts from the roof which leaks ('splash, splash, splash into the soap dish') past Mrs. Gape, the charwoman,

[1] Written in 1932

182

whose retort to the greengrocer gives me the keenest pleasure, via Miss Curtis and her odd confidence on the steps of the omnibus; to Siamese cats ('Wrap their noses in an old stocking my Aunt says if they howl'); so to the value of criticism to a writer; so to Donne; so to Gerard Hopkins; so to tombstones; so to gold-fish; and so with a sudden alarming swoop to 'Do write and tell me where poetry's going, or if it's dead?' No, your letter, because it is a true letter—one that can neither be read aloud now, nor printed in time to come—will have to be burnt. Posterity must live upon Walpole and Madame de Sévigné. The great age of letter-writing, which is, of course, the present, will leave no letters behind it. And in making my reply there is only one question that I can answer or attempt to answer in public; about poetry and its death.

But before I begin, I must own up to those defects, both natural and acquired, which, as you will find, distort and invalidate all that I have to say about poetry. The lack of a sound university training has always made it impossible for me to distinguish between an iambic and a dactyl, and if this were not enough to condemn one for ever, the practice of prose has bred in me, as in most prose writers, a foolish jealousy, a righteous indignation—anyhow, an emotion which the critic should be without. For how, we despised prose writers ask when we get together, could one say what one meant and observe the rules of poetry? Conceive dragging in 'blade' because one had mentioned 'made'; and pairing 'sorrow' with 'borrow'? Rhyme is not only childish, but dishonest, we prose writers say. Then we go on to say, And look at their rules! How easy to be a poet! How strait the path is for them, and how strict! This you must do; this you must not. I would rather be a child and walk in a crocodile down a suburban path than write poetry, I have heard prose writers say. It must be like taking the veil and entering a religious order—observing the rites and rigours of metre. That explains why they repeat the same thing over and over again. Whereas we prose writers (I am only telling you the sort of nonsense prose writers talk when they are alone) are masters of language, not its slaves; nobody can teach us; nobody can coerce us; we say what we mean; we have the whole of life for our province. We are the creators, we are the explorers . . . So we run on—nonsensically enough, I must admit.

Now that I have made a clean breast of these deficiencies, let us proceed. From certain phrases in your letter I gather that you think that poetry is in a parlous way, and that your case as a poet in this particular autumn of 1931 is a great deal harder than Shakespeare's, Dryden's, Pope's, or Tennyson's. In fact it is the hardest case that has ever been known. Here you give me an opening, which I am prompt to seize, for a little lecture. Never think yourself singular, never think your own case much harder than other people's. I admit that the age we live in makes this difficult. For the first time in history there are readers—a large body of people, occupied in business, in sport, in nursing their grandfathers, in tying up parcels behind counters—they all read now; and they want to be told how to read and what to read; and their teachers—the reviewers, the lecturers, the broadcasters—must in all humanity make reading easy for them; assure them that literature is violent and exciting, full of heroes and villains; of hostile forces perpetually in conflict; of fields strewn with bones; of solitary victors riding off on white horses wrapped in black cloaks to meet their death at the turn of the road. A pistol shot rings out. 'The age of romance was over. The age of realism had begun'—you know the sort of thing. Now of course writers themselves know very well that there is not a word of truth in all this—there are no battles, and no murders and no defeats and no victories. But as it is of the utmost importance that readers should be amused, writers acquiesce. They dress themselves up. They act their parts. One leads; the other follows. One is romantic, the other realist. One is advanced, the other out of date. There is no harm in it, so long as you take it as a joke, but once you believe in it, once you begin to take yourself seriously as a leader or as a follower, as a modern or as a conservative, then you become a self-conscious, biting, and scratching little animal whose work is not of the slightest value or importance to anybody. Think of yourself rather as something much humbler and less spectacular, but to my mind far more interesting—a poet in whom live all the poets of the past, from whom all poets in time to come will spring. You have a touch of Chaucer in you, and something of Shakespeare; Dryden, Pope, Tennyson—to mention only the respectable among your ancestors—stir in your blood and sometimes move your pen a little to the right or to the left. In short you are an immensely ancient, complex, and continuous character, for

which reason please treat yourself with respect and think twice
before you dress up as Guy Fawkes and spring out upon timid old
ladies at street corners, threatening death and demanding twopence-halfpenny.

However, as you say that you are in a fix ('it has never been so
hard to write poetry as it is today') and that poetry may be, you
think, at its last gasp in England ('the novelists are doing all the
interesting things now'), let me while away the time before the
post goes in imagining your state and in hazarding one or two
guesses which, since this is a letter, need not be taken too seriously
or pressed too far. Let me try to put myself in your place; let me
try to imagine, with your letter to help me, what it feels like to be
a young poet in the autumn of 1931. (And taking my own advice,
I shall treat you not as one poet in particular, but as several poets
in one.) On the floor of your mind, then—is it not this that makes
you a poet?—rhythm keeps up its perpetual beat. Sometimes it
seems to die down to nothing; it lets you eat, sleep, talk like other
people. Then again it swells and rises and attempts to sweep all
the contents of your mind into one dominant dance. Tonight is
such an occasion. Although you are alone, and have taken one
boot off and are about to undo the other, you cannot go on with
the process of undressing, but must instantly write at the bidding
of the dance. You snatch pen and paper; you hardly trouble to
hold the one or to straighten the other. And while you write, while
the first stanzas of the dance are being fastened down, I will withdraw a little and look out of the window. A woman passes, then a
man; a car glides to a stop and then—but there is no need to say
what I see out of the window, nor indeed is there time, for I am
suddenly recalled from my observations by a cry of rage or despair.
Your page is crumpled in a ball; your pen sticks upright by the
nib in the carpet. If there were a cat to swing or a wife to murder
now would be the time. So at least I infer from the ferocity of
your expression. You are rasped, jarred, thoroughly out of temper.
And if I am to guess the reason, it is, I should say, that the rhythm
which was opening and shutting with a force that sent shocks of
excitement from your head to your heels has encountered some
hard and hostile object upon which it has smashed itself to pieces.
Something has worked in which cannot be made into poetry;
some foreign body, angular, sharp-edged, gritty, has refused to

join in the dance. Obviously, suspicion attaches to Mrs. Gape; she has asked you to make a poem of her; then to Miss Curtis and her confidences on the omnibus; then to C., who has infected you with a wish to tell his story—and a very amusing one it was—in verse. But for some reason you cannot do their bidding. Chaucer could; Shakespeare could; so could Crabbe, Byron, and perhaps Robert Browning. But it is October 1931, and for a long time now poetry has shirked contact with—what shall we call it?—Shall we shortly and no doubt inaccurately call it life? And will you come to my help by guessing what I mean? Well then, it has left all that to the novelist. Here you see how easy it would be for me to write two or three volumes in honour of prose and in mockery of verse; to say how wide and ample is the domain of the one, how starved and stunted the little grove of the other. But it would be simpler and perhaps fairer to check these theories by opening one of the thin books of modern verse that lie on your table. I open and I find myself instantly confuted. Here are the common objects of daily prose—the bicycle and the omnibus. Obviously the poet is making his muse face facts. Listen:

> Which of you waking early and watching daybreak
> Will not hasten in heart, handsome, aware of wonder
> At light unleashed, advancing, a leader of movement,
> Breaking like surf on turf on road and roof,
> Or chasing shadow on downs like whippet racing,
> The stilled stone, halting at eyelash barrier,
> Enforcing in face a profile, marks of misuse,
> Beating impatient and importunate on boudoir shutters
> Where the old life is not up yet, with rays
> Exploring through rotting floor a dismantled mill—
> The old life never to be born again?

Yes, but how will he get through with it? I read on and find:

> Whistling as he shuts
> His door behind him, travelling to work by tube
> Or walking to the park to it to *ease the bowels*,

and read on and find again:

> As a boy lately come up from country to town
> Returns for the day to his village in *expensive shoes*—

and so on again to:

Seeking a heaven on earth he chases his shadow,
Loses his capital and his nerve in pursuing
What yachtsmen, explorers, climbers and *buggers are after.*

These lines and the words I have emphasized are enough to
confirm me in part of my guess at least. The poet is trying to
include Mrs. Gape. He is honestly of opinion that she can be
brought into poetry and will do very well there. Poetry, he feels,
will be improved by the actual, the colloquial. But though I
honour him for the attempt, I doubt that it is wholly successful.
I feel a jar. I feel a shock. I feel as if I had stubbed my toe on the
corner of the wardrobe. Am I then, I go on to ask, shocked,
prudishly and conventionally, by the words themselves? I think
not. The shock is literally a shock. The poet as I guess has strained
himself to include an emotion that is not domesticated and accli-
matized to poetry; the effort has thrown him off his balance; he
rights himself, as I am sure I shall find if I turn the page, by a
violent recourse to the poetical—he invokes the moon or the nightingale. Anyhow, the transition is sharp. The poem is cracked in
the middle. Look, it comes apart in my hands: here is reality on
one side, here is beauty on the other; and instead of acquiring a
whole object rounded and entire, I am left with broken parts in
my hands which, since my reason has been roused and my imagination has not been allowed to take entire possession of me, I contemplate coldly, critically, and with distaste.

Such at least is the hasty analysis I make of my own sensations
as a reader; but again I am interrupted. I see that you have overcome your difficulty, whatever it was; the pen is once more in
action, and having torn up the first poem you are at work upon
another. Now then if I want to understand your state of mind I
must invent another explanation to account for this return of
fluency. You have dismissed, as I suppose, all sorts of things that
would come naturally to your pen if you had been writing prose—
the charwoman, the omnibus, the incident on the Channel boat.
Your range is restricted—I judge from your expression—concentrated and intensified. I hazard a guess that you are thinking
now, not about things in general, but about yourself in particular.
There is a fixity, a gloom, yet an inner glow that seem to hint that
you are looking within and not without. But in order to consoli-
date these flimsy guesses about the meaning of an expression on a

face, let me open another of the books on your table and check it
by what I find there. Again I open at random and read this:

> To penetrate that room is my desire,
> The extreme attic of the mind, that lies
> Just beyond the last bend in the corridor.
> Writing I do it. Phrases, poems are keys.
> Loving's another way (but not so sure).
> A fire's in there, I think, there's truth at last
> Deep in a lumber chest. Sometimes I'm near,
> But draughts puff out the matches, and I'm lost.
> Sometimes I'm lucky, find a key to turn,
> Open an inch or two—but always then
> A bell rings, someone calls, or cries of 'fire'
> Arrest my hand when nothing's known or seen,
> And running down the stairs again I mourn.

And then this:

> There is a dark room,
> The locked and shuttered womb,
> Where negative's made positive.
> Another dark room,
> The blind and bolted tomb,
> Where positives change to negative.
> We may not undo that or escape this, who
> Have birth and death coiled in our bones,
> Nothing we can do
> Will sweeten the real rue,
> That we begin, and end, with groans.

And then this:

> Never being, but always at the edge of Being
> My head, like Death mask, is brought into the Sun.
> The shadow pointing finger across cheek
> I move lips for tasting, I move hands for touching,
> But never am nearer than touching,
> Though the spirit leans outward for seeing.
> Observing rose, gold, eyes, an admired landscape,
> My senses record the act of wishing
> Wishing to be
> Rose, gold, landscape or another—
> Claiming fulfilment in the act of loving.

Since these quotations are chosen at random and I have yet
found three different poets writing about nothing, if not about
the poet himself, I hold that the chances are that you too are
engaged in the same occupation. I conclude that self offers no
impediment; self joins in the dance; self lends itself to the rhythm;
it is apparently easier to write a poem about oneself than about
any other subject. But what does one mean by 'oneself'? Not the
self that Wordsworth, Keats, and Shelley have described—not the
self that loves a woman, or that hates a tyrant, or that broods over
the mystery of the world. No, the self that you are engaged in
describing is shut out from all that. It is a self that sits alone in the
room at night with the blinds drawn. In other words the poet is
much less interested in what we have in common than in what he
has apart. Hence I suppose the extreme difficulty of these poems
—and I have to confess that it would floor me completely to say
from one reading or even from two or three what these poems
mean. The poet is trying honestly and exactly to describe a world
that has perhaps no existence except for one particular person at
one particular moment. And the more sincere he is in keeping to
the precise outline of the roses and cabbages of his private
universe, the more he puzzles us who have agreed in a lazy spirit
of compromise to see roses and cabbages as they are seen, more
or less, by the twenty-six passengers on the outside of an omnibus.
He strains to describe; we strain to see; he flickers his torch; we
catch a flying gleam. It is exciting; it is stimulating; but is that a
tree, we ask, or is it perhaps an old woman tying up her shoe in
the gutter?

Well, then, if there is any truth in what I am saying—if that
is you cannot write about the actual, the colloquial, Mrs. Gape
or the Channel boat or Miss Curtis on the omnibus, without
straining the machine of poetry, if, therefore, you are driven to
contemplate landscapes and emotions within and must render
visible to the world at large what you alone can see, then indeed
yours is a hard case, and poetry, though still breathing—witness
these little books—is drawing her breath in short, sharp gasps.
Still, consider the symptoms. They are not the symptoms of death
in the least. Death in literature, and I need not tell you how
often literature has died in this country or in that, comes grace-
fully, smoothly, quietly. Lines slip easily down the accustomed

grooves. The old designs are copied so glibly that we are half-inclined to think them original, save for that very glibness. But here the very opposite is happening: here in my first quotation the poet breaks his machine because he will clog it with raw fact. In my second, he is unintelligible because of his desperate determination to tell the truth about himself. Thus I cannot help thinking that though you may be right in talking of the difficulty of the time, you are wrong to despair.

Is there not, alas, good reason to hope? I say 'alas' because then I must give my reasons, which are bound to be foolish and certain also to cause pain to the large and highly respectable society of necrophils—Mr. Peabody, and his like—who much prefer death to life and are even now intoning the sacred and comfortable words, Keats is dead, Shelley is dead, Byron is dead. But it is late: necrophily induces slumber; the old gentlemen have fallen asleep over their classics, and if what I am about to say takes a sanguine tone—and for my part I do not believe in poets dying; Keats, Shelley, Byron are alive here in this room in you and you and you—I can take comfort from the thought that my hoping will not disturb their snoring. So to continue—why should not poetry, now that it has so honestly scraped itself free from certain falsities, the wreckage of the great Victorian age, now that it has so sincerely gone down into the mind of the poet and verified its outlines—a work of renovation that has to be done from time to time and was certainly needed, for bad poetry is almost always the result of forgetting oneself—all becomes distorted and impure if you lose sight of that central reality—now, I say, that poetry has done all this, why should it not once more open its eyes, look out of the window and write about other people? Two or three hundred years ago you were always writing about other people. Your pages were crammed with characters of the most opposite and various kinds—Hamlet, Cleopatra, Falstaff. Not only did we go to you for drama, and for the subtleties of human character, but we also went to you, incredible though this now seems, for laughter. You made us roar with laughter. Then later, not more than a hundred years ago, you were lashing our follies, trouncing our hypocrisies, and dashing off the most brilliant of satires. You were Byron, remember; you wrote *Don Juan*. You were Crabbe also; you took the most sordid details of the lives of peasants for your theme. Clearly therefore you have it in you to deal with a vast variety of subjects; it is only a temporary necessity that has shut you up in one room, alone, by yourself.

But how are you going to get out, into the world of other people? That is your problem now, if I may hazard a guess—to find the right relationship, now that you know yourself, between the self that you know and the world outside. It is a difficult problem. No living poet has, I think, altogether solved it. And there are a thousand voices prophesying despair. Science, they say, has made poetry impossible; there is no poetry in motor cars and wireless. And we have no religion. All is tumultuous and transitional. Therefore, so people say, there can be no relation between the poet and the present age. But surely that is nonsense. These accidents are superficial; they do not go nearly deep enough to destroy the most profound and primitive of instincts, the instinct of rhythm. All you need now is to stand at the window and let your rhythmical sense open and shut, open and shut, boldly and freely, until one thing melts in another, until the taxis are dancing with the daffodils, until a whole has been made from all these separate fragments. I am talking nonsense, I know. What I mean is, summon all your courage, exert all your vigilance, invoke all the gifts that Nature has been induced to bestow. Then let your rhythmical sense wind itself in and out among men and women, omnibuses, sparrows— whatever comes along the street—until it has strung them together in one harmonious whole. That perhaps is your task—to find the relation between things that seem incompatible yet have a mysterious affinity, to absorb every experience that comes your way fearlessly and saturate it completely so that your poem is a whole, not a fragment; to re-think human life into poetry and so give us tragedy again and comedy by means of characters not spun out at length in the novelist's way, but condensed and synthesized in the poet's way—that is what we look to you to do now. But as I do not know what I mean by rhythm nor what I mean by life, and as most certainly I cannot tell you which objects can properly be combined together in a poem—that is entirely your affair—and as I cannot tell a dactyl from an iambic, and am therefore unable to say how you must modify and expand the rites and ceremonies of your ancient and mysterious art—I will move on to safer ground and turn again to these little books themselves.

When, then, I return to them I am, as I have admitted, filled, not with forebodings of death, but with hopes for the future. But one does not always want to be thinking of the future, if, as sometimes happens, one is living in the present. When I read these poems, now, at the present moment, I find myself—reading, you know, is rather like opening the door to a horde of rebels who swarm out attacking one in twenty places at once—hit, roused, scraped, bared, swung through the air, so that life seems to flash by; then again blinded, knocked on the head—all of which are agreeable sensations for a reader (since nothing is more dismal than to open the door and get no response), and all I believe certain proof that this poet is alive and kicking. And yet mingling with these cries of delight, of jubilation, I record also, as I read, the repetition in the bass of one word intoned over and over again by some malcontent. At last then, silencing the others, I say to this malcontent, 'Well, and what do *you* want?' Whereupon he bursts out, rather to my discomfort, 'Beauty.' Let me repeat, I take no responsibility for what my senses say when I read; I merely record the fact that there is a malcontent in me who complains that it seems to him odd, considering that English is a mixed language, a rich language; a language unmatched for its sound and colour, for its power of imagery and suggestion—it seems to him odd that these modern poets should write as if they had neither ears nor eyes, neither soles to their feet nor palms to their hands, but only honest enterprising book-fed brains, uni-sexual bodies and—but here I interrupted him. For when it comes to saying that a poet should be bi-sexual, and that I think is what he was about to say, even I, who have had no scientific training whatsoever, draw the line and tell that voice to be silent.

But how far, if we discount these obvious absurdities, do you think there is truth in this complaint? For my own part now that I have stopped reading, and can see the poems more or less as a whole, I think it is true that the eye and ear are starved of their rights. There is no sense of riches held in reserve behind the admirable exactitude of the lines I have quoted, as there is, for example, behind the exactitude of Mr. Yeats. The poet clings to his one word, his only word, as a drowning man to a spar. And if this is so, I am ready to hazard a reason for it all the more readily because I think it bears out what I have just been saying. The art of writing, and that is perhaps what my malcontent means by 'beauty', the art of having at one's beck and call every word in the language, of knowing their weights, colours, sounds, associations, and thus making them, as is so necessary in English, suggest more than they can state, can be learnt of course to some extent by reading—it is impossible to read too much; but much more drastically and effectively by imagining that one is not oneself but somebody different. How can you learn to write if you write only about one single person? To take the obvious example. Can you doubt that the reason why Shakespeare knew every sound and syllable in the language and could do precisely what he liked with grammar and syntax, was that Hamlet, Falstaff and Cleopatra rushed him into this knowledge; that the lords, officers, dependants, murderers and common soldiers of the plays insisted that he should say exactly what they felt in the words expressing their feelings? It was they who taught him to write, not the begetter of the Sonnets. So that if you want to satisfy all those senses that rise in a swarm whenever we drop a poem among them—the reason, the imagination, the eyes, the ears, the palms of the hands and the soles of the feet, not to mention a million more that the psychologists have yet to name, you will do well to embark upon a long poem in which people as unlike yourself as possible talk at the tops of their voices. And for heaven's sake, publish nothing before you are thirty.

That, I am sure, is of very great importance. Most of the faults in the poems I have been reading can be explained, I think, by the fact that they have been exposed to the fierce light of publicity while they were still too young to stand the strain. It has shrivelled them into a skeleton austerity, both emotional and verbal, which should not be characteristic of youth. The poet writes very well; he writes for the eye of a severe and intelligent public; but how much better he would have written if for ten years he had written for no eye but his own! After all, the years from twenty to thirty are years (let me refer to your letter again) of emotional excitement. The rain dripping, a wing flashing, someone passing—the commonest sounds and sights have power to fling one, as I seem to remember, from the heights of rapture to the depths of despair. And if the actual life is thus extreme, the visionary life should be free to follow. Write then, now that you are young, nonsense by the ream. Be silly, be sentimental, imitate Shelley, imitate Samuel Smiles; give the rein to every impulse; commit every fault of style, grammar, taste, and syntax; pour out; tumble over; loose anger, love, satire, in whatever words you can catch, coerce or create, in whatever metre, prose, poetry, or gibberish that comes to hand. Thus you will learn to write. But if you publish, your freedom will be checked; you will be thinking what people will say; you will write for others when you ought only to be writing for yourself. And what point can there be in curbing the wild torrent of spontaneous nonsense which is now, for a few years only, your divine gift in order to publish prim little books of experimental verses? To make money? That, we both know, is out of the question. To get criticism? But your friends will pepper your manuscripts with far more serious and searching criticism than any you will get from the reviewers. As for fame, look I implore you at famous people; see how the waters of dullness spread around them as they enter; observe their pomposity, their prophetic airs; reflect that the greatest poets were anonymous; think how Shakespeare cared nothing for fame; how Donne tossed his poems into the waste-paper basket; write an essay giving a single instance of any modern English writer who has survived the disciples and the admirers, the autograph hunters and the interviewers, the dinners and the luncheons, the celebrations and the commemorations with which English society so effectively stops the mouths of its singers and silences their songs.

But enough. I, at any rate, refuse to be necrophilus. So long as you and you and you, venerable and ancient representatives of Sappho, Shakespeare, and Shelley, are aged precisely twenty-three and propose—O enviable lot!—to spend the next fifty years of your lives in writing poetry, I refuse to think that the art is dead. And if ever the temptation to necrophilize comes over you, be warned by the fate of that old gentleman whose name I forget, but I think it was Peabody. In the very act of consigning all the arts to the grave he choked over a large piece of hot buttered toast and the consolation then offered him that he was about to join the elder Pliny in the shades gave him, I am told, no sort of satisfaction whatsoever.

And now for the intimate, the indiscreet, and indeed, the only really interesting parts of this letter . . .

Middlebrow[1]

TO THE EDITOR OF THE 'NEW STATESMAN'

SIR,

Will you allow me to draw your attention to the fact that in a review of a book by me (October) your reviewer omitted to use the word Highbrow? The review, save for that omission, gave me so much pleasure that I am driven to ask you, at the risk of appearing unduly egotistical, whether your reviewer, a man of obvious intelligence, intended to deny my claim to that title? I say 'claim', for surely I may claim that title when a great critic, who is also a great novelist, a rare and enviable combination, always calls me a highbrow when he condescends to notice my work in a great newspaper; and further, always finds space to inform not only myself, who know it already, but the whole British Empire, who hang on his words, that I live in Bloomsbury? Is your critic unaware of that fact too? Or does he, for all his intelligence, maintain that it is unnecessary in reviewing a book to add the postal address of the writer?

His answer to these questions, though of real value to me, is of no possible interest to the public at large. Of that I am well aware. But since larger issues are involved, since the Battle of the Brows troubles, I am told, the evening air, since the finest minds of our age have lately been engaged in debating, not without that passion which befits a noble cause, what a highbrow is and what a lowbrow, which is better and which is worse, may I take this opportunity to express my opinion and at the same time draw attention to certain aspects of the question which seem to me to have been unfortunately overlooked?

Now there can be no two opinions as to what a highbrow is. He is the man or woman of thoroughbred intelligence who rides his mind at a gallop across country in pursuit of an idea. That is why I have always been so proud to be called highbrow. That is why, if I could be more of a highbrow I would. I honour and

---

[1] This letter was written, but not sent to the *New Statesman*

respect highbrows. Some of my relations have been highbrows; and some, but by no means all, of my friends. To be a highbrow, a complete and representative highbrow, a highbrow like Shakespeare, Dickens, Byron, Shelley, Keats, Charlotte Brontë, Scott, Jane Austen, Flaubert, Hardy, or Henry James—to name a few highbrows from the same profession chosen at random—is of course beyond the wildest dreams of my imagination. And, though I would cheerfully lay myself down in the dust and kiss the print of their feet, no person of sense will deny that this passionate preoccupation of theirs—riding across country in pursuit of ideas—often leads to disaster. Undoubtedly, they come fearful croppers. Take Shelley—what a mess he made of his life! And Byron, getting into bed with first one woman and then with another and dying in the mud at Missolonghi. Look at Keats, loving poetry and Fanny Brawne so intemperately that he pined and died of consumption at the age of twenty-six. Charlotte Brontë again—I have been assured on good authority that Charlotte Brontë was, with the possible exception of Emily, the worst governess in the British Isles. Then there was Scott—he went bankrupt, and left, together with a few magnificent novels, one house, Abbotsford, which is perhaps the ugliest in the whole Empire. But surely these instances are enough—I need not further labour the point that highbrows, for some reason or another, are wholly incapable of dealing successfully with what is called real life. That is why, and here I come to a point that is often surprisingly ignored, they honour so wholeheartedly and depend so completely upon those who are called lowbrows. By a lowbrow is meant of course a man or a woman of thoroughbred vitality who rides his body in pursuit of a living at a gallop across life. That is why I honour and respect lowbrows—and I have never known a highbrow who did not. In so far as I am a highbrow (and my imperfections in that line are well known to me) I love lowbrows; I study them; I always sit next the conductor in an omnibus and try to get him to tell me what it is like—being a conductor. In whatever company I am I always try to know what it is like—being a conductor, being a woman with ten children and thirty-five shillings a week, being a stockbroker, being an admiral, being a bank clerk, being a dressmaker, being a duchess, being a miner, being a cook, being a prostitute. All that lowbrows do is of surpassing interest and wonder to me, because, in so far as I am a highbrow, I cannot do things myself.

This brings me to another point which is also surprisingly overlooked. Lowbrows need highbrows and honour them just as much as highbrows need lowbrows and honour them. This too is not a matter that requires much demonstration. You have only to stroll along the Strand on a wet winter's night and watch the crowds lining up to get into the movies. These lowbrows are waiting, after the day's work, in the rain, sometimes for hours, to get into the cheap seats and sit in hot theatres in order to see what their lives look like. Since they are lowbrows, engaged magnificently and adventurously in riding full tilt from one end of life to the other in pursuit of a living, they cannot see themselves doing it. Yet nothing interests them more. Nothing matters to them more. It is one of the prime necessities of life to them—to be shown what life looks like. And the highbrows, of course, are the only people who can show them. Since they are the only people who do not do things, they are the only people who can see things being done. This is so—and so it is I am certain; nevertheless we are told—the air buzzes with it by night, the Press booms with it by day, the very donkeys in the fields do nothing but bray it, the very curs in the streets do nothing but bark it—'Highbrows hate lowbrows! Lowbrows hate highbrows!' —when highbrows need lowbrows, when lowbrows need highbrows, when they cannot exist apart, when one is the complement and other side of the other! How has such a lie come into existence? Who has set this malicious gossip afloat?

There can be no doubt about that either. It is the doing of the middlebrows. They are the people, I confess, that I seldom regard with entire cordiality. They are the go-betweens; they are the busybodies who run from one to the other with their tittle tattle and make all the mischief—the middlebrows, I repeat. But what, you may ask, is a middlebrow? And that, to tell the truth, is no easy question to answer. They are neither one thing nor the other. They are not highbrows, whose brows are high; nor lowbrows, whose brows are low. Their brows are betwixt and between. They do not live in Bloomsbury which is on high ground; nor in Chelsea which is on low ground. Since they must live somewhere presumably, they live perhaps in South Kensington, which is betwixt and between. The middlebrow is the man, or woman, of middlebred intelligence who ambles and saunters now on this side of the hedge, now on that, in pursuit of no single object, neither art itself nor life itself, but both mixed indistinguishably, and rather nastily, with money, fame, power, or prestige. The middlebrow curries favour with both sides equally. He goes to the lowbrows and tells them that while he is not quite one of them, he is almost their friend. Next moment he rings up the highbrows and asks them with equal geniality whether he may not come to tea. Now there are highbrows—I myself have known duchesses who were highbrows, also charwomen, and they have both told me with that vigour of language which so often unites the aristocracy with the working classes, that they would rather sit in the coal cellar, together, than in the drawing-room with middlebrows and pour out tea. I have myself been asked—but may I, for the sake of brevity, cast this scene which is only partly fictitious, into the form of fiction?—I myself, then, have been asked to come and 'see' them—how strange a passion theirs is for being 'seen'! They ring me up, therefore, at about eleven in the morning, and ask me to come to tea. I go to my wardrobe and consider, rather lugubriously, what is the right thing to wear? We highbrows may be smart, or we may be shabby; but we never have the right thing to wear. I proceed to ask next: What is the right thing to say? Which is the right knife to use? What is the right book to praise? All these are things I do not know for myself. We highbrows read what we like and do what we like and praise what we like. We also know what we dislike—for example, thin bread and butter tea. The difficulty of eating thin bread and butter in white kid gloves has always seemed to me one of life's more insuperable problems. Then I dislike bound volumes of the classics behind plate glass. Then I distrust people who call both Shakespeare and Wordsworth equally 'Bill'—it is a habit moreover that leads to confusion. And in the matter of clothes, I like people either to dress very well; or to dress very badly; I dislike the correct thing in clothes. Then there is the question of games. Being a highbrow I do not play them. But I love watching people play who have a passion for games. These middlebrows pat balls about; they poke their bats and muff their catches at cricket. And when poor Middlebrow mounts on horseback and that animal breaks into a canter, to me there is no sadder sight in all Rotten Row. To put it in a nutshell (in order to get on with the story) that tea party was not wholly a success, nor altogether a failure; for Middlebrow, who writes, following me to the door, clapped me briskly on the back, and said, 'I'm sending you my book!' (Or did he call it 'stuff'?) And his book comes—sure enough, though called, so symbolically, *Keepaway*,[1] it comes. And I read a page here, and I read a page there (I am breakfasting, as usual, in bed). And it is not well written; nor is it badly written. It is not proper, nor is it improper—in short it is betwixt and between. Now if there is any sort of book for which I have, perhaps, an imperfect sympathy, it is the betwixt and between. And so, though I suffer from the gout of a morning—but if one's ancestors for two or three centuries have tumbled into bed dead drunk one has deserved a touch of that malady—I rise. I dress. I proceed weakly to the window. I take that book in my swollen right hand and toss it gently over the hedge into the field. The hungry sheep—did I remember to say that this part of the story takes place in the country?—the hungry sheep look up but are not fed.

But to have done with fiction and its tendency to lapse into poetry—I will now report a perfectly prosaic conversation in words of one syllable. I often ask my friends the lowbrows, over our muffins and honey, why it is that while we, the highbrows, never buy a middlebrow book, or go to a middlebrow lecture, or read, unless we are paid for doing so, a middlebrow review, they, on the contrary, take these middlebrow activities so seriously? Why, I ask (not of course on the wireless), are you so damnably modest? Do you think that a description of your lives, as they are, is too sordid and too mean to be beautiful? Is that why you prefer the middlebrow version of what they have the impudence to call real humanity?—this mixture of geniality and sentiment stuck together with a sticky slime of calves-foot jelly? The truth, if you would only believe it, is much more beautiful than any lie. Then again, I continue, how can you let the middlebrows teach *you* how to write?—you, who write so beautifully when you write naturally, that I would give both my hands to write as you do—

---

[1] *Keepaway* is the name of a preparation used to distract the male dog from the female at certain seasons.

for which reason I never attempt it, but do my best to learn the art of writing as a highbrow should. And again, I press on, brandishing a muffin on the point of a teaspoon, how dare the middlebrows teach *you* how to read—Shakespeare, for instance? All you have to do is to read him. The Cambridge edition is both good and cheap. If you find *Hamlet* difficult, ask him to tea. He is a highbrow. Ask Ophelia to meet him. She is a lowbrow. Talk to them, as you talk to me, and you will know more about Shakespeare than all the middlebrows in the world can teach you—I do not think, by the way, from certain phrases, that Shakespeare liked middlebrows, or Pope either.

To all this the lowbrows reply—but I cannot imitate their style of talking—that they consider themselves to be common people without education. It is very kind of the middlebrows to try to teach them culture. And after all, the lowbrows continue, middlebrows, like other people, have to make money. There must be money in teaching and in writing books about Shakespeare. We all have to earn our livings nowadays, my friends the lowbrows remind me. I quite agree. Even those of us whose Aunts came a cropper riding in India and left them an annual income of four hundred and fifty pounds, now reduced, thanks to the war and other luxuries, to little more than two hundred odd, even we have to do that. And we do it, too, by writing about anybody who seems amusing—enough has been written about Shakespeare—Shakespeare hardly pays. We highbrows, I agree, have to earn our livings; but when we have earned enough to live on, then we live. When the middlebrows, on the contrary, have earned enough to live on, they go on earning enough to buy—what are the things that middlebrows always buy? Queen Anne furniture (faked, but none the less expensive); first editions of dead writers—always the worst; pictures, or reproductions from pictures, by dead painters; houses in what is called 'the Georgian style'—but never anything new, never a picture by a living painter, or a chair by a living carpenter, or books by living writers, for to buy living art requires living taste. And, as that kind of art and that kind of taste are what middlebrows call 'highbrow', 'Bloomsbury', poor middlebrow spends vast sums on sham antiques, and has to keep at it scribbling away, year in, year out, while we highbrows ring each other up, and are off for a day's jaunt into the country. That is the worst of course of living in a set—one likes being with one's friends.

Have I then made my point clear, sir, that the true battle in my opinion lies not between highbrow and lowbrow, but between highbrows and lowbrows joined together in blood brotherhood against the bloodless and pernicious pest who comes between? If the B.B.C. stood for anything but the Betwixt and Between Company they would use their control of the air not to stir strife between brothers, but to broadcast the fact that highbrows and lowbrows must band together to exterminate a pest which is the bane of all thinking and living. It may be, to quote from your advertisement columns, that 'terrifically sensitive' lady novelists over-estimate the dampness and dinginess of this fungoid growth. But all I can say is that when, lapsing into that stream which people call, so oddly, consciousness, and gathering wool from the sheep that have been mentioned above, I ramble round my garden in the suburbs, middlebrow seems to me to be everywhere. 'What's that?' I cry. 'Middlebrow on the cabbages? Middlebrow infecting that poor old sheep? And what about the moon?' I look up and, behold, the moon is under eclipse. 'Middlebrow at it again!' I exclaim. 'Middlebrow obscuring, dulling, tarnishing and coarsening even the silver edge of Heaven's own scythe.' (I 'draw near to poetry', see advt.) And then my thoughts, as Freud assures us thoughts will do, rush (Middlebrow's saunter and simper, out of respect for the Censor) to sex, and I ask of the sea-gulls who are crying on desolate sea sands and of the farm hands who are coming home rather drunk to their wives, what will become of us, men and women, if Middlebrow has his way with us, and there is only a middle sex but no husbands or wives? The next remark I address with the utmost humility to the Prime Minister. 'What, sir,' I demand, 'will be the fate of the British Empire and of our Dominions Across the Seas if Middlebrows prevail? Will you not, sir, read a pronouncement of an authoritative nature from Broadcasting House?'

Such are the thoughts, such are the fancies that visit 'cultured invalidish ladies with private means' (see advt.) when they stroll in their suburban gardens and look at the cabbages and at the red brick villas that have been built by middlebrows so that middlebrows may look at the view. Such are the thoughts 'at once gay and tragic and deeply feminine' (see advt.) of one who has not yet 'been driven out of Bloomsbury' (advt. again), a place where lowbrows and highbrows live happily together on equal terms and priests are not, nor priestesses, and, to be quite frank, the adjective 'priestly' is neither often heard nor held in high esteem. Such are the thoughts of one who will stay in Bloomsbury until the Duke of Bedford, rightly concerned for the respectability of his squares, raises the rent so high that Bloomsbury is safe for middlebrows to live in. Then she will leave.

May I conclude, as I began, by thanking your reviewer for his courteous and interesting review, but may I tell him that though he did not, for reasons best known to himself, call me a highbrow, there is no name in the world that I prefer? I ask nothing better than that all reviewers, for ever, and everywhere, should call me a highbrow. I will do my best to oblige them. If they like to add Bloomsbury wc1, that is the correct postal address, and my telephone number is in the Directory. But if your reviewer, or any other reviewer, dares hint that I live in South Kensington, I will sue him for libel. If any human being, man, woman, dog, cat, or half-crushed worm dares call me 'middlebrow' I will take my pen and stab him, dead.

Yours etc.,
VIRGINIA WOOLF

Reviewing[1]

I

IN London there are certain shop windows that always attract a crowd. The attraction is not in the finished article but in the worn-out garments that are having patches inserted in them. The crowd is watching the women at work. There they sit in the shop window putting invisible stitches into moth-eaten trousers. And this familiar sight may serve as illustration to the following paper. So our poets, playwrights, and novelists sit in the shop window, doing their work under the curious eyes of reviewers. But the reviewers are not content, like the crowd in the street, to gaze in silence; they comment aloud upon the size of the holes, upon the skill of the workers, and advise the public which of the goods in the shop window is the best worth buying. The purpose of this paper is to rouse discussion as to the value of the reviewer's office—to the writer, to the public, to the reviewer, and to literature. But a reservation must first be made—by 'the reviewer' is meant the reviewer of imaginative literature—poetry, drama, fiction; not the reviewer of history, politics, economics. His is a different office, and for reasons not to be discussed here he fulfils it in the main so adequately and indeed admirably that his value is not in question. Has the reviewer, then, of imaginative literature any value at the present time to the writer, to the public, to the reviewer, and to literature? And, if so, what? And if not, how could his function be changed, and made profitable? Let us broach these involved and complicated questions by giving one quick glance at the history of reviewing, since it may help to define the nature of a review at the present moment.

Since the review came into existence with the newspaper, that history is a brief one. *Hamlet* was not reviewed, nor *Paradise Lost*. Criticism there was but criticism conveyed by word of mouth, by the audience in the theatre, by fellow writers in taverns and private workshops. Printed criticism came into existence, presumably in a crude and primitive form, in the seventeenth cen-

[1] Written in 1939

tury. Certainly the eighteenth century rings with the screams and catcalls of the reviewer and his victim. But towards the end of the eighteenth century there was a change—the body of criticism then seems to split into two parts. The critic and the reviewer divided the country between them. The critic—let Dr. Johnson represent him—dealt with the past and with principles; the reviewer took the measure of new books as they fell from the press. As the nineteenth century drew on, these functions became more and more distinct. There were the critics—Coleridge, Matthew Arnold—who took their time and their space; and there were the 'irresponsible' and mostly anonymous reviewers who had less time and less space, and whose complex task it was partly to inform the public, partly to criticize the book, and partly to advertise its existence.

Thus, though the reviewer in the nineteenth century has much resemblance to his living representative, there were certain important differences. One difference is shown by the author of the *Times History*: 'The books reviewed were fewer, but the reviews were longer than now. . . . Even a novel might get two columns and more'—he is referring to the middle of the nineteenth century. Those differences are very important, as will be seen later. But it is worth while to pause for a moment to examine other results of the review which are first manifest then, though by no means easy to sum up; the effect that is to say of the review upon the author's sales and upon the author's sensibility. A review had undoubtedly a great effect upon sales. Thackeray, for instance, said that the *Times*' review of *Esmond* 'absolutely stopped the sale of the book'. The review also had an immense though less calculable effect upon the sensibility of the author. Upon Keats the effect is notorious; also upon the sensitive Tennyson. Not only did he alter his poems at the reviewer's bidding, but actually contemplated emigration; and was thrown, according to one biographer, into such despair by the hostility of reviewers that his state of mind for a whole decade, and thus his poetry, was changed by them. But the robust and self-confident were also affected. 'How can a man like Macready,' Dickens demanded, 'fret and fume and chafe himself for such lice of literature as these?'—the 'lice' are writers in Sunday newspapers—'rotten creatures with men's forms and devils' hearts?' Yet lice as they are, when they 'discharge their pigmy arrows' even Dickens with all his genius and his magnificent vitality cannot help but mind and has to make a vow to overcome his rage and 'to gain the victory by being indifferent and bidding them whistle on'.

In their different ways then the great poet and the great novelist both admit the power of the nineteenth-century reviewer; and it is safe to assume that behind them stood a myriad of minor poets and minor novelists whether of the sensitive variety or of the robust who were all affected in much the same way. The way was complex; it is difficult to analyse. Tennyson and Dickens are both angry and hurt; they are also ashamed of themselves for feeling such emotions. The reviewer was a louse; his bite was contemptible; yet his bite was painful. His bite injured vanity; it injured reputation; it injured sales. Undoubtedly in the nineteenth century the reviewer was a formidable insect; he had considerable power over the author's sensibility; and upon the public taste. He could hurt the author; he could persuade the public either to buy or to refrain from buying.

II

The figures being thus set in position and their functions and powers roughly outlined, it must next be asked whether what was true then is true now. At first sight there seems to be little change. All the figures are still with us—critic; reviewer; author; public; and in much the same relations. The critic is separate from the reviewer; the function of the reviewer is partly to sort current literature; partly to advertise the author; partly to inform the public. Nevertheless there is a change; and it is a change of the highest importance. It seems to have made itself felt in the last part of the nineteenth century. It is summed up in the words of the *Times*' historian already quoted: '. . . the tendency was for reviews to grow shorter and to be less long delayed'. But there was another tendency; not only did the reviews become shorter and quicker, but they increased immeasurably in number. The result of these three tendencies was of the highest importance. It was catastrophic indeed; between them they have brought about the decline and fall of reviewing. Because they were quicker, shorter, and more numerous the value of reviews for all parties concerned has dwindled until—is it too much to say until it has disappeared? But let us consider. The people concerned are the author, the reader, and the publisher. Placing them in this order let us ask first how these tendencies have affected the author— why the review has ceased to have any value for him? Let us assume, for brevity's sake, that the most important value of a review to the author was its effect upon him as a writer—that it gave him an expert opinion of his work and allowed him to judge roughly how far as an artist he had failed or succeeded. That has been destroyed almost entirely by the multiplicity of reviews. Now that he has sixty reviews where in the nineteenth century he had perhaps six, he finds that there is no such thing as 'an opinion' of his work. Praise cancels blame; and blame praise. There are as many different opinions of his work as there are different reviewers. Soon he comes to discount both praise and blame; they are equally worthless. He values the review only for its effect upon his reputation and for its effect upon his sales.

The same cause has also lessened the value of the review to the reader. The reader asks the reviewer to tell him whether the poem or novel is good or bad in order that he may decide whether to buy it or not. Sixty reviewers at once assure him that it is a masterpiece—and worthless. The clash of completely contradictory opinions cancel each other out. The reader suspends judgment; waits for an opportunity of seeing the book himself; very probably forgets all about it, and keeps his seven and sixpence in his pocket.

The variety and diversity of opinion affect the publisher in the same way. Aware that the public no longer trusts either praise or blame, the publisher is reduced to printing both side by side: 'This is . . . poetry that will be remembered in hundreds of years time . . .' 'There are several passages that make me physically sick',[1] to quote an actual instance; to which he adds very naturally, in his own person: 'Why not read it yourself?' That question is enough by itself to show that reviewing as practised at present has failed in all its objects. Why bother to

[1] *The New Statesman*, April, 1939

write reviews or to read them or to quote them if in the end the reader must decide the question for himself?

III

If the reviewer has ceased to have any value either to the author or to the public it seems a public duty to abolish him. And, indeed, the recent failure of certain magazines consisting largely of reviews seems to show that whatever the reason, such will be his fate. But it is worth while to look at him in being—a flutter of little reviews is still attached to the great political dailies and weeklies—before he is swept out of existence, in order to see what he is still trying to do; why it is so difficult for him to do it; and whether perhaps there is not some element of value that ought to be preserved. Let us ask the reviewer himself to throw light upon the nature of the problem as it appears to him. Nobody is better qualified to do so than Mr. Harold Nicolson. The other day[1] he dealt with the duties and the difficulties of the reviewer as they appear to him. He began by saying that the reviewer, who is 'something quite different from the critic', is 'hampered by the hebdomadal nature of his task',—in other words, he has to write too often and too much. He went on to define the nature of that task. 'Is he to relate every book that he reads to the eternal standards of literary excellence? Were he to do that, his reviews would be one long ululation. Is he merely to consider the library public and to tell people what it may please them to read? Were he to do that, he would be subjugating his own level of taste to a level which is not very stimulating. How does he act?' Since he cannot refer to the eternal standards of literature; since he cannot tell the library public what they would like to read—that would be 'a degradation of the mind'— there is only one thing that he can do: he can hedge. 'I hedge between the two extremes. I address myself to the authors of the books which I review; I want to tell them why I either like or dislike their work; and I trust that from such a dialogue the ordinary reader will derive some information.'

That is an honest statement; and its honesty is illuminating. It shows that the review has become an expression of individual

[1] *The Daily Telegraph*, March, 1939

opinion, given without any attempt to refer to 'eternal standards' by a man who is in a hurry; who is pressed for space; who is expected to cater in that little space for many different interests; who is bothered by the knowledge that he is not fulfilling his task; who is doubtful what that task is; and who, finally, is forced to hedge. Now the public though crass is not such an ass as to invest seven and sixpence on the advice of a reviewer writing under such conditions; and the public though dull is not such a gull as to believe in the great poets, great novelists, and epoch-making works that are weekly discovered under such conditions. Those are the conditions however; and there is good reason to think that they will become more drastic in the course of the next few years. The reviewer is already a distracted tag on the tail of the political kite. Soon he will be conditioned out of existence altogether. His work will be done—in many newspapers it is already done—by a competent official armed with scissors and paste who will be called (it may be) The Gutter. The Gutter will write out a short statement of the book; extract the plot (if it is a novel); choose a few verses (if it is a poem); quote a few anecdotes (if it is a biography). To this what is left of the reviewer —perhaps he will come to be known as the Taster—will fix a stamp—an asterisk to signify approval, a dagger to signify disapproval. This statement—this Gutter and Stamp production— will serve instead of the present discordant and distracted twitter. And there is no reason to think that it will serve two of the parties concerned worse than the present system. The library public will be told what it wishes to know—whether the book is the kind of book to order from the library; and the publisher will collect asterisks and daggers instead of going to the pains to copy out alternate phrases of praise and abuse in which neither he nor the public has any faith. Each perhaps will save a little time and a little money. There remain, however, two other parties to be considered—that is the author and the reviewer. What will the Gutter and Stamp system mean to them?

To deal first with the author—his case is the more complex, for his is the more highly developed organism. During the two centuries or so in which he has been exposed to reviewers he has undoubtedly developed what may be called a reviewer consciousness. There is present in his mind a figure who is known as 'the reviewer'. To Dickens he was a louse armed with pigmy arrows, having the form of a man and the heart of a devil. To Tennyson he was even more formidable. It is true that the lice are so many today and they bite so innumerably that the author is compara- tively immune from their poison—no author now abuses re- viewers as violently as Dickens or obeys them as submissively as Tennyson. Still, there are eruptions even now in the press which lead us to believe that the reviewer's fang is still poisoned. But what part is affected by his bite?—what is the true nature of the emotion he causes? That is a complex question; but perhaps we can discover something that will serve as answer by submitting the author to a simple test. Take a sensitive author and place before him a hostile review. Symptoms of pain and anger rapidly develop. Next tell him that nobody save himself will read those abusive remarks. In five or ten minutes the pain which, if the attack had been delivered in public, would have lasted a week and bred bitter rancour, is completely over. The temperature falls; indifference returns. This proves that the sensitive part is the reputation; what the victim feared was the effect of abuse upon the opinion that other people had of him. He is afraid, too, of the effect of abuse upon his purse. But the purse sensibility is in most cases far less highly-developed than the reputation sensibility. As for the artist's sensibility—his own opinion of his own work—that is not touched by anything good or bad that the reviewer says about it. The reputation sensibility however is still lively; and it will thus take some time to persuade authors that the Gutter and Stamp system is as satisfactory as the present reviewing system. They will say that they have 'reputations'— bladders of opinion formed by what other people think about them; and that these bladders are inflated or deflated by what is said of them in print. Still, under present conditions the time is at hand when even the author will believe that nobody thinks the better or the worse of him because he is praised or blamed in print. Soon he will come to realize that his interests—his desire for fame and money—are as effectively catered for by the Gutter and Stamp system as by the present reviewing system.

But even when this stage is reached, the author may still have some ground for complaint. The reviewer did serve some end besides that of inflating reputations and stimulating sales. And

Mr. Nicolson has put his finger on it. 'I want to tell them why I either like or dislike their work.' The author wants to be told why Mr. Nicolson likes or dislikes his work. This is a genuine desire. It survives the test of privacy. Shut doors and windows; pull the curtains. Ensure that no fame accrues or money; and still it is a matter of the very greatest interest to a writer to know what an honest and intelligent reader thinks about his work.

IV

At this point let us turn once more to the reviewer. There can be no doubt that his position at the present moment, judging both from the outspoken remarks of Mr. Nicolson and from the internal evidence of the reviews themselves, is extremely unsatisfactory. He has to write in haste and to write shortly. Most of the books he reviews are not worth the scratch of a pen upon paper—it is futile to refer them to 'eternal standards'. He knows further, as Matthew Arnold has stated, that even if the conditions were favourable, it is impossible for the living to judge the works of the living. Years, many years, according to Matthew Arnold, have to pass before it is possible to deliver an opinion that is not 'only personal, but personal with passion'. And the reviewer has one week. And authors are not dead but living. And the living are friends or enemies; have wives and families; personalities and politics. The reviewer knows that he is hampered, distracted, and prejudiced. Yet knowing all this and having proof in the wild contradictions of contemporary opinion that it is so, he has to submit a perpetual succession of new books to a mind as incapable of taking a fresh impression or of making a dispassionate statement as an old piece of blotting paper on a post office counter. He has to review; for he has to live; and he has to live, since most reviewers come of the educated class, according to the standards of that class. Thus he has to write often, and he has to write much. There is, it seems, only one alleviation of the horror, that he enjoys telling authors why he likes or dislikes their books.

V

The one element in reviewing that is of value to the reviewer himself (independently of the money earned) is the one element that is of value to the author. The problem then is how to preserve this value—the value of the dialogue as Mr. Nicolson calls it— and to bring both parties together in a union that is profitable, to the minds and purses of both. It should not be a difficult problem to solve. The medical profession has shown the way. With some differences the medical custom might be imitated— there are many resemblances between doctor and reviewer, between patient and author. Let the reviewers then abolish themselves or what relic remains of them, as reviewers, and resurrect themselves as doctors. Another name might be chosen— consultant, expositor or expounder; some credentials might be given, the books written rather than the examinations passed; and a list of those ready and authorized to practise made public. The writer then would submit his work to the judge of his choice; an appointment would be made; an interview arranged. In strict privacy, and with some formality—the fee, however, would be enough to ensure that the interview did not degenerate into tea-table gossip—doctor and writer would meet; and for an hour they would consult upon the book in question. They would talk, seriously and privately. This privacy in the first place would be an immeasurable advantage to them both. The consultant would speak honestly and openly, because the fear of affecting sales and of hurting feelings would be removed. Privacy would lessen the shop-window temptation to cut a figure, to pay off scores. The consultant would have no library public to inform and consider; no reading public to impress and amuse. He could thus concentrate upon the book itself, and upon telling the author why he likes or dislikes it. The author would profit equally. An hour's private talk with a critic of his own choosing would be incalculably more valuable than the five hundred words of criticism mixed with extraneous matter that is now allotted him. He could state his case. He could point to his difficulties. He would no longer feel, as so often at present, that the critic is talking about something that he has not written. Further, he would have the advantage of coming into touch with a well-stored mind, housing other books and even other literatures, and thus other standards; with a live human being, not with a man in a mask. Many bogies would lose their horns. The louse would become a man. By degrees the writer's 'reputation' would drop off. He would become quit of that tiresome appendage and its irritable consequences—such are a few of the obvious and indisputable advantages that privacy would ensure.

Next there is the financial question—would the profession of expositor be as profitable as the profession of reviewer? How many authors are there who would wish to have an expert opinion on their work? The answer to this is to be heard crying daily and crying loudly in any publisher's office or in any author's post-bag. 'Give me advice,' they repeat, 'give me criticism.' The number of authors seeking criticism and advice genuinely, not for advertising purposes but because their need is acute, is an abundant proof of the demand. But would they pay the doctor's fee of three guineas? When they discovered, as certainly they would, how much more an hour of talk holds, even if it costs three guineas, than the hurried letter which they now extort from the harassed publisher's reader, or the five hundred words which is all they can count on from the distracted reviewer, even the indigent would think it an investment worth making. Nor is it only the young and needy who seek advice. The art of writing is difficult; at every stage the opinion of an impersonal and dis-interested critic would be of the highest value. Who would not spout the family teapot in order to talk with Keats for an hour about poetry, or with Jane Austen about the art of fiction?

VI

There remains finally the most important, but the most difficult of all these questions—what effect would the abolition of the reviewer have upon literature? Some reasons for thinking that the smashing of the shop window would make for the better health of that remote goddess have already been implied. The writer would withdraw into the darkness of the workshop; he would no longer carry on his difficult and delicate task like a trouser mender in Oxford Street, with a horde of reviewers pressing their noses to the glass and commenting to a curious crowd upon each stitch. Hence his self-consciousness would diminish and his reputation would shrivel. No longer puffed this way and that, now elated, now depressed, he could attend to his work. That might make for better writing. Again the reviewer, who must now earn his pence by cutting shop window capers to amuse the public and to advertise his skill, would have only the book to think of and the writer's needs. That might make for better criticism.

But there might be other and more positive advantages. The Gutter and Stamp system by eliminating what now passes for literary criticism—those few words devoted to 'why I like or dislike this book'—will save space. Four or five thousand words, possibly, might be saved in the course of a month or two. And an editor with that space at his disposal might not only express his respect for literature, but actually prove it. He might spend that space, even in a political daily or weekly, not upon stars and snippets, but upon unsigned and uncommercial literature—upon essays, upon criticism. There may be a Montaigne among us—a Montaigne now severed into futile slices of one thousand to fifteen hundred words weekly. Given time and space he might revive, and with him an admirable and now almost extinct form of art. Or there may be a critic among us—a Coleridge, a Matthew Arnold. He is now frittering himself away, as Mr. Nicolson has shown, upon a miscellaneous heap of poems, plays, novels, all to be reviewed in one column by Wednesday next. Given four thousand words, even twice a year, the critic might emerge, and with him those standards, those 'eternal standards', which if they are never referred to, far from being eternal cease to exist. Do we not all know that Mr. A writes better or it may be worse than Mr. B? But is that all we want to know? Is that all we ought to ask?

But to sum up, or rather to heap a little cairn of conjectures and conclusions at the end of these scattered remarks for somebody else to knock down. The review, it is contended, increases selfconsciousness and diminishes strength. The shop window and the looking-glass inhibit and confine. By putting in their place discussion—fearless and disinterested discussion—the writer would gain in range, in depth, in power. And this change would tell eventually upon the public mind. Their favourite figure of fun, the author, that hybrid between the peacock and the ape, would be removed from their derision, and in his place would be an obscure workman doing his job in the darkness of the workshop and not unworthy of respect. A new relationship might come into being, less petty and less personal than the old. A new interest in literature, a new respect for literature might follow. And, financial advantages apart, what a ray of light that would bring, what a ray of pure sunlight a critical and hungry public would bring into the darkness of the workshop!

Note

By Leonard Woolf

This pamphlet raises questions of considerable importance to literature, journalism, and the reading public. With many of its arguments I agree, but some of its conclusions seem to me doubtful because the meaning of certain facts has been ignored or their weight under-estimated. The object of this note is to draw attention to these facts and to suggest how they may modify the conclusions.

In the eighteenth century a revolution took place in the reading public and in the economic organization of literature as a profession. Goldsmith, who lived through the revolution, has given us a clear picture of what took place and an admirable analysis of its effects. There was an enormous expansion of the reading public. Hitherto the writer had written and the publisher published for a small, cultured, literary public. The author and publisher depended economically upon a patron or patrons, and books were luxury articles produced for a small, luxury-consuming class. The expansion of the reading public destroyed this system and substituted another. It became economically possible for the publisher to publish books for 'the public'; to sell a sufficient number of copies to pay his expenses, including a living wage to the author, and make a profit for himself. This killed the patronage system and eliminated the patron. It opened the way to the cheap book, read by thousands instead of by tens. The author, if he wanted to make a living by writing, now had to write for 'the public' instead of for the patron. Whether this change of system was on the whole good or bad for literature and the writer may be a subject of dispute; it is, however, to be noted that Goldsmith, who had experienced both systems and is generally considered to have produced at least one 'work of art', was wholeheartedly in favour of the new. The new system inevitably produced the reviewer, just as it produced modern journalism, of which the reviewer is only a small and particular phase. As the number of readers increased and with them the number of books and writers and publishers, two things happened: writing and publishing became highly competitive trades or professions and a need arose of giving to the vast reading public information regarding the contents and quality of the books published so that each person would have something to go on in making his selection of the books to read out of the thousands published.

Modern journalism saw its opportunity to meet this demand for information about new books and invented reviewing and the reviewer. As the size, differentiation, and quality of the reading public has changed, so too have the number, variety, and quality of books changed. This has entailed, no doubt, a change in the number, the variety, and the quality of reviewers. But the function of the reviewer remains fundamentally the same: it is to give to readers a description of the book and an estimate of its quality in order that he may know whether or not it is the kind of book which he may want to read.

Reviewing is therefore quite distinct from literary criticism. The reviewer, unlike the critic, in 999 cases out of 1,000 has nothing to say to the author; he is talking to the reader. On the rare occasions when he finds that he is reviewing a real work of art, if he is honest and intelligent, he will have to warn his readers against the fact and descend or ascend for a short time into the regions of true criticism. But to assume that, because of this, the art of reviewing is easy and mechanical is a complete misapprehension. I can speak with the experience of a journalist who was responsible for years for getting reviews and reviewers on a reputable paper. Reviewing is a highly-skilled profession. There are incompetent and dishonest reviewers, just as there are incompetent and dishonest politicians, carpenters, and writers; but the standard of competence and honesty is as high in reviewing as in any other trade or profession of which I have had inside knowledge. It is not at all an easy thing to give a clear, intelligent, and honest analysis of a novel or a book of poems. The fact that in the exceptional cases in which the book reviewed may have some claims to be a new work of art two reviewers take sometimes diametrically opposite views is really irrelevant and does not alter the fact that the vast majority of reviews give an accurate and often interesting account of the book reviewed.

Literary magazines have failed because they have fallen between two stools. The modern reading public is not interested in literary criticism and you cannot sell it to them. The monthly or quarterly which hopes to print literary criticism and pay is doomed to disappointment. Most of them have therefore tried to butter the bread of criticism with reviewing. But the public which wants reviewing will not pay 2s. 6d., 3s. 6d., or 5s. for it monthly or quarterly when they can get it just as good in the dailies and weeklies.

So much for the reviewer, the reading public, and the critic. One word about the writer. The writer who wants to write works of art and make a living by doing so is in a difficult position. As an artist the critic and criticism may be of immense value or interest to him. But he has no right to complain that the reviewer does not perform the function of critic for him. If he wants criticism, he should adopt the ingenious suggestion made in this pamphlet. But that will not make the reviewer unnecessary or unimportant to him. If he wants to sell his books to the great reading public and the circulating libraries, he will still need the reviewer—and that is why he will probably, like Tennyson and Dickens, continue to abuse the reviewer when the review is not favourable.

The Narrow Bridge of Art[1]

FAR the greater number of critics turn their backs upon the present and gaze steadily into the past. Wisely, no doubt, they make no comment upon what is being actually written at the moment; they leave that duty to the race of reviewers whose very title seems to imply transiency in themselves and in the objects they survey. But one has sometimes asked oneself, must the duty of the critic always be to the past, must his gaze always be fixed backward? Could he not sometimes turn round and, shading his eyes in the manner of Robinson Crusoe on the desert island, look into the future and trace on its mist the faint lines of the land which some day perhaps we may reach? The truth of such speculations can never be proved, of course, but in an age like ours there is a great temptation to indulge in them. For it is an age clearly when we are not fast anchored where we are; things are moving round us; we are moving ourselves. Is it not the critic's duty to tell us, or to guess at least, where we are going?

Obviously the inquiry must narrow itself very strictly, but it might perhaps be possible in a short space to take one instance of dissatisfaction and difficulty, and, having examined into that, we might be the better able to guess the direction in which, when we have surmounted it, we shall go.

Nobody indeed can read much modern literature without being aware that some dissatisfaction, some difficulty, is lying in our way. On all sides writers are attempting what they cannot achieve, are forcing the form they use to contain a meaning which is strange to it. Many reasons might be given, but here let us select only one, and that is the failure of poetry to serve us as it has served so many generations of our fathers. Poetry is not lending her services to us nearly as freely as she did to them. The great channel of expression which has carried away so much energy, so much genius, seems to have narrowed itself or to have turned aside.

That is true only within certain limits of course; our age is rich in lyric poetry; no age perhaps has been richer. But for our

[1] *New York Herald Tribune,* August 14, 1927

generation and the generation that is coming the lyric cry of ecstasy or despair, which is so intense, so personal, and so limited, is not enough. The mind is full of monstrous, hybrid, unmanageable emotions. That the age of the earth is 3,000,000,000 years; that human life lasts but a second; that the capacity of the human mind is nevertheless boundless; that life is infinitely beautiful yet repulsive; that one's fellow creatures are adorable but disgusting; that science and religion have between them destroyed belief; that all bonds of union seem broken, yet some control must exist—it is in this atmosphere of doubt and conflict that writers have now to create, and the fine fabric of a lyric is no more fitted to contain this point of view than a rose leaf to envelop the rugged immensity of a rock.

But when we ask ourselves what has in the past served to express such an attitude as this—an attitude which is full of contrast and collision; an attitude which seems to demand the conflict of one character upon another, and at the same time to stand in need of some general shaping power, some conception which lends the whole harmony and force, we must reply that there was a form once, and it was not the form of lyric poetry; it was the form of the drama, of the poetic drama of the Elizabethan age. And that is the one form which seems dead beyond all possibility of resurrection today.

For if we look at the state of the poetic play we must have grave doubts that any force on earth can now revive it. It has been practised and is still practised by writers of the highest genius and ambition. Since the death of Dryden every great poet it seems has had his fling. Wordsworth and Coleridge, Shelley and Keats, Tennyson, Swinburne, and Browning (to name the dead only) have all written poetic plays, but none has succeeded. Of all the plays they wrote, probably only Swinburne's *Atalanta* and Shelley's *Prometheus* are still read, and they less frequently than other works by the same writers. All the rest have climbed to the top shelves of our bookcases, put their heads under their wings, and gone to sleep. No one will willingly disturb those slumbers.

Yet it is tempting to try to find some explanation of this failure in case it should throw light upon the future which we are considering. The reason why poets can no longer write poetic plays lies somewhere perhaps in this direction.

There is a vague, mysterious thing called an attitude toward life. We all know people—if we turn from literature to life for a moment—who are at loggerheads with existence; unhappy people who never get what they want; are baffled, complaining, who stand at an uncomfortable angle whence they see everything askew. There are others again who, though they appear perfectly content, seem to have lost all touch with reality. They lavish all their affections upon little dogs and old china. They take interest in nothing but the vicissitudes of their own health and the ups and downs of social snobbery. There are, however, others who strike us, why precisely it would be difficult to say, as being by nature or circumstances in a position where they can use their faculties to the full upon things that are of importance. They are not necessarily happy or successful, but there is a zest in their presence, an interest in their doings. They seem alive all over. This may be partly the result of circumstances—they have been born into surroundings that suit them—but much more is the result of some happy balance of qualities in themselves so that they see things not at an awkward angle, all askew; nor distorted through a mist; but four square, in proportion; they grasp something hard; when they come into action they cut real ice.

A writer too has in the same way an attitude toward life, though it is a different life from the other. They too can stand at an uncomfortable angle; can be baffled, frustrated, unable to get at what they want as writers. This is true, for example, of the novels of George Gissing. Then, again, they can retire to the suburbs and lavish their interest upon pet dogs and duchesses— prettinesses, sentimentalities, snobberies, and this is true of some of our most highly successful novelists. But there are others who seem by nature or circumstances so placed that they can use their faculties freely upon important things. It is not that they write quickly or easily, or become at once successful or celebrated. One is rather trying to analyse a quality which is present in most of the great ages of literature and is most marked in the work of Elizabethan dramatists. They seem to have an attitude toward life, a position which allows them to move their limbs freely; a view which, though made up of all sorts of different things, falls into the right perspective for their purposes.

In part, of course, this was the result of circumstances. The public appetite, not for books, but for the drama, the smallness of the towns, the distance which separated people, the ignorance in which even the educated then lived, all made it natural for the Elizabethan imagination to fill itself with lions and unicorns, dukes and duchesses, violence and mystery. This was reinforced by something which we cannot explain so simply, but which we can certainly feel. They had an attitude toward life which made them able to express themselves freely and fully. Shakespeare's plays are not the work of a baffled and frustrated mind; they are the perfectly elastic envelope of his thought. Without a hitch he turns from philosophy to a drunken brawl; from love songs to an argument; from simple merriment to profound speculation. And it is true of all the Elizabethan dramatists that though they may bore us—and they do—they never make us feel that they are afraid or self-conscious, or that there is anything hindering, hampering, inhibiting the full current of their minds.

Yet our first thought when we open a modern poetic play— and this applies to much modern poetry—is that the writer is not at his ease. He is afraid, he is forced, he is self-conscious. And with what good reason! we may exclaim, for which of us is perfectly at his ease with a man in a toga called Xenocrates, or with a woman in a blanket called Eudoxa? Yet for some reason the modern poetic play is always about Xenocrates and not about Mr. Robinson; it is about Thessaly and not about Charing Cross Road. When the Elizabethans laid their scenes in foreign parts and made their heroes and heroines princes and princesses they only shifted the scene from one side to the other of a very thin veil. It was a natural device which gave depth and distance to their figures. But the country remained English; and the Bohemian prince was the same person as the English noble. Our modern poetic playwrights, however, seem to seek the veil of the past and of distance for a different reason. They want not a veil that heightens but a curtain that conceals; they lay their scene in the past because they are afraid of the present. They are aware that if they tried to express the thoughts, the visions, the sympathies and antipathies which are actually turning and tumbling in their brains in this year of grace 1927 the poetic decencies would be violated; they could only stammer and stumble and perhaps have to sit down or to leave the room. The Elizabethans had an attitude

which allowed them complete freedom; the modern playwright
has either no attitude at all, or one so strained that it cramps his
limbs and distorts his vision. He has therefore to take refuge with
Xenocrates, who says nothing or only what blank verse can with
decency say.

But can we explain ourselves a little more fully? What has
changed, what has happened, what has put the writer now at
such an angle that he cannot pour his mind straight into the old
channels of English poetry? Some sort of answer may be suggested
by a walk through the streets of any large town. The long avenue
of brick is cut up into boxes, each of which is inhabited by a
different human being who has put locks on his doors and bolts
on his windows to ensure some privacy, yet is linked to his
fellows by wires which pass overhead, by waves of sound which
pour through the roof and speak aloud to him of battles and
murders and strikes and revolutions all over the world. And if
we go in and talk to him we shall find that he is a wary, secretive,
suspicious animal, extremely self-conscious, extremely careful not
to give himself away. Indeed, there is nothing in modern life
which forces him to do it. There is no violence in private life; we
are polite, tolerant, agreeable, when we meet. War even is con-
ducted by companies and communities rather than by individuals.
Duelling is extinct. The marriage bond can stretch indefinitely
without snapping. The ordinary person is calmer, smoother, more
self-contained than he used to be.

But again we should find if we took a walk with our friend that
he is extremely alive to everything—to ugliness, sordidity, beauty,
amusement. He follows every thought careless where it may lead
him. He discusses openly what used never to be mentioned even
privately. And this very freedom and curiosity are perhaps the
cause of what appears to be his most marked characteristic—the
strange way in which things that have no apparent connection
are associated in his mind. Feelings which used to come single
and separate do so no longer. Beauty is part ugliness; amusement
part disgust; pleasure part pain. Emotions which used to enter
the mind whole are now broken up on the threshold.

For example: It is a spring night, the moon is up, the nightingale
singing, the willows bending over the river. Yes, but at the same
time a diseased old woman is picking over her greasy rags on a

hideous iron bench. She and the spring enter his mind together; they blend but do not mix. The two emotions, so incongruously coupled, bite and kick at each other in unison. But the emotion which Keats felt when he heard the song of the nightingale is one and entire, though it passes from joy in beauty to sorrow at the unhappiness of human fate. He makes no contrast. In his poem sorrow is the shadow which accompanies beauty. In the modern mind beauty is accompanied not by its shadow but by its opposite. The modern poet talks of the nightingale who sings 'jug jug to dirty ears'. There trips along by the side of our modern beauty some mocking spirit which sneers at beauty for being beautiful; which turns the looking-glass and shows us that the other side of her cheek is pitted and deformed. It is as if the modern mind, wishing always to verify its emotions, had lost the power of accepting anything simply for what it is. Undoubtedly this sceptical and testing spirit has led to a great freshening and quickening of soul. There is a candour, an honesty in modern writing which is salutary if not supremely delightful. Modern literature, which had grown a little sultry and scented with Oscar Wilde and Walter Pater, revived instantly from her nineteenth-century languor when Samuel Butler and Bernard Shaw began to burn their feathers and apply their salts to her nose. She awoke; she sat up; she sneezed. Naturally, the poets were frightened away.

For of course poetry has always been overwhelmingly on the side of beauty. She has always insisted on certain rights, such as rhyme, metre, poetic diction. She has never been used for the common purpose of life. Prose has taken all the dirty work on to her own shoulders; has answered letters, paid bills, written articles, made speeches, served the needs of businessmen, shop-keepers, lawyers, soldiers, peasants.

Poetry has remained aloof in the possession of her priests. She has perhaps paid the penalty for this seclusion by becoming a little stiff. Her presence with all her apparatus—her veils, her garlands, her memories, her associations—affects us the moment she speaks. Thus when we ask poetry to express this discord, this incongruity, this sneer, this contrast, this curiosity, the quick, queer emotions which are bred in small separate rooms, the wide, general ideas which civilization teaches, she cannot move quickly enough, simply enough, or broadly enough to do it. Her accent is too marked; her manner too emphatic. She gives us instead lovely lyric cries of passion; with a majestic sweep of her arm she bids us take refuge in the past; but she does not keep pace with the mind and fling herself subtly, quickly, passionately into its various sufferings and joys. Byron in *Don Juan* pointed the way; he showed how flexible an instrument poetry might become, but none has followed his example or put his tool to further use. We remain without a poetic play.

Thus we are brought to reflect whether poetry is capable of the task which we are now setting her. It may be that the emotions here sketched in such rude outline and imputed to the modern mind submit more readily to prose than to poetry. It may be possible that prose is going to take over—has, indeed, already taken over—some of the duties which were once discharged by poetry.

If, then, we are daring and risk ridicule and try to see in what direction we who seem to be moving so fast are going, we may guess that we are going in the direction of prose and that in ten or fifteen years' time prose will be used for purposes for which prose has never been used before. That cannibal, the novel, which has devoured so many forms of art will by then have devoured even more. We shall be forced to invent new names for the different books which masquerade under this one heading. And it is possible that there will be among the so-called novels one which we shall scarcely know how to christen. It will be written in prose, but in prose which has many of the characteristics of poetry. It will have something of the exaltation of poetry, but much of the ordinariness of prose. It will be dramatic, and yet not a play. It will be read, not acted. By what name we are to call it is not a matter of very great importance. What is important is that this book which we see on the horizon may serve to express some of those feelings which seem at the moment to be balked by poetry pure and simple and to find the drama equally inhospitable to them. Let us try, then, to come to closer terms with it and to imagine what may be its scope and nature.

In the first place, one may guess that it will differ from the novel as we know it now chiefly in that it will stand further back from life. It will give, as poetry does, the outline rather than the detail. It will make little use of the marvellous fact-recording power, which is one of the attributes of fiction. It will tell us very little about the houses, incomes, occupations of its characters; it will have little kinship with the sociological novel or the novel of environment. With these limitations it will express the feeling and ideas of the characters closely and vividly, but from a different angle. It will resemble poetry in this that it will give not only or mainly people's relations to each other and their activities together, as the novel has hitherto done, but it will give the relation of the mind to general ideas and its soliloquy in solitude. For under the dominion of the novel we have scrutinized one part of the mind closely and left another unexplored. We have come to forget that a large and important part of life consists in our emotions toward such things as roses and nightingales, the dawn, the sunset, life, death, and fate; we forget that we spend much time sleeping, dreaming, thinking, reading, alone; we are not entirely occupied in personal relations; all our energies are not absorbed in making our livings. The psychological novelist has been too prone to limit psychology to the psychology of personal intercourse; we long sometimes to escape from the incessant, the remorseless analysis of falling into love and falling out of love, of what Tom feels for Judith and Judith does or does not altogether feel for Tom. We long for some more impersonal relationship. We long for ideas, for dreams, for imaginations, for poetry.

And it is one of the glories of the Elizabethan dramatists that they give us this. The poet is always able to transcend the particularity of Hamlet's relation to Ophelia and to give us his questioning not of his own personal lot alone but of the state and being of all human life. In *Measure for Measure*, for example, passages of extreme psychological subtlety are mingled with profound reflections, tremendous imaginations. Yet it is worth noticing that if Shakespeare gives us this profundity, this psychology, at the same time Shakespeare makes no attempt to give us certain other things. The plays are of no use whatever as 'applied sociology'. If we had to depend upon them for a knowledge of the social and economic conditions of Elizabethan life, we should be hopelessly at sea.

In these respects then the novel or the variety of the novel which will be written in time to come will take on some of the attributes of poetry. It will give the relations of man to nature, to fate; his imagination; his dreams. But it will also give the sneer, the contrast, the question, the closeness and complexity of life. It will take the mould of that queer conglomeration of incongruous things—the modern mind. Therefore it will clasp to its breast the precious prerogatives of the democratic art of prose; its freedom, its fearlessness, its flexibility. For prose is so humble that it can go anywhere; no place is too low, too sordid, or too mean for it to enter. It is infinitely patient, too, humbly acquisitive. It can lick up with its long glutinous tongue the most minute fragments of fact and mass them into the most subtle labyrinths, and listen silently at doors behind which only a murmur, only a whisper, is to be heard. With all the suppleness of a tool which is in constant use it can follow the windings and record the changes which are typical of the modern mind. To this, with Proust and Dostoevsky behind us, we must agree.

But can prose, we may ask, adequate though it is to deal with the common and the complex—can prose say the simple things which are so tremendous? Give the sudden emotions which are so surprising? Can it chant the elegy, or hymn the love, or shriek in terror, or praise the rose, the nightingale, or the beauty of the night? Can it leap at one spring at the heart of its subject as the poet does? I think not. That is the penalty it pays for having dispensed with the incantation and the mystery, with rhyme and metre. It is true that prose writers are daring; they are constantly forcing their instrument to make the attempt. But one has always a feeling of discomfort in the presence of the purple patch or the prose poem. The objection to the purple patch, however, is not that it is purple but that it is a patch. Recall for instance Meredith's 'Diversion on a Penny Whistle' in *Richard Feverel*. How awkwardly, how emphatically, with a broken poetic metre it begins: 'Golden lie the meadows; golden run the streams; red-gold is on the pine-stems. The sun is coming down to earth and walks the fields and the waters.' Or recall the famous description of the storm at the end of Charlotte Brontë's *Villette*. These passages are eloquent, lyrical, splendid; they read very well cut out and stuck in an anthology; but in the context of the novel they make us uncomfortable. For both Meredith and Charlotte Brontë called themselves novelists; they stood close up to life;

226

they led us to expect the rhythm, the observation, and the perspective of prose. We feel the jerk and the effort; we are half woken from that trance of consent and illusion in which our submission to the power of the writer's imagination is most complete.

But let us now consider another book, which though written in prose and by way of being called a novel, adopts from the start a different attitude, a different rhythm, which stands back from life, and leads us to expect a different perspective—*Tristram Shandy*. It is a book full of poetry, but we never notice it; it is a book stained deep purple, which is yet never patchy. Here though the mood is changing always, there is no jerk, no jolt in that change to waken us from the depths of consent and belief. In the same breath Sterne laughs, sneers, cuts some indecent ribaldry, and passes on to a passage like this:

> Time wastes too fast: every letter I trace tells me with what rapidity life follows my pen; the days and hours of it more precious—my dear Jenny—than the rubies about thy neck, are flying over our heads like light clouds of a windy day, never to return more; everything presses on—whilst thou are twisting that lock—see! it grows gray; and every time I kiss thy hand to bid adieu, and every absence which follows it, are preludes to that eternal separation which we are shortly to make.—Heaven have mercy upon us both!
>
> CHAP. IX
> Now, for what the world thinks of that ejaculation—I would not give a groat.

And he goes on to my Uncle Toby, the Corporal, Mrs. Shandy, and the rest of them.

There, one sees, is poetry changing easily and naturally into prose, prose into poetry. Standing a little aloof, Sterne lays his hands lightly upon imagination, wit, fantasy; and reaching high up among the branches where these things grow, naturally and no doubt willingly forfeits his right to the more substantial vegetables that grow on the ground. For, unfortunately, it seems true that some renunciation is inevitable. You cannot cross the narrow bridge of art carrying all its tools in your hands. Some you must leave behind, or you will drop them in midstream or, what is worse, overbalance and be drowned yourself.

So, then, this unnamed variety of the novel will be written standing back from life, because in that way a larger view is to be obtained of some important features of it; it will be written in prose, because prose, if you free it from the beast-of-burden work which so many novelists necessarily lay upon it, of carrying loads of details, bushels of fact—prose thus treated will show itself capable of rising high from the ground, not in one dart, but in sweeps and circles, and of keeping at the same time in touch with the amusements and idiosyncrasies of human character in daily life.

There remains, however, a further question. Can prose be dramatic? It is obvious, of course, that Shaw and Ibsen have used prose dramatically with the highest success, but they have been faithful to the dramatic form. This form one may prophesy is not the one which the poetic dramatist of the future will find fit for his needs. A prose play is too rigid, too limited, too emphatic for his purposes. It lets slip between its meshes half the things that he wants to say. He cannot compress into dialogue all the comment, all the analysis, all the richness that he wants to give. Yet he covets the explosive emotional effect of the drama; he wants to draw blood from his readers, and not merely to stroke and tickle their intellectual susceptibilities. The looseness and freedom of *Tristram Shandy*, wonderfully though they encircle and float off such characters as Uncle Toby and Corporal Trim, do not attempt to range and marshal these people in dramatic contrast together. Therefore it will be necessary for the writer of this exacting book to bring to bear upon his tumultuous and contradictory emotions the generalizing and simplifying power of a strict and logical imagination. Tumult is vile; confusion is hateful; everything in a work of art should be mastered and ordered. His effort will be to generalize and split up. Instead of enumerating details he will mould blocks. His characters thus will have a dramatic power which the minutely realized characters of contemporary fiction often sacrifice in the interests of psychology. And then, though this is scarcely visible, so far distant it lies on the rim of the horizon—one can imagine that he will have extended the scope of his interest so as to dramatize some of those influences which play so large a part in life, yet have so far escaped the novelist—the power of music, the stimulus of sight, the effect on us of the shape of trees or the play of colour, the emotions bred in us by crowds, the obscure terrors and hatreds which come so irrationally in certain places or from certain people, the delight of movement, the intoxication of wine. Every moment is the centre and meeting-place of an extraordinary number of perceptions which have not yet been expressed. Life is always and inevitably much richer than we who try to express it.

But it needs no great gift of prophecy to be certain that whoever attempts to do what is outlined above will have need of all his courage. Prose is not going to learn a new step at the bidding of the first comer. Yet if the signs of the times are worth anything the need of fresh developments is being felt. It is certain that there are scattered about in England, France, and America writers who are trying to work themselves free from a bondage which has become irksome to them; writers who are trying to readjust their attitude so that they may once more stand easily and naturally in a position where their powers have full play upon important things. And it is when a book strikes us as the result of that attitude rather than by its beauty or its brilliancy that we know that it has in it the seeds of an enduring existence.

The Artist and Politics

I HAVE been asked by the Artists' International Association to explain as shortly as I can why it is that the artist at present is interested, actively and genuinely, in politics. For it seems that there are some people to whom this interest is suspect.

That the writer is interested in politics needs no saying. Every publisher's list, almost every book that is now issued, brings proof of the fact. The historian today is writing not about Greece and Rome in the past, but about Germany and Spain in the present; the biographer is writing lives of Hitler and Mussolini, not of Henry the Eighth and Charles Lamb; the poet introduces communism and fascism into his lyrics; the novelist turns from the private lives of his characters to their social surroundings and their political opinions. Obviously the writer is in such close touch with human life that any agitation in his subject matter must change his angle of vision. Either he focuses his sight upon the immediate problem; or he brings his subject matter into relation with the present; or in some cases, so paralysed is he by the agitations of the moment that he remains silent.

But why should this agitation affect the painter and the sculptor? it may be asked. He is not concerned with the feelings of his model but with its form. The rose and the apple have no political views. Why should he not spend his time contemplating them, as he has always done, in the cold north light that still falls through his studio window?

To answer this question shortly is not easy, for to understand why the artist—the plastic artist—is affected by the state of society, we must try to define the relations of the artist to society, and this is difficult, partly because no such definition has ever been made. But that there is some sort of understanding between them, most people would agree; and in times of peace it may be said roughly to run as follows. The artist on his side held that since the value of his work depended upon freedom of mind, security of person, and immunity from practical affairs—for to mix art with politics, he held, was to adulterate it—he was absolved from political duties; sacrificed many of the privileges that the active citizen enjoyed; and in return created what is called a work of art. Society on its side bound itself to run the state in such a manner that it paid the artist a living wage; asked no active help from him; and considered itself repaid by those works of art which have always formed one of its chief claims to distinction. With many lapses and breaches on both sides, the contract has been kept; society has accepted the artist's work in lieu of other services, and the artist, living for the most part precariously on a pittance, has written or painted without regard for the political agitations of the moment. Thus it would be impossible, when we read Keats, or look at the pictures of Titian and Velasquez, or listen to the music of Mozart or Bach, to say what was the political condition of the age or the country in which these works were created. And if it were otherwise—if the *Ode to a Nightingale* were inspired by hatred of Germany; if *Bacchus and Ariadne* symbolized the conquest of Abyssinia; if *Figaro* expounded the doctrines of Hitler, we should feel cheated and imposed upon, as if, instead of bread made with flour, we were given bread made with plaster.

But if it is true that some such contract existed between the artist and society, in times of peace, it by no means follows that the artist is independent of society. Materially of course he depends upon it for his bread and butter. Art is the first luxury to be discarded in times of stress; the artist is the first of the workers to suffer. But intellectually also he depends upon society. Society is not only his paymaster but his patron. If the patron becomes too busy or too distracted to exercise his critical faculty, the artist will work in a vacuum and his art will suffer and perhaps perish from lack of understanding. Again, if the patron is neither poor nor indifferent, but dictatorial—if he will only buy pictures that flatter his vanity or serve his politics—then again the artist is impeded and his work becomes worthless. And even if there are some artists who can afford to disregard the patron, either because they have private means or have learnt in the course of time to form their own style and to depend upon tradition, these are for the most part only the older artists whose work is already done. Even they, however, are by no means immune. For though it would be easy to stress the point absurdly, still it is a fact that the practice of art, far from making the artist out of touch with his kind, rather increases his sensibility. It breeds in him a feeling for the passions and needs of mankind in the mass which the citizen whose duty it is to work for a particular country or for a particular party has no time and perhaps no need to cultivate. Thus even if he be ineffective, he is by no means apathetic. Perhaps indeed he suffers more than the active citizen because he has no obvious duty to discharge.

For such reasons then it is clear that the artist is affected as powerfully as other citizens when society is in chaos, although the disturbance affects him in different ways. His studio now is far from being a cloistered spot where he can contemplate his model or his apple in peace. It is besieged by voices, all disturbing, some for one reason, some for another. First there is the voice which cries: 'I cannot protect you; I cannot pay you. I am so tortured and distracted that I can no longer enjoy your works of art.' Then there is the voice which asks for help. 'Come down from your ivory tower, leave your studio,' it cries, 'and use your gifts as doctor, as teacher, not as artist.' Again there is the voice which warns the artist that unless he can show good cause why art benefits the state he will be made to help it actively—by making aeroplanes, by firing guns. And finally there is the voice which many artists in other countries have already heard and had to obey—the voice which proclaims that the artist is the servant of the politician. 'You shall only practise your art,' it says, 'at our bidding. Paint us pictures, carve us statues that glorify our gospels. Celebrate fascism; celebrate communism. Preach what we bid you preach. On no other terms shall you exist.'

With all these voices crying and conflicting in his ears, how can the artist still remain at peace in his studio, contemplating his model or his apple in the cold light that comes through the studio window? He is forced to take part in politics; he must form himself into societies like the Artists' International Association. Two causes of supreme importance to him are in peril. The first is his own survival; the other is the survival of his art.

Walter Sickert

THOUGH talk is a common habit and much enjoyed, those who try to record it are aware that it runs hither and thither, seldom sticks to the point, abounds in exaggeration and inaccuracy, and has frequent stretches of extreme dullness. Thus when seven or eight people dined together the other night the first ten minutes went in saying how very difficult it is to get about London nowadays; was it quicker to walk or to drive; did the new system of coloured lights help or hinder? Just as dinner was announced, somebody asked: 'But when were picture galleries invented?', a question naturally arising, for the discussing about the value of coloured lights had led somebody to say that in the eyes of a motorist red is not a colour but simply a danger signal. We shall very soon lose our sense of colour, another added, exaggerating, of course. Colours are used so much as signals now that they will very soon suggest action merely—that is the worst of living in a highly organized community. Other instances of the change wrought upon our senses by modern conditions were then cited; how buildings are changing their character because no one can stand still to look at them; how statues and mosaics removed from their old stations and confined to the insides of churches and private houses lose the qualities proper to them in the open air. This naturally led to the question when picture galleries were first opened, and as no precise answer was forthcoming the speaker went on to sketch a fancy picture of an inventive youth having to wait his turn to cross Ludgate Circus in the reign of Queen Anne. 'Look,' he said to himself, 'how the coaches cut across the corner! That poor old boy,' he said, 'positively had to put his hand to his pigtail. Nobody any longer stops to look at St. Paul's. Soon all these swinging signboards will be dismantled. Let me take time by the forelock,' he said, and, going to his bank, which was near at hand, drew out what remained of his patrimony, and invested it in a neat set of rooms in Bond Street, where he hung the first show of pictures ever to be displayed to the public. Perhaps that is the origin of the House of Agnew's; perhaps their gallery stands on the site of the house that was leased, so foreseeingly, by the young man over two hundred years ago. Perhaps, said the others; but nobody troubled to verify the statement, for it was a bitter cold night in December and the soup stood upon the table.

In course of time the talk turned, as talk has a way of turning, back on itself—to colour; how different people see colour differently; how painters are affected by their place of birth, whether in the blue South or the grey North; how colour blazes, unrelated to any object, in the eyes of children; how politicians and businessmen are blind, days spent in an office leading to atrophy of the eye; and so, by contrast, to those insects, said still to be found in the primeval forests of South America, in whom the eye is so developed that they are all eye, the body a tuft of leather, serving merely to connect the two great chambers of vision. Somebody had met a man whose business it was to explore the wilder parts of the world in search of cactuses, and from him had heard of these insects who are born with the flowers and die when the flowers fade. A hard-headed man, used to roughing it in all parts of the world, yet there was something moving to him in the sight of these little creatures drinking crimson until they became crimson; then flitting on to violet; then to a vivid green, and becoming for the moment the thing they saw—red, green, blue, whatever the colour of the flower might be. At the first breath of winter, he said, when the flowers died, the life went out of them, and you might mistake them as they lay on the grass for shrivelled air-balls. Were we once insects like that, too, one of the diners asked; all eye? Do we still preserve the capacity for drinking, eating, indeed becoming colour furled up in us, waiting proper conditions to develop? For as the rocks hide fossils, so we hide tigers, baboons, and perhaps insects, under our coats and hats. On first entering a picture gallery, whose stillness, warmth and seclusion from the perils of the street reproduce the conditions of the primeval forest, it often seems as if we reverted to the insect stage of our long life.

'On first entering a picture gallery'—there was silence for a moment. Many pictures were being shown in London at that time. There was the famous Holbein; there were pictures by Picasso and Matisse; young English painters were holding an exhibition in Burlington Gardens, and there was a show of

Sickert's pictures at Agnew's. When I first went into Sickert's show, said one of the diners, I became completely and solely an insect—all eye. I flew from colour to colour, from red to blue, from yellow to green. Colours went spirally through my body lighting a flare as if a rocket fell through the night and lit up greens and browns, grass and trees, and there in the grass a white bird. Colour warmed, thrilled, chafed, burnt, soothed, fed and finally exhausted me. For though the life of colour is a glorious life it is a short one. Soon the eye can hold no more; it shuts itself in sleep, and if the man who looks for cactuses had come by he would only have seen a shrivelled air-ball on a red plush chair.

That is an exaggeration, a dramatization, the others said. Nobody, who can walk down Bond Street in the year 1933, without exciting suspicion in the heart of the policeman, can simplify sufficiently to see colour only. One must be a fly in order to die in aromatic pain. And it is many ages now since we lost 'the microscopic eye'. Ages ago we left the forest and went into the world, and the eye shrivelled and the heart grew, and the liver and the intestines and the tongue and the hands and the feet. Sickert's show proves the truth of that soon enough. Look at his portraits: Charles Bradlaugh at the Bar of the House of Commons; the Right Honourable Winston Churchill, M.P.; Rear-Admiral Lumsden, C.I.E., C.V.O.; and Dr. Cobbledick. These gentlemen are by no means simple flowers. In front of Sickert's portraits of them we are reminded of all that we have done with all our organs since we left the jungle. The face of a civilized human being is a summing-up, an epitome of a million acts, thoughts, statements and concealments. Yes, Sickert is a great biographer, said one of them; when he paints a portrait I read a life. Think of his picture of the disillusioned lady in full evening-dress sitting on a balcony in Venice. She has seen every sort of sunrise and sunset whether dressed in diamonds or white night-gown; now all is ruin and shipwreck; and yet the tattered ship in the background still floats. For though Sickert is a realist he is by no means a pessimist . . . Laughter drowned the last words. The portrait of the lady on the balcony had suggested nothing of the kind to most of the others. Had she lovers or not—it did not matter; did the ship sail or did it sink—they did not care. And they fetched a book of photographs from Sickert's paintings and began cutting off a hand or a head, and made them connect or separate, not as a hand or a head but as if they had some quite different relationship.

Now they are going into the silent land; soon they will be out of reach of the human voice, two of the diners said, watching them. They are seeing things that we cannot see, just as a dog bristles and whines in a dark lane when nothing is visible to human eyes. They are making passes with their hands, to express what they cannot say; what excites them in those photographs is something so deeply sunk that they cannot put words to it. But we, like most English people, have been trained not to see but to talk. Yet it may be, they went on, that there is a zone of silence in the middle of every art. The artists themselves live in it. Coleridge could not explain *Kubla Khan*—that he left to the critics. And those who are almost on a par with the artists, like our friends who are looking at the pictures, cannot impart what they feel when they go beyond the outskirts. They can only open and shut their fingers. We must resign ourselves to the fact that we are outsiders, condemned for ever to haunt the borders and margins of this great art. Nevertheless that is a region of very strong sensations. First, on entering a picture gallery, the violent rapture of colour; then, when we have soused our eyes sufficiently in that, there is the complexity and intrigue of character. I repeat, said one of them, that Sickert is among the best of biographers. When he sits a man or woman down in front of him he sees the whole of the life that has been lived to make that face. There it is —stated. None of our biographers make such complete and flaw-less statements. They are tripped up by those miserable impedi-ments called facts; was he born on such a day; was his mother's name Jane or Mary; then the affair with the barmaid has to be suppressed out of deference to family feeling; and there is always, brooding over him with its dark wings and hooked beak, the Law of Libel. Hence the three or four hundred pages of compromise, evasion, understatement, overstatement, irrelevance and down-right falsehood which we call biography. But Sickert takes his brush, squeezes his tube, looks at the face; and then, cloaked in the divine gift of silence, he paints—lies, paltriness, splendour, depravity, endurance, beauty—it is all there and nobody can say, 'But his mother's name was Jane not Mary.' Not in our time will anyone write a life as Sickert paints it. Words are an impure medium; better far to have been born into the silent kingdom of paint.

But to me Sickert always seems more of a novelist than a biographer, said the other. He likes to set his characters in motion, to watch them in action. As I remember it, his show was full of pictures that might be stories, as indeed their names suggest—*Rose et Marie*; *Christine buys a house*; *A difficult moment*. The figures are motionless, of course, but each has been seized in a moment of crisis; it is difficult to look at them and not to invent a plot, to hear what they are saying. You remember the picture of the old publican, with his glass on the table before him and a cigar gone cold at his lips, looking out of his shrewd little pig's eyes at the intolerable wastes of desolation in front of him? A fat woman lounges, her arm on a cheap yellow chest of drawers, behind him. It is all over with them, one feels. The accumulated weariness of innumerable days has discharged its burden on them. They are buried under an avalanche of rubbish. In the street beneath, the trams are squeaking, children are shrieking. Even now somebody is tapping his glass impatiently on the bar counter. She will have to bestir herself; to pull her heavy, indolent body together and go and serve him. The grimness of that situation lies in the fact that there is no crisis; dull minutes are mounting, old matches are accumulating and dirty glasses and dead cigars; still on they must go, up they must get.

And yet it is beautiful, said the other; satisfactory; complete in some way. Perhaps it is the flash of the stuffed birds in the glass case, or the relation of the chest of drawers to the woman's body; anyhow, there is a quality in that picture which makes me feel that though the publican is done for, and his disillusion complete, still in the other world, of which he is mysteriously a part without knowing it, beauty and order prevail; all is right there —or does that convey nothing to you? Perhaps that is one of the things that is better said with a flick of the fingers, said the other. But let us go on living in the world of words a little longer. Do you remember the picture of the girl sitting on the edge of her bed half naked? Perhaps it is called *Nuit d'Amour*. Anyhow, the night is over. The bed, a cheap iron bed, is tousled and tumbled; she has to face the day, to get her breakfast, to see about the rent. As she sits there with her night-gown slipping from her shoulders, just for a moment the truth of her life comes over her; she sees in a flash the little garden in Wales and the dripping tunnel in the Adelphi where she began, where she will end, her days. So be it, she says, and yawns and shrugs and stretches a hand for her stockings and chemise. Fate has willed it so. Now a novelist who told that story would plunge—how obviously—into the depths of sentimentality. How is he to convey in words the mixture of innocence and sordidity, pity and squalor? Sickert merely takes his brush and paints a tender green light on the faded wallpaper. Light is beautiful falling through green leaves. He has no need of explanation; green is enough. Then again there is the story of Marie and Rose—a grim, a complex, a moving and at the same time a heartening and rousing story. Marie on the chair has been sobbing out some piteous plaint of vows betrayed and hearts broken to the woman in the crimson petticoat. 'Don't be a damned fool, my dear,' says Rose, standing before her with her arms akimbo. 'I know all about it,' she says, standing there in the intimacy of undress, experienced, seasoned, a woman of the world. And Marie looks up at her with all her illusions tearfully exposed and receives the full impact of the other's knowledge, which, however, perhaps because of the glow of the crimson petticoat, does not altogether wither her. There is too much salt and savour in it. She takes heart again. Down she trips past the one-eyed char with a pail, out into the street, a wiser woman than she went in. 'So that's what life is,' she says, brushing the tear from her eye and hailing the omnibus. There are any number of stories and three-volume novels in Sickert's exhibition.

But to what school of novelists does he belong? He is a realist, of course, nearer to Dickens than to Meredith. He has something in common with Balzac, Gissing and the earlier Arnold Bennett. The life of the lower middle class interests him most—of inn-keepers, shopkeepers, music-hall actors and actresses. He seems to care little for the life of the aristocracy whether of birth or of intellect. The reason may be that people who inherit beautiful things sit much more loosely to their possessions than those who have bought them off barrows in the street with money earned by their own hands. There is a gusto in the spending of the poor; they are very close to what they possess. Hence the intimacy that seems to exist in Sickert's pictures between his people and their rooms. The bed, the chest of drawers, the one picture and the vase on the mantelpiece are all expressive of the owner. Merely by process of use and fitness the cheap furniture has rubbed its varnish off; the grain shows through; it has the expressive quality that expensive furniture always lacks; one must call it beautiful, though outside the room in which it plays its part it would be hideous in the extreme. Diamonds and Sheraton tables never submit to use like that. But whatever Sickert paints has to submit; it has to lose its separateness; it has to compose part of his scene. He chooses, therefore, the casual clothes of daily life that have taken the shape of the body; the felt hat with one feather that a girl has bought with sixpence off a barrow in Berwick Market. He likes bodies that work, hands that work, faces that have been lined and suppled and seamed by work, because, in working, people take unconscious gestures, and their faces have the expressiveness of unconsciousness—a look that the very rich, the very beautiful and the very sophisticated seldom possess. And of course Sickert composes his picture down to the very castors on the chairs and the fire-irons in the grate just as carefully as Turgenev, of whom he sometimes reminds me, composes his scene.

There are many points one could argue in that statement, said the other. But certainly it would seem to be true that Sickert is the novelist of the middle class. At the same time, though he prefers to paint people who use their hands rather than the leisured, he never sinks below a certain level in the social scale. Like most painters, he has a profound love of the good things of life; well-cooked food, good wine, fine cigars. His world abounds in richness and succulence and humour. He could not draw breath in a starved, a stunted or a puritanical universe. His people are always well fed in body and mind; they excel in mother wit and shrewd knowledge of the world. Some of their sayings are really a little broad; I have always wondered that the censor has let them pass. There is always good company in his pictures. Nothing could be more enjoyable than to sit behind the shop with the French innkeeper—that formidable man in the frock-coat whose name I forget. He would offer us a very fine cigar; uncork a bottle kept for his private use; and Madame would join us from the glass-house where she keeps accounts, and we should sit and talk and sing songs and crack jokes.

Yes, and in the middle of our songs we should look up and see red-gold light dripping down into the green waters of the canal. We should suddenly become aware of a grey church looming over us and one pink cloud riding down the bosom of the west. We should see it suddenly over the shoulders of the innkeeper; and then we should go on talking. That is how Sickert makes us aware of beauty—over the shoulders of the innkeeper; for he is a true poet, of course, one in the long line of English poets, and not the least. Think of his Venice, of his landscapes; or of those pictures of music-halls, of circuses, of street markets, where the acute drama of human character is cut off; and we no longer make up stories but behold—is it too much to say a vision? But it would be absurd to class Sickert among the visionaries; he is not a rhapsodist; he does not gaze into the sunset; he does not lead us down glorious vistas to blue horizons and remote ecstasies. He is not a Shelley or a Blake. We see his Venice from a little table on the Piazza, just as we are lifting a glass to our lips. Then we go on talking. His paint has a tangible quality; it is made not of air and star-dust but of oil and earth. We long to lay hands on his clouds and his pinnacles; to feel his columns round and his pillars hard beneath our touch. One can almost hear his gold and red dripping with a little splash into the waters of the canal. Moreover, human nature is never exiled from his canvas—there is always a woman with a parasol in the foreground, or a man selling cabbages in the shadow of the arch. Even when he paints a formal eighteenth-century town like Bath, he puts a great cart-wheel in the middle of the road. And those long French streets of pale pink and yellow stucco are all patched and peeled; a child's pink frock hangs out to dry; there are marble-topped tables at the corner. He never goes far from the sound of the human voice, from the mobility and idiosyncrasy of the human figure. As a poet, then, we must liken him to the poets who haunt taverns and sea beaches where the fishermen are tumbling their silver catch into wicker baskets. Crabbe, Wordsworth, Cowper are the names that come to mind, the poets who have kept close to the earth, to the house, to the sound of the natural human voice.

But here the speakers fell silent. Perhaps they were thinking that there is a vast distance between any poem and any picture; and that to compare them stretches words too far. At last, said one of them, we have reached the edge where painting breaks off and takes her way into the silent land. We shall have to set foot there soon, and all our words will fold their wings and sit huddled like rooks on the tops of the trees in winter. But since we love words let us dally for a little on the verge, said the other. Let us hold painting by the hand a moment longer, for though they must part in the end, painting and writing have much to tell each other: they have much in common. The novelist after all wants to make us see. Gardens, rivers, skies, clouds changing, the colour of a woman's dress, landscapes that bask beneath lovers, twisted woods that people walk in when they quarrel— novels are full of pictures like these. The novelist is always saying to himself how can I bring the sun on to my page? How can I show the night and the moon rising? And he must often think that to describe a scene is the worst way to show it. It must be done with one word, or with one word in skilful contrast with another. For example, there is Shakespeare's 'Dear as the ruddy drops that visit this sad heart'. Does not 'ruddy' shine out partly because 'sad' comes after it; does not 'sad' convey to us a double sense of the gloom of the mind and the dullness of colour? They both speak at once, striking two notes to make one chord, stimulating the eye of the mind and of the body. Then again there is Herrick's

> *More white than are the whitest creams,*
> *Or moonlight tinselling the streams.*

where the word 'tinselling' adds to the simplicity of 'white' the glittering, sequined, fluid look of moonlit water. It is a very complex business, the mixing and marrying of words that goes on, probably unconsciously, in the poet's mind to feed the reader's eye. All great writers are great colourists, just as they are musicians into the bargain; they always contrive to make their scenes glow and darken and change to the eye. Each of Shakespeare's plays has its dominant colour. And each writer differs of course as a colourist. Pope has no great range of colours; he is more draughtsman than colourist; clear washes of indigo, discreet blacks and violets best suit his exquisite sharp outlines— save that in the *Elegy to an Unfortunate Lady* there is a mass of funeral black; and the great image of the Eastern King glows, fantastically, if you like, dark crimson. Keats uses colour lavishly, lusciously, like a Venetian. In the *Eve of St. Agnes* he paints for lines at a time, dipping his pen in mounds of pure reds and blues. Tennyson on the other hand is never luscious; he uses the hard brush and the pure bright tints of a miniature painter. *The Princess* is illuminated like a monk's manuscript; there are whole landscapes in the curves of the capital letters. You almost need a magnifying glass to see the minuteness of the detail.

Undoubtedly, they agreed, the arts are closely united. What poet sets pen to paper without first hearing a tune in his head? And the prose-writer, though he makes believe to walk soberly, in obedience to the voice of reason, excites us by perpetual changes of rhythm following the emotions with which he deals. The best critics, Dryden, Lamb, Hazlitt, were acutely aware of the mixture of elements, and wrote of literature with music and painting in their minds. Nowadays we are all so specialized that critics keep their brain fixed to the print, which accounts for the starved condition of criticism in our time, and the attenuated and partial manner in which it deals with its subject.

But we have gossiped long enough, they said; it is time to make an end. The silent land lies before us. We have come within sight of it many times while we were talking; when, for example, we said that Rose's red petticoat satisfied us; when we said that the chest of drawers and the arm convinced us that all was well with the world as a whole. Why did the red petticoat, the yellow chest of drawers, make us feel something that had nothing to do with the story? We could not say; we could not express in words the effect of those combinations of line and colour. And, thinking back over the show, we have to admit that there is a great stretch of silent territory in Sickert's pictures. Consider once more the picture of the music-hall. At first it suggests the husky voice of Marie Lloyd singing a song about the ruins that Cromwell knocked about a bit; then the song dies away, and we see a scooped-out space filled curiously with the curves of fiddles, bowler hats, and shirt fronts converging into a pattern with a lemon-coloured splash in the centre. It is extraordinarily satisfying. Yet the description is so formal, so superficial, that we can hardly force our lips to frame it; while the emotion is distinct, powerful, and satisfactory.

Yes, said the other, it is not a description at all; it leaves out the meaning. But what sort of meaning is that which cannot be expressed in words? What is a picture when it has rid itself of the companionship of language and of music. Let us ask the critics.

But the critics were still talking with their fingers. They were still bristling and shivering like dogs in dark lanes when something passes that we cannot see.

They have gone much farther into the forest than we shall ever go, said one of the talkers, sadly. We only catch a glimpse now and then of what lives there; we try to describe it and we cannot; and then it vanishes, and having seen it and lost it, exhaustion and depression overcome us; we recognize the limitations which Nature has put upon us, and so turn back to the sunny margin where the arts flirt and joke and pay each other compliments.

But do not let us fall into despair, said the other. I once read a letter from Walter Sickert in which he said, 'I have always been a literary painter, thank goodness, like all the decent painters.' Perhaps then he would not altogether despise us. When we talk of his biographies, his novels, and his poems we may not be so foolish as it seems. Among the many kinds of artists, it may be that there are some who are hybrid. Some, that is to say, bore deeper and deeper into the stuff of their own art; others are always making raids into the lands of others. Sickert it may be is among the hybrids, the raiders. His name itself suggests that he is of mixed birth. I have read that he is part German, part English, part Scandinavian perhaps; he was born in Munich, was educated at Reading, and lived in France. What more likely than that his mind is also cosmopolitan; that he sings a good song, writes a fine style, and reads enormously in four or five different languages? All this filters down into his brush. That is why he draws so many different people to look at his pictures. From his photograph you might take him for a highly distinguished

lawyer with a nautical bent; the sort of man who settles a complicated case at the Law Courts, then changes into an old serge
suit, pulls a yachting-cap with a green peak over his eyes and
buffets about the North Sea with a volume of Aeschylus in his
pocket. In the intervals of hauling up and down the mainsail he
wipes the salt from his eyes, whips out a canvas and paints a
divinely lovely picture of Dieppe, Harwich, or the cliffs of Dover.
That is the sort of man I take Walter Sickert to be. You should
call him Richard Sickert, said the other—Richard Sickert, R.A.
But since he is probably the best painter now living in England,
whether he is called Richard or Walter, whether he has all the
letters in the alphabet after his name or none, scarcely matters.
Upon that they were all agreed.

Craftsmanship[1]

THE title of this series is 'Words Fail Me', and this particular talk is called 'Craftsmanship'. We must suppose, therefore, that the talker is meant to discuss the craft of words—the craftsmanship of the writer. But there is something incongruous, unfitting, about the term 'craftsmanship' when applied to words. The English dictionary, to which we always turn in moments of dilemma, confirms us in our doubts. It says that the word 'craft' has two meanings; it means in the first place making useful objects out of solid matter—for example, a pot, a chair, a table. In the second place, the word 'craft' means cajolery, cunning, deceit. Now we know little that is certain about words, but this we do know—words never make anything that is useful; and words are the only things that tell the truth and nothing but the truth. Therefore, to talk of craft in connexion with words is to bring together two incongruous ideas, which if they mate can only give birth to some monster fit for a glass case in a museum. Instantly, therefore, the title of the talk must be changed, and for it substituted another—A Ramble round Words, perhaps. For when you cut off the head of a talk it behaves like a hen that has been decapitated. It runs round in a circle till it drops dead—so people say who have killed hens. And that must be the course, or circle, of this decapitated talk. Let us then take for our starting point the statement that words are not useful. This happily needs little proving, for we are all aware of it. When we travel on the Tube, for example, when we wait on the platform for a train, there, hung up in front of us, on an illuminated signboard, are the words 'Passing Russell Square'. We look at those words; we repeat them; we try to impress that useful fact upon our minds; the next train will pass Russell Square. We say over and over again as we pace. 'Passing Russell Square, passing Russell Square'. And then as we say them, the words shuffle and change, and we find ourselves saying 'Passing away saith the world, passing away . . . The leaves decay and fall, the vapours weep

[1] A broadcast on April 20, 1937

245

their burthen to the ground. Man comes . . .' And then we wake up and find ourselves at King's Cross.

Take another example. Written up opposite us in the railway carriage are the words: 'Do not lean out of the window'. At the first reading the useful meaning, the surface meaning, is conveyed; but soon, as we sit looking at the words, they shuffle, they change; and we begin saying, 'Windows, yes windows—casements opening on the foam of perilous seas in faery lands forlorn.' And before we know what we are doing, we have leant out of the window; we are looking for Ruth in tears amid the alien corn. The penalty for that is twenty pounds or a broken neck.

This proves, if it needs proving, how very little natural gift words have for being useful. If we insist on forcing them against their nature to be useful, we see to our cost how they mislead us, how they fool us, how they land us a crack on the head. We have been so often fooled in this way by words, they have so often proved that they hate being useful, that it is their nature not to express one simple statement but a thousand possibilities—they have done this so often that at last, happily, we are beginning to face the fact. We are beginning to invent another language—a language perfectly and beautifully adapted to express useful statements, a language of signs. There is one great living master of this language to whom we are all indebted, that anonymous writer—whether man, woman or disembodied spirit nobody knows—who describes hotels in the Michelin Guide. He wants to tell us that one hotel is moderate, another good, and a third the best in the place. How does he do it? Not with words; words would at once bring into being shrubberies and billiard tables, men and women, the moon rising and the long splash of the summer sea—all good things, but all here beside the point. He sticks to signs; one gable; two gables; three gables. That is all he says and all he needs to say. Baedeker carries the sign language still further into the sublime realms of art. When he wishes to say that a picture is good, he uses one star; if very good, two stars; when, in his opinion, it is a work of transcendent genius, three black stars shine on the page, and that is all. So with a handful of stars and daggers the whole of art criticism, the whole of literary criticism could be reduced to the size of a sixpenny bit—there are moments when one could wish it. But this suggests that in time to

246

come writers will have two languages at their service; one for fact, one for fiction. When the biographer has to convey a useful and necessary fact, as, for example, that Oliver Smith went to college and took a third in the year 1892, he will say so with a hollow O on top of the figure five. When the novelist is forced to inform us that John rang the bell; after a pause the door was opened by a parlourmaid who said, 'Mrs. Jones is not at home,' he will to our great gain and his own comfort convey that repulsive statement not in words, but in signs—say, a capital H on top of the figure three. Thus we may look forward to the day when our biographies and novels will be slim and muscular; and a railway company that says: 'Do not lean out of the window' in words will be fined a penalty not exceeding five pounds for the improper use of language.

Words, then, are not useful. Let us now inquire into their other quality, their positive quality, that is, their power to tell the truth. According once more to the dictionary there are at least three kinds of truth: God's or gospel truth; literary truth; and home truth (generally unflattering). But to consider each separately would take too long. Let us then simplify and assert that since the only test of truth is length of life, and since words survive the chops and changes of time longer than any other substance, therefore they are the truest. Buildings fall; even the earth perishes. What was yesterday a cornfield is today a bungalow. But words, if properly used, seem able to live for ever. What, then, we may ask next, is the proper use of words? Not, so we have said, to make a useful statement; for a useful statement is a statement that can mean only one thing. And it is the nature of words to mean many things. Take the simple sentence 'Passing Russell Square'. That proved useless because besides the surface meaning it contained so many sunken meanings. The word 'passing' suggested the transiency of things, the passing of time and the changes of human life. Then the word 'Russell' suggested the rustling of leaves and the skirt on a polished floor; also the ducal house of Bedford and half the history of England. Finally the word 'Square' brings in the sight, the shape of an actual square combined with some visual suggestion of the stark angularity of stucco. Thus one sentence of the simplest kind rouses the imagination, the memory, the eye and the ear—all combine in reading it.

But they combine—they combine unconsciously together. The moment we single out and emphasize the suggestions as we have done here they become unreal; and we, too, become unreal—specialists, word mongers, phrase finders, not readers. In reading we have to allow the sunken meanings to remain sunken, suggested, not stated; lapsing and flowing into each other like reeds on the bed of a river. But the words in that sentence—Passing Russell Square—are of course very rudimentary words. They show no trace of the strange, of the diabolical power which words possess when they are not tapped out by a typewriter but come fresh from a human brain—the power that is to suggest the writer; his character, his appearance, his wife, his family, his house—even the cat on the hearthrug. Why words do this, how they do it, how to prevent them from doing it nobody knows. They do it without the writer's will; often against his will. No writer presumably wishes to impose his own miserable character, his own private secrets and vices upon the reader. But has any writer, who is not a typewriter, succeeded in being wholly impersonal? Always, inevitably, we know them as well as their books. Such is the suggestive power of words that they will often make a bad book into a very lovable human being, and a good book into a man whom we can hardly tolerate in the room. Even words that are hundreds of years old have this power; when they are new they have it so strongly that they deafen us to the writer's meaning—it is them we see, them we hear. That is one reason why our judgments of living writers are so wildly erratic. Only after the writer is dead do his words to some extent become disinfected, purified of the accidents of the living body.

Now, this power of suggestion is one of the most mysterious properties of words. Everyone who has ever written a sentence must be conscious or half-conscious of it. Words, English words, are full of echoes, of memories, of associations—naturally. They have been out and about, on people's lips, in their houses, in the streets, in the fields, for so many centuries. And that is one of the chief difficulties in writing them to-day—that they are so stored with meanings, with memories, that they have contracted so many famous marriages. The splendid word 'incarnadine', for example—who can use it without remembering also 'multitudinous seas'? In the old days, of course, when English was a new

language, writers could invent new words and use them. Nowadays it is easy enough to invent new words—they spring to the
lips whenever we see a new sight or feel a new sensation—but we
cannot use them because the language is old. You cannot use a
brand new word in an old language because of the very obvious
yet mysterious fact that a word is not a single and separate entity,
but part of other words. It is not a word indeed until it is part of
a sentence. Words belong to each other, although, of course, only
a great writer knows that the word 'incarnadine' belongs to
'multitudinous seas'. To combine new words with old words is
fatal to the constitution of the sentence. In order to use new
words properly you would have to invent a new language; and
that, though no doubt we shall come to it, is not at the moment
our business. Our business is to see what we can do with the
English language as it is. How can we combine the old words in
new orders so that they survive, so that they create beauty, so
that they tell the truth? That is the question.

And the person who could answer that question would deserve
whatever crown of glory the world has to offer. Think what it
would mean if you could teach, if you could learn, the art of
writing. Why, every book, every newspaper would tell the truth,
would create beauty. But there is, it would appear, some obstacle
in the way, some hindrance to the teaching of words. For though
at this moment at least a hundred professors are lecturing upon
the literature of the past, at least a thousand critics are reviewing
the literature of the present, and hundreds upon hundreds of
young men and women are passing examinations in English
literature with the utmost credit, still—do we write better, do
we read better than we read and wrote four hundred years ago
when we were unlectured, uncriticized, untaught? Is our
Georgian literature a patch on the Elizabethan? Where then are
we to lay the blame? Not on our professors; not on our reviewers;
not on our writers; but on words. It is words that are to blame.
They are the wildest, freest, most irresponsible, most unteachable
of all things. Of course, you can catch them and sort them and
place them in alphabetical order in dictionaries. But words do
not live in dictionaries; they live in the mind. If you want proof
of this, consider how often in moments of emotion when we most
need words we find none. Yet there is the dictionary; there at

our disposal are some half a million words all in alphabetical order. But can we use them? No, because words do not live in dictionaries; they live in the mind. Look again at the dictionary. There beyond a doubt lie plays more splendid than *Antony and Cleopatra*; poems more lovely than the *Ode to a Nightingale*; novels beside which *Pride and Prejudice* or *David Copperfield* are the crude bunglings of amateurs. It is only a question of finding the right words and putting them in the right order. But we cannot do it because they do not live in dictionaries; they live in the mind. And how do they live in the mind? Variously and strangely, much as human beings live, by ranging hither and thither, by falling in love, and mating together. It is true that they are much less bound by ceremony and convention than we are. Royal words mate with commoners. English words marry French words, German words, Indian words, Negro words, if they have a fancy. Indeed, the less we inquire into the past of our dear Mother English the better it will be for that lady's reputation. For she has gone a-roving, a-roving fair maid.

Thus to lay down any laws for such irreclaimable vagabonds is worse than useless. A few trifling rules of grammar and spelling are all the constraint we can put on them. All we can say about them, as we peer at them over the edge of that deep, dark and fitfully illuminated cavern in which they live—the mind—all we can say about them is that they seem to like people to think and to feel before they use them, but to think and to feel not about them, but about something different. They are highly sensitive, easily made self-conscious. They do not like to have their purity or their impurity discussed. If you start a Society for Pure English, they will show their resentment by starting another for impure English—hence the unnatural violence of much modern speech; it is a protest against the puritans. They are highly democratic, too; they believe that one word is as good as another; uneducated words are as good as educated words, uncultivated words as cultivated words, there are no ranks or titles in their society. Nor do they like being lifted out on the point of a pen and examined separately. They hang together, in sentences, in paragraphs, sometimes for whole pages at a time. They hate being useful; they hate making money; they hate being lectured about in public. In short, they hate anything that stamps them with one meaning or confines them to one attitude, for it is their nature to change.

Perhaps that is their most striking peculiarity—their need of change. It is because the truth they try to catch is many-sided, and they convey it by being themselves many-sided, flashing this way, then that. Thus they mean one thing to one person, another thing to another person; they are unintelligible to one generation, plain as a pikestaff to the next. And it is because of this complexity that they survive. Perhaps then one reason why we have no great poet, novelist, or critic writing today is that we refuse words their liberty. We pin them down to one meaning, their useful meaning, the meaning which makes us catch the train, the meaning which makes us pass the examination. And when words are pinned down they fold their wings and die. Finally, and most emphatically, words, like ourselves, in order to live at their ease, need privacy. Undoubtedly they like us to think, and they like us to feel, before we use them; but they also like us to pause; to become unconscious. Our unconsciousness is their privacy; our darkness is their light . . . That pause was made, that veil of darkness was dropped, to tempt words to come together in one of those swift marriages which are perfect images and create everlasting beauty. But no—nothing of that sort is going to happen tonight. The little wretches are out of temper; disobliging; disobedient; dumb. What is it that they are muttering? 'Time's up! Silence!'

An Essay in Criticism[1]

HUMAN credulity is indeed wonderful. There may be good reasons for believing in a King or a Judge or a Lord Mayor. When we see them go sweeping by in their robes and their wigs, with their heralds and their outriders, our knees begin to shake and our looks to falter. But what reason there is for believing in critics it is impossible to say. They have neither wigs nor outriders. They differ in no way from other people if one sees them in the flesh. Yet these insignificant fellow creatures have only to shut themselves up in a room, dip a pen in the ink, and call themselves 'we', for the rest of us to believe that they are somehow exalted, inspired, infallible. Wigs grow on their heads. Robes cover their limbs. No greater miracle was ever performed by the power of human credulity. And, like most miracles, this one, too, has had a weakening effect upon the mind of the believer. He begins to think that critics, because they call themselves so, must be right. He begins to suppose that something actually happens to a book when it has been praised or denounced in print. He begins to doubt and conceal his own sensitive, hesitating apprehensions when they conflict with the critics' decrees.

And yet, barring the learned (and learning is chiefly useful in judging the work of the dead), the critic is rather more fallible than the rest of us. He has to give us his opinion of a book that has been published two days, perhaps, with the shell still sticking to its head. He has to get outside that cloud of fertile, but unrealized, sensation which hangs about a reader, to solidify it, to sum it up. The chances are that he does this before the time is ripe; he does it too rapidly and too definitely. He says that it is a great book or a bad book. Yet, as he knows, when he is content to read only, it is neither. He is driven by force of circumstances and some human vanity to hide those hesitations which beset him as he reads, to smooth out all traces of that crab-like and crooked path by which he has reached what he chooses to call 'a conclusion'. So the crude trumpet blasts of critical opinion blow

[1] *New York Herald Tribune*, October 9, 1927

loud and shrill, and we, humble readers that we are, bow our submissive heads.

But let us see whether we can do away with these pretences for a season and pull down the imposing curtain which hides the critical process until it is complete. Let us give the mind a new book, as one drops a lump of fish into a cage of fringed and eager sea anemones, and watch it pausing, pondering, considering its attack. Let us see what prejudices affect it; what influences tell upon it. And if the conclusion becomes in the process a little less conclusive, it may, for that very reason, approach nearer to the truth. The first thing that the mind desires is some foothold of fact upon which it can lodge before it takes flight upon its speculative career. Vague rumours attach themselves to people's names. Of Mr. Hemingway, we know that he is an American living in France, an 'advanced' writer, we suspect, connected with what is called a movement, though which of the many we own that we do not know. It will be well to make a little more certain of these matters by reading first Mr. Hemingway's earlier book, *The Sun Also Rises*, and it soon becomes clear from this that, if Mr. Hemingway is 'advanced', it is not in the way that is to us most interesting. A prejudice of which the reader would do well to take account is here exposed; the critic is a modernist. Yes, the excuse would be because the moderns make us aware of what we feel subconsciously; they are truer to our own experience; they even anticipate it, and this gives us a particular excitement. But nothing new is revealed about any of the characters in *The Sun Also Rises*. They come before us shaped, proportioned, weighed, exactly as the characters of Maupassant are shaped and proportioned. They are seen from the old angle; the old reticences, the old relations between author and character are observed.

But the critic has the grace to reflect that this demand for new aspects and new perspectives may well be overdone. It may become whimsical. It may become foolish. For why should not art be traditional as well as original? Are we not attaching too much importance to an excitement which, though agreeable, may not be valuable in itself, so that we are led to make the fatal mistake of overriding the writer's gift?

At any rate, Mr. Hemingway is not modern in the sense given; and it would appear from his first novel that this rumour of modernity must have sprung from his subject matter and from his treatment of it rather than from any fundamental novelty in his conception of the art of fiction. It is a bare, abrupt, outspoken book. Life as people live it in Paris in 1927 or even in 1928 is described as we of this age do describe life (it is here that we steal a march upon the Victorians) openly, frankly, without prudery, but also without surprise. The immoralities and moralities of Paris are described as we are apt to hear them spoken of in private life. Such candour is modern and it is admirable. Then, for qualities grow together in art as in life, we find attached to this admirable frankness an equal bareness of style. Nobody speaks for more than a line or two. Half a line is mostly sufficient. If a hill or a town is described (and there is always some reason for its description) there it is, exactly and literally built up of little facts, literal enough, but chosen, as the final sharpness of the outline proves, with the utmost care. Therefore, a few words like these: 'The grain was just beginning to ripen and the fields were full of poppies. The pasture land was green and there were fine trees, and sometimes big rivers and chateaux off in the trees' —which have a curious force. Each word pulls its weight in the sentence. And the prevailing atmosphere is fine and sharp, like that of winter days when the boughs are bare against the sky. (But if we had to choose one sentence with which to describe what Mr. Hemingway attempts and sometimes achieves, we should quote a passage from a description of a bullfight: 'Romero never made any contortions, always it was straight and pure and natural in line. The others twisted themselves like corkscrews, their elbows raised and leaned against the flanks of the bull after his horns had passed, to give a faked look of danger. Afterwards, all that was faked turned bad and gave an unpleasant feeling. Romero's bullfighting gave real emotion, because he kept the absolute purity of line in his movements and always quietly and calmly let the horns pass him close each time.') Mr. Hemingway's writing, one might paraphrase, gives us now and then a real emotion, because he keeps absolute purity of line in his movements and lets the horns (which are truth, fact, reality) pass him close each time. But there is something faked, too, which turns bad and gives an unpleasant feeling—that also we must face in course of time.

And here, indeed, we may conveniently pause and sum up what point we have reached in our critical progress. Mr. Hemingway is not an advanced writer in the sense that he is looking at life from a new angle. What he sees is a tolerably familiar sight. Common objects like beer bottles and journalists figure largely in the foreground. But he is a skilled and conscientious writer. He has an aim and makes for it without fear or circumlocution. We have, therefore, to take his measure against somebody of substance, and not merely line him, for form's sake, beside the indistinct bulk of some ephemeral shape largely stuffed with straw. Reluctantly we reach this decision, for this process of measurement is one of the most difficult of a critic's tasks. He has to decide which are the most salient points of the book he has just read; to distinguish accurately to what kind they belong, and then, holding them against whatever model is chosen for comparison, to bring out their deficiency or their adequacy.

Recalling *The Sun Also Rises*, certain scenes rise in memory: the bullfight, the character of the Englishman, Harris; here a little landscape which seems to grow behind the people naturally; here a long, lean phrase which goes curling round a situation like the lash of a whip. Now and again this phrase evokes a character brilliantly, more often a scene. Of character, there is little that remains firmly and solidly elucidated. Something indeed seems wrong with the people. If we place them (the comparison is bad) against Tchekov's people, they are flat as cardboard. If we place them (the comparison is better) against Maupassant's people they are crude as a photograph. If we place them (the comparison may be illegitimate) against real people, the people we liken them to are of an unreal type. They are people one may have seen showing off at some café; talking a rapid, high-pitched slang, because slang is the speech of the herd, seemingly much at their ease, and yet if we look at them a little from the shadow not at their ease at all, and, indeed, terribly afraid of being themselves, or they would say things simply in their natural voices. So it would seem that the thing that is faked is character; Mr. Hemingway leans against the flanks of that particular bull after the horns have passed.

After this preliminary study of Mr. Hemingway's first book, we come to the new book, *Men Without Women*, possessed of certain views or prejudices. His talent plainly may develop along different lines. It may broaden and fill out; it may take a little more time and go into things—human beings in particular—rather more deeply. And even if this meant the sacrifice of some energy and point, the exchange would be to our private liking. On the other hand, his is a talent which may contract and harden still further, it may come to depend more and more upon the emphatic moment; make more and more use of dialogue, and cast narrative and description overboard as an encumbrance.

The fact that *Men Without Women* consists of short stories, makes it probable that Mr. Hemingway has taken the second line. But, before we explore the new book, a word should be said which is generally left unsaid, about the implications of the title. As the publisher puts it . . . 'the softening feminine influence is absent—either through training, discipline, death, or situation'. Whether we are to understand by this that women are incapable of training, discipline, death, or situation, we do not know. But it is undoubtedly true, if we are going to persevere in our attempt to reveal the processes of the critic's mind, that any emphasis laid upon sex is dangerous. Tell a man that this is a woman's book, or a woman that this is a man's, and you have brought into play sympathies and antipathies which have nothing to do with art. The greatest writers lay no stress upon sex one way or the other. The critic is not reminded as he reads them that he belongs to the masculine or the feminine gender. But in our time, thanks to our sexual perturbations, sex consciousness is strong, and shows itself in literature by an exaggeration, a protest of sexual characteristics which in either case is disagreeable. Thus Mr. Lawrence, Mr. Douglas, and Mr. Joyce partly spoil their books for women readers by their display of self-conscious virility; and Mr. Hemingway, but much less violently, follows suit. All we can do, whether we are men or women, is to admit the influence, look the fact in the face, and so hope to stare it out of countenance.

To proceed then—*Men Without Women* consists of short stories in the French rather than in the Russian manner. The great French masters, Mérimée and Maupassant, made their stories as self-conscious and compact as possible. There is never a thread left hanging; indeed, so contracted are they that when the last sentence of the last page flares up, as it so often does, we see by its light the whole circumference and significance of the story revealed. The Tchekov method is, of course, the very opposite of this. Everything is cloudy and vague, loosely trailing rather than tightly furled. The stories move slowly out of sight like clouds in the summer air, leaving a wake of meaning in our minds which gradually fades away. Of the two methods, who shall say which is the better? At any rate, Mr. Hemingway, enlisting under the French masters, carries out their teaching up to a point with considerable success.

There are in *Men Without Women* many stories which, if life were longer, one would wish to read again. Most of them indeed are so competent, so efficient, and so bare of superfluity that one wonders why they do not make a deeper dent in the mind than they do. Take the pathetic story of the Major whose wife died—'In Another Country'; or the sardonic story of a conversation in a railway carriage—'A Canary for One'; or stories like 'The Undefeated' and 'Fifty Grand' which are full of the sordidness and heroism of bull-fighting and boxing—all of these are good trenchant stories, quick, terse, and strong. If one had not summoned the ghosts of Tchekov, Mérimée, and Maupassant, no doubt one would be enthusiastic. As it is, one looks about for something, fails to find something, and so is brought again to the old familiar business of ringing impressions on the counter, and asking what is wrong?

For some reason the book of short stories does not seem to us to go as deep or to promise as much as the novel. Perhaps it is the excessive use of dialogue, for Mr. Hemingway's use of it is surely excessive. A writer will always be chary of dialogue because dialogue puts the most violent pressure upon the reader's attention. He has to hear, to see, to supply the right tone, and to fill in the background from what the characters say without any help from the author. Therefore, when fictitious people are allowed to speak it must be because they have something so important to say that it stimulates the reader to do rather more than his share of the work of creation. But, although Mr. Hemingway keeps us under the fire of dialogue constantly, his people, half the time, are saying what the author could say much more economically for them. At last we are inclined to cry out with the little girl in 'Hills Like White Elephants': 'Would you please please please please please please please stop talking?'

And probably it is this superfluity of dialogue which leads to that other fault which is always lying in wait for the writer of short stories: the lack of proportion. A paragraph in excess will make these little craft lopsided and will bring about that blurred effect which, when one is out for clarity and point, so baffles the reader. And both these faults, the tendency to flood the page with unnecessary dialogue and the lack of sharp, unmistakable points by which we can take hold of the story, come from the more fundamental fact that, though Mr. Hemingway is brilliantly and enormously skilful, he lets his dexterity, like the bullfighter's cloak, get between him and the fact. For in truth story-writing has much in common with bullfighting. One may twist one's self like a corkscrew and go through every sort of contortion so that the public thinks one is running every risk and displaying superb gallantry. But the true writer stands close up to the bull and lets the horns—call them life, truth, reality, whatever you like—pass him close each time.

Mr. Hemingway, then, is courageous; he is candid; he is highly skilled; he plants words precisely where he wishes; he has moments of bare and nervous beauty; he is modern in manner but not in vision; he is self-consciously virile; his talent has contracted rather than expanded; compared with his novel his stories are a little dry and sterile. So we sum him up. So we reveal some of the prejudices, the instincts and the fallacies out of which what it pleases us to call criticism is made.

Modern Letters[1]

AMONG the commonplaces, this one takes a prominent place
—that the art of letter writing is dead; that it flourished in
the days of the frank, dwindled under the penny post, and was
dealt its death blow by the telephone—now it lies feebly expiring.
Once in a way it might be well to look into this truism, to
examine the day's post, to compare the flimsy sheets of today,
rapidly written over in such various hands, with those statelier
compositions that were a week, or perhaps a month, on the road,
and were, therefore, written in much better hands upon paper
that still lies crisp between thumb and finger.

There, of course, lie some of the chief distinctions between the
old letters and the new, more care, more time went to their
composition. But need we take it for granted that care and time
are wholly to the good? A letter then was written to be read and
not by one person only. It was a composition that did its best to
deserve the expense it cost. The arrival of the post was an occasion. The sheets were not for the waste-paper basket in five
minutes, but for handing round, and reading aloud and then for
deposit in some family casket as a record. These undoubtedly
were inducements to careful composition, to the finishing of
sentences, the artful disposition of trifles, the polish of phrases,
the elaboration of arguments and the arts of the writing master.
But whether Sir William Temple, who wished to know if Dorothy
was well and happy and to be assured that she loved him, enjoyed her letters as much as we enjoy them is perhaps doubtful.
Sir Horace Mann or West or Gray did not, one guesses, break
the seals of Walpole's thick packets in a hurry. One can imagine
that they waited for a good fire, and a bottle of wine, and a group
of friends and then read the witty and delightful pages aloud, in
perfect confidence that nothing was going to be said that was too
private for another ear—indeed, the very opposite was the case—
such wit, such polish, such a budget of news was too good for a
single person and demanded to be shared with others. Often,
more often than not, the great letter-writers were suppressed

[1] Written in 1930

259

novelists, frustrated essayists born before their time. In our day, Dorothy Osborne would have been an admirable biographer, and Walpole one of our most distinguished and prolific journalists —whether to the profit or loss of the world it is impossible to say. Indisputably they practised to perfection a peculiar art, born of special circumstances, but to go on, as we in our rash condemnatory mood so often do, to say that their art was the art of letter writing and that we have lost it, and that our art, because it differs from theirs, is not art at all, seems an unnecessary act of pessimism and self-depreciation.

Here, of course, there should be laid down once and for all the principles of letter-writing. But since Aristotle never got so far and since the art has always been an anonymous and hand-to-mouth practice, whose chief adepts would have been scandalized had they been convicted of design or intention, it will be more convenient to leave those principles obscure. Let us turn, therefore, without a yard measure to examine the morning's post, and those posts of other mornings that have been thrust pell-mell into old drawers more from laziness than from any desire to preserve a record for posterity. These pages came by post, were addressed by one person to one person, fell into the letterbox, and were laid on the breakfast table—that is all. In the first place, they are very badly written. Whether the invention of the fountain pen is to blame, certainly a well-formed handwriting is now the rarest of happy discoveries. Moreover, no common style of writing prevails. Here it slants, here it bends back; it is rapid, and running in almost every case. The paper too is of all sizes and coloured blue, green, yellow; much of it is shoddy enough, and coated with some smooth glaze which will no doubt turn traitor before fifty years are passed. This haphazard harum scarum individuality is reflected in the style. There is none at first showing—each writer makes his own. Urgent need is the begetter of most of these pages. The writers have forgotten, or want to know, or wish to be sure, or must remind one. A sentence about the weather may be thrown in as make weight; an initial is scrawled, the stamp stuck on upside down, and so off it goes. The whole affair is purely utilitarian.

Besides these, however, though not so common, are letters written mostly from abroad with the old wish to get into touch

with a friend, to give news, to communicate in short what would
be said in a private conversation. A friend marooned in a Spanish
inn, one travelling in Italy, one who has taken up his residence
in India, these are now the nearest representatives of Cowper at
Olney writing to Lady Hesketh at Bath. But with what a difference! In the first place nobody would be so rash as to read a
modern letter, even from Rangoon, in mixed company. One does
not know what is coming next. Modern letter-writers are highly
indiscreet. Almost certainly there is some phrase that will cause
pain. Very careful editing is needed before a letter can be read
aloud to friends. And then our conventions allow of so much
freedom of speech—language is so colloquial, slap-dash, and
unpruned that the presence of someone of another generation
would be a grave deterrent. What is sincerity might be mistaken
for coarseness. Further, the modern letter-writer is so casual, and
so careless of the forms and ceremonies of literature, that the
pages do not stand the ordeal of reading aloud well. But then,
on the other hand, the privacy, the intimacy of these letters make
them far more immediately interesting and exciting than the
old letters. There is no news for the whole world in them, because
newspapers have made that unneeded. Only one person is written
to, and the writer had some reason for wishing to write to him
or her in particular. Its meaning is private, its news intimate.
For these reasons it is a rash incriminating document and the
proper place for it is not between the pages of the family Bible
but in a drawer with a key.

There then, pell-mell, with all their imperfections thick upon
them, they are stuffed—today's post on top of yesterday's post
and so on, undocketed, unsorted, as they came. And as the years
pass so they accumulate. The drawers are almost bursting with
letters; some of the writers are dead, others have vanished; others
write no more. What is to be done with them? Let us look quickly
through them and see whether the time has not come to burn
them. But once begin dipping and diving, reading this and reading that, and what to do with them is completely forgotten. Page
after page is turned. Here are invitations to parties ten years old.
Here are postcards demanding the return of lost umbrellas. Here
are childish sheets thanking for boxes of water-colour paints.
Here are calculations about the cost of building a house. Here are

long, wild, profuse letters, all about somebody who did not want,
it seems, to marry somebody else. The effect is indescribable.
One could swear one heard certain voices, smelt certain flowers,
was in Italy, was in Spain, was horribly bored, terribly unhappy,
tremendously excited all over again. If the art of letter-writing
consists in exciting the emotions, in bringing back the past, in
reviving a day, a moment, nay a very second, of past time, then
these obscure correspondents, with their hasty haphazard ways,
their gibes and flings, their irreverence and mockery, their careful
totting up of days and dates, their general absorption in the
moment and entire carelessness what posterity will think of them,
beat Cowper, Walpole, and Edward Fitzgerald hollow. Yes, but
what to do with them? The question remains, for as one reads it
becomes perfectly plain that the art of letter writing has now
reached a stage, thanks to the penny post and telephone, where
it is not dead—that is the last word to apply to it—but so much
alive as to be quite unprintable. The best letters of our time are
precisely those that can never be published.

All about Books[1]

YOUR last letter ends with the following sentence: 'The cold profile of Mont Blanc; falling snow; peasants and pine trees; a string of stout fellows roped together with alpenstocks—such is the prospect from my window; so for pity's sake draw your chair to the fire, take your pen in your hand and write me a long, long letter all about books.' But you must realize that a long, long letter is apt to be exaggerated, inaccurate, and full of those irreticences and hyperboles which the voice of the speaker corrects in talk. A letter is not a review; it is not a considered judgment, but, on condition that you do not believe a word I say, I will scribble for an hour or two whatever comes into my head about books.

That it has been a very bad season goes without saying. The proof of it is that old Mr. Baddeley had read *Guy ·Mannering* for the fifty-eighth time. Never was Jane Austen in greater demand. Trollope, Dickens, Carlyle, and Macaulay are all providing that solace, that security, that sense that the human heart does not change which our miserable age requires and our living authors so woefully fail to provide. When, therefore, the rumour spread that the diary of an old clergyman called Cole, who had gone to Paris in the autumn of 1765, was about to be published, and that Miss Waddell had put her brilliance and her erudition at our service, a purr of content and anticipation rose from half the armchairs of England. This Cole, moreover, was not anybody's Cole; he was Horace Walpole's Cole; nor does it need any pedantic familiarity with history to be aware that the autumn of 1765 was for one old blind woman in Paris the most excruciating, the most humiliating, the most ecstatic of her life. At last Horace Walpole had come—after what snubs, what humiliations, what bitter disappointments! At last Madame du Deffand would —not indeed see him in the flesh, but feel him with the spirit. He would be in the same room with her; he would talk his broken French; she would feel come over her that strange delight, that

[1] Written in January 1931

abasement, that ecstasy—call it not love, for love he would not have it called—which the presence of the elderly and elegant Horace never failed to inspire in a heart that had long outlived any sensation but boredom, despair, and disgust. It was in that very autumn that Cole chose to visit Paris. Cole, it seemed probable since Walpole liked him, would have eyes in his head; certainly he had a diary in his portmanteau. What revelations might one not expect? What confidences from one Englishman to another? And Horace Walpole was willing. Every day he sent his servant to ask Cole to dinner. And every day—it is incredible what the dead will do, but it is true—Cole preferred to go sight-seeing. He went to Notre Dame; he went to the Sorbonne; he went to the Convent of that Virgin, to the Cathedral of this Saint. When he came home he sat down to digest and methodize what he had seen. He was too tired to dine with Mr. Walpole. So instead of revelations we have information. 'On the right hand of the High Altar as one enters. . . . The dome of this church is very beautiful. . . . Over the door is a curious alto-relievo representing the Last Supper. . . .' That is what he writes about, and, of course, about the habits of the natives. The habits of the natives are disgusting; the women hawk on the floor; the forks are dirty; the trees are poor, the Pont Neuf is not a patch on London Bridge; the cows are skinny; morals are licentious; polish is good; cabbages cost so much; bread is made of coarse flour; Mr. Drumgold could not with patience mention the character of John James Rousseau; the Coles are distantly related to the Herberts; and a French turkey is about the size of an English hen. How natural it all is! How admirable Mr. Cole would be at home in his own parish! How gladly we will read sixteen volumes about life in Bletchley if Miss Waddell will print them! But the present volume is nothing short of torture. 'Cole,' one is inclined to cry, 'if you don't give up sightseeing to-day, if you don't dine with Mr. Walpole, if you don't report every word he says, leaving Drumgold out of it altogether, if you don't turn the talk somehow upon Madame du Deffand, if you don't some-how tell us more about one of the most curious affairs of the heart that was ever transacted, or failing that, rake up a few odds and ends of interest about that amazing society that was playing spillikins on the verge of revolution, we will——' But what can we do? The dead have no sense whatever of what is due to posterity. Mr. Cole imperturbably pulls on his boots and proceeds to visit the Sorbonne.

Must one then read *Guy Mannering*, or take Jane Austen from the bookshelf? No, the advantage of belonging to a good library is that it is only upon very exceptional occasions that one need have recourse to the classics. New books, in fresh jackets, are delivered daily, and good books, too—*Things I Remember*, by the Grand Duchess Marie of Russia, for instance, a very terrible book; *The Diary of a Somersetshire Parson*—a very absorbing book; *By Guess and by God*—a very exciting yet infinitely childish book; and *Scrutinies*, a collection of critical essays by various writers. But what kind of book is *Scrutinies*? That, indeed, I cannot tell you at the moment for the good reason that I have not read it; but you can guess from the title and a glance at the table of contents that it consists of articles by the tolerably young— Messrs. Alec Brown, B. Higgins, Mary Butts, Jack Lindsay, P. Quennell, Sherard Vines, C. Saltmarshe, and so on, upon the tolerably old—Messrs. Eliot, Huxley, Joyce, Lawrence, Sitwell, Strachey, and so on. And if I hesitate to read beyond the title page at present it is for the very sound and simple reason that it is so much pleasanter to look upon the young than upon the old, the young who are fresh and pliable, who have not stood out in the storm and stiffened into attitudes and hardened into wrinkles. Beauty is theirs now, as soon the future will be theirs also. Let us, therefore, leave the figures of the elders where they stand and turn our bull's eye upon the advancing and victorious hordes of youth.

And what is our first impression as we look? A very strange one. How orderly they come! One could swear that they are all arrayed in troops, and all march in step, and all halt, charge and otherwise behave themselves under the command of officers mounted upon chargers. As far as one can see—a bull's eye, it must be admitted, is not a very steady or comprehensive weapon —there is not a single straggler or deserter among them; there is no dancing or disorder; no wild voice cries alone; no man or woman breaks the ranks and leaves the troop and takes to the wilderness stirring desire and unrest among the hearts of his companions. All is orderly, all is preconcerted. If division there is, even that is regular. Camp is opposed to camp; the hostile parties separate, form, meet, fight, leave each other for dead upon the ground; rise, form and fight again. Classic is opposed to romantic; naturalist to metaphysic. Never was there such a sight since the world began. Never—as they come nearer this too becomes certain—were the young so well-equipped as at present. No more respectable army has ever issued from the portals of the two great Universities—none more courageous, more instructed, more outspoken, more intolerant of humbug in all its forms, better fitted to deal pretence its death and falsity its finish —and yet (for all these flowers, of course, conceal a viper) there is a fatal defect; they do not lead, they follow. Where is the adventurous, the intolerant, the immensely foolish young man or woman who dares to be himself? He or she must, of course, be there. He or she will in time to come make himself known. But at present, since he always keeps the ranks, since if he fights he is careful, like Sir Walter Blunt in *Henry the Fourth*, to wear the armour of his king, there is no knowing him at present from the seven hundred and fifty-five others who are similarly disguised.

If this is true, if there is now a uniformity and a drill and a discretion unknown before, what do you think can be the reason? In one word, and I have room for one only, and that is murmured in your private ear—education. Some years since, for reasons unknown, but presumably of value, it must have occurred to someone that the arts of reading and of writing can be taught. Degrees were given at the universities to those who showed proficiency in their native tongue. And the teachers of the living language were not old and hoary; as fitted their subject they were young and supple. Persuasion sat on their tongues, and the taught, instead of mocking, loved their teachers. And the teachers took the manuscripts of the young and drew circles of blue chalk round this adjective and circles of red chalk round that adverb. They added in purple ink what Pope would have thought and what Wordsworth would have said. And the young, since they loved their teachers, believed them. Hence it came about that, instead of knowing that the sun was in the sky and the bird on the branch, the young knew the whole course of English literature from one end to another; how one age follows another; and one influence cancels another; and one style is derived from another; and one phrase is better than another. They took service under their teachers instead of riding into battle alone. All their marriages—and what are the five years between twenty and twenty-five in the life of a writer but years of courtship and wedding, of falling in love with words and learning their nature, how to mate them by one's own decree in sentences of one's own framing?—all their marriages were arranged in public; tutors introduced the couples; lecturers supervised the amours; and examiners finally pronounced whether the fruit of the union was blessed or the reverse. Such methods, of course, produce an erudite and eugenic offspring. But, one asks, turning over the honest, the admirable, the entirely sensible and unsentimental pages, where is love? Meaning by that, where is the sound of the sea and the red of the rose; where is music, imagery, and a voice speaking from the heart?

That this is all great nonsense I am well aware. But what else can you expect in a letter? The time has come to open *Scrutinies* and begin to read—no, the time has come to rake out the cinders and go to bed.

The Cinema[1]

PEOPLE say that the savage no longer exists in us, that we are at the fag-end of civilization, that everything has been said already, and that it is too late to be ambitious. But these philosophers have presumably forgotten the movies. They have never seen the savages of the twentieth century watching the pictures. They have never sat themselves in front of the screen and thought how for all the clothes on their backs and the carpets at their feet, no great distance separates them from those bright-eyed naked men who knocked two bars of iron together and heard in that clangour a foretaste of the music of Mozart.

The bars in this case, of course, are so highly wrought and so covered over with accretions of alien matter that it is extremely difficult to hear anything distinctly. All is hubble-bubble, swarm and chaos. We are peering over the edge of a cauldron in which fragments of all shapes and savours seem to simmer; now and again some vast form heaves itself up and seems about to haul itself out of chaos. Yet at first sight the art of the cinema seems simple, even stupid. There is the king shaking hands with a football team; there is Sir Thomas Lipton's yacht; there is Jack Horner winning the Grand National. The eye licks it all up instantaneously, and the brain, agreeably titillated, settles down to watch things happening without bestirring itself to think. For the ordinary eye, the English unæsthetic eye, is a simple mechanism which takes care that the body does not fall down coal-holes, provides the brain with toys and sweetmeats to keep it quiet, and can be trusted to go on behaving like a competent nursemaid until the brain comes to the conclusion that it is time to wake up. What is its purpose, then, to be roused suddenly in the midst of its agreeable somnolence and asked for help? The eye is in difficulties. The eye wants help. The eye says to the brain, 'Something is happening which I do not in the least understand. You are needed.' Together they look at the king, the boat, the horse, and the brain sees at once that they have taken on a quality which does not belong to the simple photograph of real life.

[1] Written in 1926

They have become not more beautiful in the sense in which pictures are beautiful, but shall we call it (our vocabulary is miserably insufficient) more real, or real with a different reality from that which we perceive in daily life? We behold them as they are when we are not there. We see life as it is when we have no part in it. As we gaze we seem to be removed from the pettiness of actual existence. The horse will not knock us down. The king will not grasp our hands. The wave will not wet our feet. From this point of vantage, as we watch the antics of our kind, we have time to feel pity and amusement, to generalize, to endow one man with the attributes of the race. Watching the boat sail and the wave break, we have time to open our minds wide to beauty and register on top of it the queer sensation—this beauty will continue, and this beauty will flourish whether we behold it or not. Further, all this happened ten years ago, we are told. We are beholding a world which has gone beneath the waves. Brides are emerging from the abbey—they are now mothers; ushers are ardent—they are now silent; mothers are tearful; guests are joyful; this has been won and that has been lost, and it is over and done with. The war sprung its chasm at the feet of all this innocence and ignorance but it was thus that we danced and pirouetted, toiled and desired, thus that the sun shone and the clouds scudded, up to the very end.

But the picture-makers seem dissatisfied with such obvious sources of interest as the passage of time and the suggestiveness of reality. They despise the flight of gulls, ships on the Thames, the Prince of Wales, the Mile End Road, Piccadilly Circus. They want to be improving, altering, making an art of their own—naturally, for so much seems to be within their scope. So many arts seemed to stand by ready to offer their help. For example, there was literature. All the famous novels of the world, with their well-known characters and their famous scenes, only asked, it seemed, to be put on the films. What could be easier and simpler? The cinema fell upon its prey with immense rapacity, and to the moment largely subsists upon the body of its unfortunate victim. But the results are disastrous to both. The alliance is unnatural. Eye and brain are torn asunder ruthlessly as they try vainly to work in couples. The eye says 'Here is Anna Karenina.' A voluptuous lady in black velvet wearing pearls comes before us. But the brain says, 'That is no more Anna Karenina than it is Queen Victoria.' For the brain knows Anna almost entirely by the inside of her mind—her charm, her passion, her despair. All the emphasis is laid by the cinema upon her teeth, her pearls, and her velvet. Then 'Anna falls in love with Vronsky'—that is to say, the lady in black velvet falls into the arms of a gentleman in uniform and they kiss with enormous succulence, great deliberation, and infinite gesticulation, on a sofa in an extremely well-appointed library, while a gardener incidentally mows the lawn. So we lurch and lumber through the most famous novels of the world. So we spell them out in words of one syllable, written, too, in the scrawl of an illiterate schoolboy. A kiss is love. A broken cup is jealousy. A grin is happiness. Death is a hearse. None of these things has the least connexion with the novel that Tolstoy wrote, and it is only when we give up trying to connect the pictures with the book that we guess from some accidental scene—like the gardener mowing the lawn—what the cinema might do if left to its own devices.

But what, then, are its devices? If it ceased to be a parasite, how would it walk erect? At present it is only from hints that one can frame any conjecture. For instance, at a performance of *Dr. Caligari* the other day a shadow shaped like a tadpole suddenly appeared at one corner of the screen. It swelled to an immense size, quivered, bulged, and sank back again into nonentity. For a moment it seemed to embody some monstrous diseased imagination of the lunatic's brain. For a moment it seemed as if thought could be conveyed by shape more effectively than by words. The monstrous quivering tadpole seemed to be fear itself, and not the statement 'I am afraid'. In fact, the shadow was accidental and the effect unintentional. But if a shadow at a certain moment can suggest so much more than the actual gestures and words of men and women in a state of fear, it seems plain that the cinema has within its grasp innumerable symbols for emotions that have so far failed to find expression. Terror has besides its ordinary forms the shape of a tadpole; it burgeons, bulges, quivers, disappears. Anger is not merely rant and rhetoric, red faces and clenched fists. It is perhaps a black line wriggling upon a white sheet. Anna and Vronsky need no longer scowl and grimace. They have at their command—but what? Is there, we ask, some secret language which we feel and see, but never speak, and, if so, could this be made visible to the eye? Is there any characteristic which thought possesses that can be rendered visible without the help of words? It has speed and slowness; dartlike directness and vaporous circumlocution. But it has, also, especially in moments of emotion, the picture-making power, the need to lift its burden to another bearer; to let an image run side by side along with it. The likeness of the thought is for some reason more beautiful, more comprehensible, more available, than the thought itself. As everybody knows, in Shakespeare the most complex ideas form chains of images through which we mount, changing and turning, until we reach the light of day. But obviously the images of a poet are not to be cast in bronze or traced by pencil. They are compact of a thousand suggestions of which the visual is only the most obvious or the uppermost. Even the simplest image 'My luve's like a red, red rose, that's newly-sprung in June' presents us with impressions of moisture and warmth and the glow of crimson and the softness of petals inextricably mixed and strung upon the lift of a rhythm which is itself the voice of the passion and hesitation of the lover. All this, which is accessible to words and to words alone, the cinema must avoid.

Yet if so much of our thinking and feeling is connected with seeing, some residue of visual emotion which is of no use either to painter or to poet may still await the cinema. That such symbols will be quite unlike the real objects which we see before us seems highly probable. Something abstract, something which moves with controlled and conscious art, something which calls for the very slightest help from words or music to make itself intelligible, yet justly uses them subserviently—of such movements and abstractions the films may in time to come be composed. Then indeed when some new symbol for expressing thought is found, the film-maker has enormous riches at his command. The exactitude of reality and its surprising power of suggestion are to be had for the asking. Annas and Vronskys—there they are in the flesh. If into this reality he could breathe emotion, could animate the perfect form with thought, then his booty could be hauled in hand over hand. Then, as smoke pours from Vesuvius, we should be able to see thought in its wildness, in its beauty, in its oddity, pouring from men with their elbows on a table; from women with their little handbags slipping to the floor. We should see these emotions mingling together and affecting each other.

We should see violent changes of emotion produced by their collision. The most fantastic contrasts could be flashed before us with a speed which the writer can only toil after in vain; the dream architecture of arches and battlements, of cascades falling and fountains rising, which sometimes visits us in sleep or shapes itself in half-darkened rooms, could be realized before our waking eyes. No fantasy could be too far-fetched or insubstantial. The past could be unrolled, distances annihilated, and the gulfs which dislocate novels (when, for instance, Tolstoy has to pass from Levin to Anna and in doing so jars his story and wrenches and arrests our sympathies) could by the sameness of the background, by the repetition of some scene, be smoothed away.

How all this is to be attempted, much less achieved, no one at the moment can tell us. We get intimations only in the chaos of the streets, perhaps, when some momentary assembly of colour, sound, movement, suggests that here is a scene waiting a new art to be transfixed. And sometimes at the cinema in the midst of its immense dexterity and enormous technical proficiency, the curtain parts and we behold, far off, some unknown and unexpected beauty. But it is for a moment only. For a strange thing has happened—while all the other arts were born naked, this, the youngest, has been born fully-clothed. It can say everything before it has anything to say. It is as if the savage tribe, instead of finding two bars of iron to play with, had found scattering the seashore fiddles, flutes, saxophones, trumpets, grand pianos by Erard and Bechstein, and had begun with incredible energy, but without knowing a note of music, to hammer and thump upon them all at the same time.

Personalities

'I MUST have Keats's "Love Letters" out; though I confess there is something in the personality of Keats, some sort of semi-physical aroma wafted from it, which I cannot endure.' Such was the opinion of J. A. Symonds—one highly unfashionable at the present moment, and, apart from that circumstance, sufficiently remarkable in itself. For most people will exclaim that if ever there was a lovable human being, one whom one would wish to live with, walk with, go on foreign travels with, it was Keats. He was rather below middle height; his shoulders were perhaps a little broad for his size; his eyes glowed with inspiration, but at the same time expressed the greatest consideration for the feelings of others. He was vigorous but gentle in all his movements, wearing neat black shoes, trousers strapped under his insteps, and a coat that was a little shabby at the seams. His eyes were of a warm yet searching brown, his hands were broad, and the fingers, unlike those of most artists, square at the tip. So we could go on making it up, page after page, whether accurately or not does not for our present purpose very much matter. For the point we wish to make is that we are ready supplied with a picture of Keats, and have the same liking or disliking for him personally that we have for a friend last seen half an hour ago in the corner of the omnibus that plies between Holborn and Ludgate Hill. Symonds also received an impression of extreme vividness, though of a distasteful kind; and both our impressions, though they affect our feelings for the poetry, are not directly caused by it, though from what they rise it would be hard to say. 'What a curious thing is that undefinable flavour of personality,' Symonds continues, 'suggestion of physical quality, odour of the man in his unconscious and spontaneous self-determination, which attracts or repels so powerfully, and is at the very root of love or dislike.' How much of it, we go on to consider, enters into our feelings for books, and how difficult it is to be certain that a sense of the physical presence of the writer, with all which that implies, is not colouring our judgment of his work. Yet the critics tell us that we should be impersonal when we write, and therefore impersonal when we read. Perhaps that is true, and it may be that the greatest passages in literature have about them something of the impersonality which belongs to our own emotions at their strongest. The great poet and the lover are both representative—in some way anonymous. But these are high matters. My purpose in dwelling upon this old-fashioned view of Keats is to confess similar prejudices, partly as an act of atonement for critical malpractices, and partly in order to see whether, when they are set out, any sense can be made of them.

It seems to me possible that our attitude to Greek literature, so queer in its reverence, servility, boredom, querulousness, and uneasiness, may be due to the fact that we have either no sense or a very weak one of the personality of the Greek dramatists. The scholars may contradict this. To them Aeschylus may be as real as a man in an omnibus—as real as Keats himself; but if that is so they have been singularly unsuccessful in impressing what they feel upon the popular imagination. I shut my eyes and summon Aeschylus before me, and all I see is a venerable old man wrapped in a blanket sitting on a marble plinth in the sun. An eagle soars high in the blue. Suddenly from his beak drops a large stone. It catches Aeschylus on the back of the head, splits his skull open, and that is all. Similarly with Sappho—she leapt from a high rock into the sea. Both anecdotes have something barren and academical about them, something detached and unilluminating. If we transpose them to our own day and imagine Tennyson killed on the steps of St. Paul's by an escaped eagle—but that is too fantastic—let us suppose him run over by a taxi-cab; or George Eliot gathering her skirts about her and leaping from a cliff, the difference between our attitude to Greek and our attitude to English literature is at once apparent. If these catastrophes had happened to our great writers, we should know a multitude of additional facts—how it happened, what they said, wore, and looked like; libraries of comment and psychology would have been spun from them, and it is through that veil that we should have been forced to read *In Memoriam* and *Middlemarch*. It cannot be denied that the Greeks have a pull over us in this as in other respects. The ordinary reader resents the bareness of their literature. There is nothing in the way of anecdote to browse upon, nothing handy and personal to help oneself up by; nothing is left but the literature itself, cut off from us by time and language, unvulgarized by association, pure from contamination, but steep and isolated. That is a happy fate for a literature, if it did not follow that very few people read it and that those who do become a little priest-like—inevitably solitary and pure, reading with more ingenuity but with less humanity than the ordinary person, and thus leaving out something—is it the character, the personality 'which is at the very root of love and dislike'—which we guess to be there, but which, save for glimpses, we can never find for ourselves. We are intolerably exacting. A few patient scholars, shut up in their studies—what can they do for us? Perhaps one must read collectively, learned side by side with the unlearned, for generations, as we have read Shakespeare, to work through to that kind of contact.

But directly Shakespeare is mentioned there comes to mind the popular opinion that he, of all great men, is the least familiar. Indeed very little is known of him biographically, but it is evident that most people have precisely that personal feeling for him which I think they have not for Aeschylus. There is never an essay upon Hamlet which does not make out with some confidence the author's view of what he calls 'Shakespeare the man'. Yet Shakespeare is a very queer case. Undoubtedly one has the certainty of knowing him; but it is as fleeting as it is intense. You think you have fixed him for ever; you look again, and something seems withheld. All your preconceptions are falsified. What was Shakespeare may, after all, have been Hamlet; or yourself; or poetry. These great artists who manage to infuse the whole of themselves into their works, yet contrive to universalize their identity so that, though we feel Shakespeare everywhere about, we cannot catch him at the moment in any particular spot. But it is simpler to take a much smaller example of the same quality. There is Jane Austen, thumbed, scored, annotated, magnified, living almost within the memory of man, and yet as inscrutable in her small way as Shakespeare in his vast one. She flatters and cajoles you with the promise of intimacy and then, at the last moment, there is the same blankness. Are those Jane Austen's eyes or is it a glass, a mirror, a silver spoon held up in the sun? The people whom we admire most as writers, then, have something elusive, enigmatic, impersonal about them. They rise slowly to their heights; and there they shine. They do not win fame directly, nor are they exposed to the alternations of praise and blame which rise from the passions and prejudices of our hearts. In ransacking their drawers we shall find out little about them. All has been distilled into their books. The life is thin, modest, colourless, like blue skimmed milk at the bottom of the jar. It is the imperfect artists who never manage to say the whole thing in their books who wield the power of personality over us.

This would be all very well if we could make it square with the facts, but unfortunately with Keats as an example of the kind of writer whose personality affects us we can do no such thing. We must then go humbly and confess that our likings and dislikings for authors in their books are as varied and as little accountable as our likings for people in the flesh. Some show themselves, others hide themselves, irrespective of their greatness. Here is Jane Austen, a great writer as we all agree, but, for my own part, I would rather not find myself alone in the room with her. A sense of meaning withheld, a smile at something unseen, an atmosphere of perfect control and courtesy mixed with something finely satirical, which, were it not directed against things in general rather than against individuals, would be almost malicious, would, so I feel, make it alarming to find her at home. On the other hand Charlotte Brontë, so easily stirred by timely mention of the Duke of Wellington, so vehement, irrational, and caustic, would be far easier to know, easier, it seems to me, to love. Her very faults make a breach through which one steps into intimacy. It is the fact that one likes people in spite of their faults, and then likes the faults because they are theirs, that makes one distrust criticism, and wake, after attempting it, in horror at dead of night. It will be remembered that Charlotte Brontë made herself ridiculous when she introduced a Baroness and a footman into the pages of *Jane Eyre*. Mrs. Humphry Ward points out the absurdity of the scene; and into what bottomless pit of iniquity do we not drop Mrs. Humphry Ward eternally for that very just observation? Again, no one has written worse English than Mr. Hardy in some of his novels—cumbrous, stilted, ugly, and inexpressive—yes, but at the same time so strangely expressive of something attractive to us in Mr. Hardy himself that we would not change it for the perfection of Sterne at his best. It becomes coloured by its surroundings; it becomes literature. These are the passages that admirers tend to imitate; and when untinged by his character one sees clearly enough how bad they are. But we need not apologize for injustice to writers of this calibre. It is when we find ourselves swayed by passion in judging the work of contemporaries that we must be on our guard. How we, who cannot hold the reader's attention and maunder on through chapter after chapter of colourless disquisition, yet contrive to impress him with such a distaste for our personality that he bristles at the mere mention of our names, I know not. But it is a fact. The legacy of a negligible novel is often an oddly vivid sense of the writer's character, a fancy sketch of his circumstances, a disposition to like or dislike which works its way into the text and possibly falsifies its meaning. Or do we only read with all our faculties when we seize this impression too?

Why?

WHEN the first number of *Lysistrata* appeared, I confess that
I was deeply disappointed. It was so well printed, on such
good paper. It looked established, prosperous. As I turned the
pages it seemed to me that wealth must have descended upon
Somerville, and I was about to answer the request of the editor
for an article with a negative, when I read, greatly to my relief,
that one of the writers was badly dressed, and gathered from
another that the women's colleges still lack power and prestige.
At this I plucked up heart, and a crowd of questions that have
been pressing to be asked rushed to my lips saying: 'Here is our
chance.'

I should explain that like so many people nowadays I am
pestered with questions. I find it impossible to walk down the
street without stopping, it may be in the middle of the road, to
ask: Why? Churches, public houses, parliaments, shops, loudspeakers, motor-cars, the drone of an aeroplane in the clouds,
and men and women all inspire questions. Yet what is the point
of asking questions of oneself? They should be asked openly in
public. But the great obstacle to asking questions openly in
public is, of course, wealth. The little twisted sign that comes at
the end of a question has a way of making the rich writhe; power
and prestige come down upon it with all their weight. Questions,
therefore, being sensitive, impulsive and often foolish, have a way
of picking their asking place with care. They shrivel up in an
atmosphere of power, prosperity, and time-worn stone. They die
by the dozen on the threshold of great newspaper offices. They
slink away to less favoured, less flourishing quarters where people
are poor and therefore have nothing to give, where they have no
power and therefore have nothing to lose. Now the questions that
have been pestering me to ask them decided, whether rightly or
wrongly, that they could be asked in *Lysistrata*. They said: 'We
do not expect you to ask us in —,' here they named some of our
most respectable dailies and weeklies; 'nor in —,' here they
named some of our most venerable institutions. 'But, thank
Heaven!' they exclaimed, 'are not women's colleges poor and

young? Are they not inventive, adventurous? Are they not out
to create a new——'

'The editor forbids feminism,' I interposed severely.

'What is feminism?' they screamed with one accord, and as I
did not answer at once, a new question was flung at me: 'Don't
you think it high time that a new——'

But I stopped them by reminding them that they had only
two thousand words at their disposal. Upon that, they withdrew,
consulted together, and finally put forward the request that I
should introduce one or two of them of the simplest, tamest, and
most obvious. For example, there is the question that always bobs
up at the beginning of term when societies issue their invitations
and universities open their doors—why lecture, why be lectured?

In order to place this question fairly before you, I will describe,
for memory has kept the picture bright, one of those rare but,
as Queen Victoria would have put it, never-to-be-sufficiently-
lamented occasions when in deference to friendship, or in a desperate attempt to acquire information about, perhaps, the French
Revolution, it seemed necessary to attend a lecture. The room
to begin with had a hybrid look—it was not for sitting in, nor
yet for eating in. Perhaps there was a map on the wall; certainly
there was a table on a platform, and several rows of rather small,
rather hard, comfortless little chairs. These were occupied intermittently, as if they shunned each other's company, by people
of both sexes, and some had notebooks and were tapping their
fountain pens, and some had none and gazed with the vacancy
and placidity of bullfrogs at the ceiling. A large clock displayed
its cheerless face, and when the hour struck in strode a harried-
looking man, a man from whose face nervousness, vanity, or
perhaps the depressing and impossible nature of his task had
removed all traces of ordinary humanity. There was a momentary
stir. He had written a book, and for a moment it is interesting to
see people who have written books. Everybody gazed at him. He
was bald and not hairy; had a mouth and a chin; in short he
was a man like another, although he had written a book. He
cleared his throat and the lecture began. Now the human voice
is an instrument of varied power; it can enchant and it can
soothe; it can rage and it can despair; but when it lectures it
almost always bores. What he said was sensible enough; there

was learning in it and argument and reason; but as the voice went on attention wandered. The face of the clock seemed abnormally pale; the hands too suffered from some infirmity. Had they the gout? Were they swollen? They moved so slowly. They reminded one of the painful progress of a three-legged fly that has survived the winter. How many flies on an average survive the English winter, and what would be the thoughts of such an insect on waking to find itself being lectured on the French Revolution? The inquiry was fatal. A link had been lost —a paragraph dropped. It was useless to ask the lecturer to repeat his words; on he plodded with dogged pertinacity. The origin of the French Revolution was being sought for—also the thoughts of flies. Now there came one of those flat stretches of discourse when minute objects can be seen coming for two or three miles ahead. 'Skip!' we entreated him—vainly. He did not skip. There was a joke. Then the voice went on again; then it seemed that the windows wanted washing; then a woman sneezed; then the voice quickened; then there was a peroration; and then—thank Heaven!—the lecture was over.

Why, since life holds only so many hours, waste one of them on being lectured? Why, since printing presses have been invented these many centuries, should he not have printed his lecture instead of speaking it? Then, by the fire in winter, or under an apple tree in summer, it could have been read, thought over, discussed; the difficult ideas pondered, the argument debated. It could have been thickened and stiffened. There would have been no need of those repetitions and dilutions with which lectures have to be watered down and brightened up, so as to attract the attention of a miscellaneous audience too apt to think about noses and chins, women sneezing and the longevity of flies.

It may be, I told these questions, that there is some reason, imperceptible to outsiders, which makes lectures an essential part of university discipline. But why—here another rushed to the forefront—why, if lectures are necessary as a form of education, should they not be abolished as a form of entertainment? Never does the crocus flower or the beech tree redden but there issues simultaneously from all the universities of England, Scotland, and Ireland a shower of notes from desperate secretaries entreating So-and-so and So-and-so and So-and-so to come down and address them upon art or literature or politics or morality—and why?

In the old days when newspapers were scarce and carefully lent about from hall to rectory, such laboured methods of rubbing up minds and imparting ideas were no doubt essential. But now, when every day of the week scatters our tables with articles and pamphlets in which every shade of opinion is expressed, far more tersely than by word of mouth, why continue an obsolete custom which not merely wastes time and temper, but incites the most debased of human passions—vanity, ostentation, self-assertion, and the desire to convert? Why encourage your elders to turn themselves into prigs and prophets, when they are ordinary men and women? Why force them to stand on a platform for forty minutes while you reflect upon the colour of their hair and the longevity of flies? Why not let them talk to you and listen to you, naturally and happily, on the floor? Why not create a new form of society founded on poverty and equality? Why not bring together people of all ages and both sexes and all shades of fame and obscurity so that they can talk, without mounting platforms or reading papers or wearing expensive clothes or eating expensive food? Would not such a society be worth, even as a form of education, all the papers on art and literature that have ever been read since the world began? Why not abolish prigs and prophets? Why not invent human intercourse? Why not try?

Here, being sick of the word 'why', I was about to indulge myself with a few reflections of a general nature upon society as it was, as it is, as it might be, with a few fancy pictures of Mrs. Thrale entertaining Dr. Johnson, Lady Holland amusing Lord Macaulay thrown in, when such a clamour arose among the questions that I could hardly hear myself think. The cause of the clamour was soon apparent. I had incautiously and foolishly used the word 'literature'. Now if there is one word that excites questions and puts them in a fury it is this word 'literature'. There they were, screaming and crying, asking questions about poetry and fiction and criticism, each demanding to be heard, each certain that his was the only question that deserved an answer. At last, when they had destroyed all my fancy pictures of Lady Holland and Dr. Johnson, one insisted, for he said that foolish and rash as he might be he was less so than the others, that he should be asked. And his question was, why learn English literature at universities when you can read it for yourselves in books? But I said that it is foolish to ask a question that has already been answered—English literature is, I believe, already taught at the universities. Besides, if we are going to start an argument about it, we should need at least twenty volumes, whereas we have only about seven hundred words remaining. Still, as he was importunate, I said I would ask the question and introduce it to the best of my ability, without expressing any opinion of my own, by copying down the following fragment of dialogue.

The other day I went to call upon a friend of mine who earns her living as a publisher's reader. The room was a little dark, it seemed to me, when I went in. Yet, as the window was open and it was a fine spring day, the darkness must have been spiritual— the effect of some private sorrow I feared. Her first words as I came in confirmed my fears:

'Alas, poor boy!' she exclaimed, tossing the manuscript she was reading to the ground with a gesture of despair. Had some accident happened to one of her relations, I asked, motoring or climbing?

'If you call three hundred pages on the evolution of the Elizabethan sonnet an accident,' she said.

'Is that all?' I replied with relief.

'All?' she retaliated. 'Isn't it enough?' And, beginning to pace up and down the room she exclaimed: 'Once he was a clever boy; once he was worth talking to; once he cared about English literature. But now——' She threw out her hands as if words failed her—but not at all. There followed such a flood of lamentation and vituperation—but reflecting how hard her life was, reading manuscripts day in, day out, I excused her—that I could not follow the argument. All I could gather was that this lecturing about English literature—'if you want to teach them to read English,' she threw in, 'teach them to read Greek'—all this passing of examinations in English literature, which led to all this writing about English literature, was bound in the end to be the death and burial of English literature. 'The tombstone,' she was proceeding, 'will be a bound volume of——' when I stopped her and told her not to talk such nonsense. 'Then tell me,' she said, standing over me with her fists clenched, 'do they write any better for it? Is poetry better, is fiction better, is criticism better now that they have been taught how to read English literature?' As if to answer her own question she read a passage from the manuscript on the floor. 'And each the spit and image of the other!' she groaned, lifting it wearily to its place with the manuscripts on the shelf.

'But think of all they must know,' I tried to argue.

'Know?' she echoed me. 'Know? What d'you mean by "know"?' As that was a difficult question to answer offhand, I passed it over by saying: 'Well, at any rate they'll be able to make their livings and teach other people.' Whereupon she lost her temper and, seizing the unfortunate work upon the Elizabethan sonnet, whizzed it across the room. The rest of the visit passed in picking up the fragments of a teapot that had belonged to her grandmother.

Now of course a dozen other questions clamour to be asked; about churches and parliaments and public houses and shops and loudspeakers and men and women; but mercifully time is up; silence falls.

Professions for Women[1]

WHEN your secretary invited me to come here, she told me that your Society is concerned with the employment of women and she suggested that I might tell you something about my own professional experiences. It is true I am a woman; it is true I am employed; but what professional experiences have I had? It is difficult to say. My profession is literature; and in that profession there are fewer experiences for women than in any other, with the exception of the stage—fewer, I mean, that are peculiar to women. For the road was cut many years ago—by Fanny Burney, by Aphra Behn, by Harriet Martineau, by Jane Austen, by George Eliot—many famous women, and many more unknown and forgotten, have been before me, making the path smooth, and regulating my steps. Thus, when I came to write, there were very few material obstacles in my way. Writing was a reputable and harmless occupation. The family peace was not broken by the scratching of a pen. No demand was made upon the family purse. For ten and sixpence one can buy paper enough to write all the plays of Shakespeare—if one has a mind that way. Pianos and models, Paris, Vienna, and Berlin, masters and mistresses, are not needed by a writer. The cheapness of writing paper is, of course, the reason why women have succeeded as writers before they have succeeded in the other professions.

But to tell you my story—it is a simple one. You have only got to figure to yourselves a girl in a bedroom with a pen in her hand. She had only to move that pen from left to right—from ten o'clock to one. Then it occurred to her to do what is simple and cheap enough after all—to slip a few of those pages into an envelope, fix a penny stamp in the corner, and drop the envelope into the red box at the corner. It was thus that I became a journalist; and my effort was rewarded on the first day of the following month—a very glorious day it was for me—by a letter from an editor containing a cheque for one pound ten shillings and sixpence. But to show you how little I deserve to be called a professional woman, how little I know of the struggles and diffi-

[1] A paper read to the Women's Service League

culties of such lives, I have to admit that instead of spending that sum upon bread and butter, rent, shoes and stockings, or butcher's bills, I went out and bought a cat—a beautiful cat, a Persian cat, which very soon involved me in bitter disputes with my neighbours.

What could be easier than to write articles and to buy Persian cats with the profits? But wait a moment. Articles have to be about something. Mine, I seem to remember, was about a novel by a famous man. And while I was writing this review, I discovered that if I were going to review books I should need to do battle with a certain phantom. And the phantom was a woman, and when I came to know her better I called her after the heroine of a famous poem, The Angel in the House. It was she who used to come between me and my paper when I was writing reviews. It was she who bothered me and wasted my time and so tormented me that at last I killed her. You who come of a younger and happier generation may not have heard of her— you may not know what I mean by The Angel in the House. I will describe her as shortly as I can. She was intensely sympathetic. She was immensely charming. She was utterly unselfish. She excelled in the difficult arts of family life. She sacrificed herself daily. If there was chicken, she took the leg; if there was a draught she sat in it—in short she was so constituted that she never had a mind or a wish of her own, but preferred to sympathize always with the minds and wishes of others. Above all—I need not say it—she was pure. Her purity was supposed to be her chief beauty—her blushes, her great grace. In those days—the last of Queen Victoria—every house had its Angel. And when I came to write I encountered her with the very first words. The shadow of her wings fell on my page; I heard the rustling of her skirts in the room. Directly, that is to say, I took my pen in my hand to review that novel by a famous man, she slipped behind me and whispered: 'My dear, you are a young woman. You are writing about a book that has been written by a man. Be sympathetic; be tender; flatter; deceive; use all the arts and wiles of our sex. Never let anybody guess that you have a mind of your own. Above all, be pure.' And she made as if to guide my pen. I now record the one act for which I take some credit to myself, though the credit rightly belongs to some excellent ancestors of mine who left me a certain sum of money—shall we say five hundred pounds a year?—so that it was not necessary for me to depend solely on charm for my living. I turned upon her and caught her by the throat. I did my best to kill her. My excuse, if I were to be had up in a court of law, would be that I acted in self-defence. Had I not killed her she would have killed me. She would have plucked the heart out of my writing. For, as I found, directly I put pen to paper, you cannot review even a novel without having a mind of your own, without expressing what you think to be the truth about human relations, morality, sex. And all these questions, according to the Angel of the House, cannot be dealt with freely and openly by women; they must charm, they must conciliate, they must—to put it bluntly—tell lies if they are to succeed. Thus, whenever I felt the shadow of her wing or the radiance of her halo upon my page, I took up the inkpot and flung it at her. She died hard. Her fictitious nature was of great assistance to her. It is far harder to kill a phantom than a reality. She was always creeping back when I thought I had despatched her. Though I flatter myself that I killed her in the end, the struggle was severe; it took much time that had better have been spent upon learning Greek grammar; or in roaming the world in search of adventures. But it was a real experience; it was an experience that was bound to befall all women writers at that time. Killing the Angel in the House was part of the occupation of a woman writer.

But to continue my story. The Angel was dead; what then remained? You may say that what remained was a simple and common object—a young woman in a bedroom with an inkpot. In other words, now that she had rid herself of falsehood, that young woman had only to be herself. Ah, but what is 'herself'? I mean, what is a woman? I assure you, I do not know. I do not believe that you know. I do not believe that anybody can know until she has expressed herself in all the arts and professions open to human skill. That indeed is one of the reasons why I have come here—out of respect for you, who are in process of showing us by your experiments what a woman is, who are in process of providing us, by your failures and successes, with that extremely important piece of information.

But to continue the story of my professional experiences. I

made one pound ten and six by my first review; and I bought a Persian cat with the proceeds. Then I grew ambitious. A Persian cat is all very well, I said; but a Persian cat is not enough. I must have a motor-car. And it was thus that I became a novelist—for it is a very strange thing that people will give you a motor-car if you will tell them a story. It is a still stranger thing that there is nothing so delightful in the world as telling stories. It is far pleasanter than writing reviews of famous novels. And yet, if I am to obey your secretary and tell you my professional experiences as a novelist, I must tell you about a very strange experience that befell me as a novelist. And to understand it you must try first to imagine a novelist's state of mind. I hope I am not giving away professional secrets if I say that a novelist's chief desire is to be as unconscious as possible. He has to induce in himself a state of perpetual lethargy. He wants life to proceed with the utmost quiet and regularity. He wants to see the same faces, to read the same books, to do the same things day after day, month after month, while he is writing, so that nothing may break the illusion in which he is living—so that nothing may disturb or disquiet the mysterious nosings about, feelings round, darts, dashes, and sudden discoveries of that very shy and illusive spirit, the imagination. I suspect that this state is the same both for men and women. Be that as it may, I want you to imagine me writing a novel in a state of trance. I want you to figure to yourselves a girl sitting with a pen in her hand, which for minutes, and indeed for hours, she never dips into the inkpot. The image that comes to my mind when I think of this girl is the image of a fisherman lying sunk in dreams on the verge of a deep lake with a rod held out over the water. She was letting her imagination sweep unchecked round every rock and cranny of the world that lies submerged in the depths of our unconscious being. Now came the experience that I believe to be far commoner with women writers than with men. The line raced through the girl's fingers. Her imagination had rushed away. It had sought the pools, the depths, the dark places where the largest fish slumber. And then there was a smash. There was an explosion. There was foam and confusion. The imagination had dashed itself against something hard. The girl was roused from her dream. She was indeed in a state of the most acute and difficult distress. To speak without figure, she had thought of something, something about the body, about the passions which it was unfitting for her as a woman to say. Men, her reason told her, would be shocked. The consciousness of what men will say of a woman who speaks the truth about her passions had roused her from her artist's state of unconsciousness. She could write no more. The trance was over. Her imagination could work no longer. This I believe to be a very common experience with women writers—they are impeded by the extreme conventionality of the other sex. For though men sensibly allow themselves great freedom in these respects, I doubt that they realize or can control the extreme severity with which they condemn such freedom in women.

These then were two very genuine experiences of my own. These were two of the adventures of my professional life. The first—killing the Angel in the House—I think I solved. She died. But the second, telling the truth about my own experiences as a body, I do not think I solved. I doubt that any woman has solved it yet. The obstacles against her are still immensely powerful—and yet they are very difficult to define. Outwardly, what is simpler than to write books? Outwardly, what obstacles are there for a woman rather than for a man? Inwardly, I think, the case is very different; she has still many ghosts to fight, many prejudices to overcome. Indeed it will be a long time still, I think, before a woman can sit down to write a book without finding a phantom to be slain, a rock to be dashed against. And if this is so in literature, the freest of all professions for women, how is it in the new professions which you are now for the first time entering?

Those are the questions that I should like, had I time, to ask you. And indeed, if I have laid stress upon these professional experiences of mine, it is because I believe that they are, though in different forms, yours also. Even when the path is nominally open—when there is nothing to prevent a woman from being a doctor, a lawyer, a civil servant—there are many phantoms and obstacles, as I believe, looming in her way. To discuss and define them is I think of great value and importance; for thus only can the labour be shared, the difficulties be solved. But besides this, it is necessary also to discuss the ends and the aims for which we are fighting, for which we are doing battle with these formidable obstacles. Those aims cannot be taken for granted; they must be perpetually questioned and examined. The whole position, as I see it—here in this hall surrounded by women practising for the first time in history I know not how many different professions —is one of extraordinary interest and importance. You have won rooms of your own in the house hitherto exclusively owned by men. You are able, though not without great labour and effort, to pay the rent. You are earning your five hundred pounds a year. But this freedom is only a beginning; the room is your own, but it is still bare. It has to be furnished; it has to be decorated; it has to be shared. How are you going to furnish it, how are you going to decorate it? With whom are you going to share it, and upon what terms? These, I think are questions of the utmost importance and interest. For the first time in history you are able to ask them; for the first time you are able to decide for yourselves what the answers should be. Willingly would I stay and discuss those questions and answers—but not tonight. My time is up; and I must cease.

Evening over Sussex:
Reflections in a Motor-car

EVENING is kind to Sussex, for Sussex is no longer young, and she is grateful for the veil of evening as an elderly woman is glad when a shade is drawn over a lamp, and only the outline of her face remains. The outline of Sussex is still very fine. The cliffs stand out to sea, one behind another. All Eastbourne, all Bexhill, all St. Leonards, their parades and their lodging houses, their bead shops and their sweet shops and their placards and their invalids and char-à-bancs, are all obliterated. What remains is what there was when William came over from France ten centuries ago: a line of cliffs running out to sea. Also the fields are redeemed. The freckle of red villas on the coast is washed over by a thin lucid lake of brown air, in which they and their redness are drowned. It was still too early for lamps; and too early for stars.

But, I thought, there is always some sediment of irritation when the moment is as beautiful as it is now. The psychologists must explain; one looks up, one is overcome by beauty extravagantly greater than one could expect—there are now pink clouds over Battle; the fields are mottled, marbled—one's perceptions blow out rapidly like air balls expanded by some rush of air, and then, when all seems blown to its fullest and tautest, with beauty and beauty and beauty, a pin pricks; it collapses. But what is the pin? So far as I could tell, the pin had something to do with one's own impotency. I cannot hold this—I cannot express this—I am overcome by it—I am mastered. Somewhere in that region one's discontent lay; and it was allied with the idea that one's nature demands mastery over all that it receives; and mastery here meant the power to convey what one saw now over Sussex so that another person could share it. And further, there was another prick of the pin: one was wasting one's chance; for beauty spread at one's right hand, at one's left; at one's back too; it was escaping all the time; one could only offer a thimble to a torrent that could fill baths, lakes.

But relinquish, I said (it is well known how in circumstances like these the self splits up and one self is eager and dissatisfied and the other stern and philosophical), relinquish these impossible aspirations; be content with the view in front of us, and believe me when I tell you that it is best to sit and soak; to be passive; to accept; and do not bother because nature has given you six little pocket knives with which to cut up the body of a whale.

While these two selves then held a colloquy about the wise course to adopt in the presence of beauty, I (a third party now declared itself) said to myself, how happy they were to enjoy so simple an occupation. There they sat as the car sped along, noticing everything: a haystack; a rust red roof; a pond; an old man coming home with his sack on his back; there they sat, matching every colour in the sky and earth from their colour box, rigging up little models of Sussex barns and farm-houses in the red light that would serve in the January gloom. But I, being somewhat different, sat aloof and melancholy. While they are thus busied, I said to myself: Gone, gone; over, over; past and done with, past and done with. I feel life left behind even as the road is left behind. We have been over that stretch, and are already forgotten. There, windows were lit by our lamps for a second; the light is out now. Others come behind us.

Then suddenly a fourth self (a self which lies in ambush, apparently dormant, and jumps upon one unawares. Its remarks are often entirely disconnected with what has been happening, but must be attended to because of their very abruptness) said: 'Look at that.' It was a light; brilliant, freakish; inexplicable. For a second I was unable to name it. 'A star'; and for that second it held its odd flicker of unexpectedness and danced and beamed. 'I take your meaning,' I said. 'You, erratic and impulsive self that you are, feel that the light over the downs there emerging, dangles from the future. Let us try to understand this. Let us reason it out. I feel suddenly attached not to the past but to the future. I think of Sussex in five hundred years to come. I think much grossness will have evaporated. Things will have been scorched up, eliminated. There will be magic gates. Draughts fan-blown by electric power will cleanse houses. Lights intense and firmly directed will go over the earth, doing the work. Look at the moving light on that hill; it is the headlight of a car. By day and by night Sussex in five centuries will be full of charming thoughts, quick, effective beams.'

The sun was now low beneath the horizon. Darkness spread rapidly. None of my selves could see anything beyond the tapering light of our headlamps on the hedge. I summoned them together. 'Now,' I said, 'comes the season of making up our accounts. Now we have got to collect ourselves; we have got to be one self. Nothing is to be seen any more, except one wedge of road and bank which our lights repeat incessantly. We are perfectly provided for. We are warmly wrapped in a rug; we are protected from wind and rain. We are alone. Now is the time of reckoning. Now I, who preside over the company, am going to arrange in order the trophies which we have all brought in. Let me see; there was a great deal of beauty brought in today: farmhouses; cliffs standing out to sea; marbled fields; mottled fields; red feathered skies; all that. Also there was disappearance and the death of the individual. The vanishing road and the window lit for a second and then dark. And then there was the sudden dancing light, that was hung in the future. What we have made then today,' I said, 'is this: that beauty; death, of the individual; and the future. Look, I will make a little figure for your satisfaction; here he comes. Does this little figure advancing through beauty, through death, to the economical, powerful, and efficient future when houses will be cleansed by a puff of hot wind satisfy you? Look at him; there on my knee.' We sat and looked at the figure we had made that day. Great sheer slabs of rock, tree tufted, surrounded him. He was for a second very, very solemn. Indeed, it seemed as if the reality of things were displayed there on the rug. A violent thrill ran through us; as if a charge of electricity had entered into us. We cried out together: 'Yes, yes,' as if affirming something, in a moment of recognition.

And then the body who had been silent up to now began its song, almost at first as low as the rush of the wheels: 'Eggs and bacon; toast and tea; fire and a bath; fire and a bath; jugged hare,' it went on, 'and red-currant jelly; a glass of wine; with coffee to follow, with coffee to follow—and then to bed; and then to bed.'

'Off with you,' I said to my assembled selves. 'Your work is done. I dismiss you. Good-night.'

And the rest of the journey was performed in the delicious society of my own body.

The Moment: Summer's Night

THE night was falling so that the table in the garden among the trees grew whiter and whiter; and the people round it more indistinct. An owl, blunt, obsolete looking, heavy weighted, crossed the fading sky with a black spot between its claws. The trees murmured. An aeroplane hummed like a piece of plucked wire. There was also, on the roads, the distant explosion of a motor cycle, shooting further and further away down the road. Yet what composed the present moment? If you are young, the future lies upon the present, like a piece of glass, making it tremble and quiver. If you are old, the past lies upon the present, like a thick glass, making it waver, distorting it. All the same, everybody believes that the present is something, seeks out the different elements in this situation in order to compose the truth of it, the whole of it.

To begin with: it is largely composed of visual and of sense impressions. The day was very hot. After heat, the surface of the body is opened, as if all the pores were open and everything lay exposed, not sealed and contracted, as in cold weather. The air wafts cold on the skin under one's clothes. The soles of the feet expand in slippers after walking on hard roads. Then the sense of the light sinking back into darkness seems to be gently putting out with a damp sponge the colour in one's own eyes. Then the leaves shiver now and again, as if a ripple of irresistible sensation ran through them, as a horse suddenly ripples its skin.

But this moment is also composed of a sense that the legs of the chair are sinking through the centre of the earth, passing through the rich garden earth; they sink, weighted down. Then the sky loses its colour perceptibly and a star here and there makes a point of light. Then changes, unseen in the day, coming in succession seem to make an order evident. One becomes aware that we are spectators and also passive participants in a pageant. And as nothing can interfere with the order, we have nothing to do but accept, and watch. Now little sparks, which are not steady, but fitful as if somebody were doubtful, come across the field. Is it time to light the lamp, the farmers' wives are saying:

can I see a little longer? The lamp sinks down; then it burns up.
All doubt is over. Yes the time has come in all cottages, in all
farms, to light the lamps. Thus then the moment is laced about
with these weavings to and fro, these inevitable downsinkings,
flights, lamp lightings.

But that is the wider circumference of the moment. Here in
the centre is a knot of consciousness; a nucleus divided up into
four heads, eight legs, eight arms, and four separate bodies. They
are not subject to the law of the sun and the owl and the lamp.
They assist it. For sometimes a hand rests on the table; sometimes a leg is thrown over a leg. Now the moment becomes
shot with the extraordinary arrow which people let fly from their
mouths—when they speak.

'He'll do well with his hay.'

The words let fall this seed, but also, coming from that obscure
face, and the mouth, and the hand so characteristically holding
the cigarette, now hit the mind with a wad, then explode like a
scent suffusing the whole dome of the mind with its incense,
flavour; let fall, from their ambiguous envelope, the self-confi-
dence of youth, but also its urgent desire, for praise, and assurance; if they were to say: 'But you're no worse looking than
many—you're no different—people don't mark you out to laugh
at you': that he should be at once so cock-a-hoop and so ungainly
makes the moment rock with laughter, and with the malice that
comes from overlooking other people's motives; and seeing what
they keep hid; and so that one takes sides; he will succeed; or
no he won't; and then again, this success, will it mean my defeat;
or won't it? All this shoots through the moment, makes it quiver
with malice and amusement; and the sense of watching and
comparing; and the quiver meets the shore, when the owl flies
out, and puts a stop to this judging, this overseeing, and with our
wings spread, we too fly, take wing, with the owl, over the earth
and survey the quietude of what sleeps, folded, slumbering, arm
stretching in the vast dark and sucking its thumb too; the amorous
and the innocent; and a sigh goes up. Could we not fly too, with
broad wings and with softness; and be all one wing; all embrac-
ing, all gathering, and these boundaries, these pryings over hedge
into hidden compartments of different colours be all swept into
one colour by the brush of the wing; and so visit in splendour,

augustly, peaks; and there lie exposed, bare, on the spine, high up, to the cold light of the moon rising, and when the moon rises, single, solitary, behold her, one, eminent over us?

Ah, yes, if we could fly, fly, fly. . . . Here the body is gripped; and shaken; and the throat stiffens; and the nostrils tingle; and like a rat shaken by a terrier one sneezes; and the whole universe is shaken; mountains, snows, meadows; moon; higgledly, piggledy, upside down, little splinters flying; and the head is jerked up, down. 'Hay fever—what a noise!—there's no cure. Except spending hay time on a boat. Perhaps worse than the disease, though that's what a man did—crossing and recrossing, all the summer.'

Issuing from a white arm, a long shape, lying back, in a film of black and white, under the tree, which, down sweeping, seems a part of that curving, that flowing, the voice, with its ridicule and its sense, reveals to the shaken terrier its own insignificance. No longer part of the snow; no part of the mountain; not in the least venerable to other human beings; but ridiculous; a little accident; a thing to be laughed at; discriminated out; seen clearly cut out, sneezing, sneezing, judged and compared. Thus into the moment steals self-assertion; ah, the sneeze again; the desire to sneeze with conviction; masterfully; making oneself heard; felt; if not pitied, then somebody of importance; perhaps to break away and go. But no; the other shape has sent from its arrow another fine binding thread, 'Shall I fetch my Vapex?' She, the observant, the discriminating, who keeps in mind always other instances, so that there is nothing singular in any special case—who refuses to be jumped into extravagance; and so sceptical withal; cannot believe in miracles; sees the vanity of effort there; perhaps then it would be well to try here; yet if she isolates cases from the mists of hugeness, sees what is there all the more definitely; refuses to be bamboozled; yet in this definite discrimination shows some amplitude. That is why the moment becomes harder, is intensified, diminished, begins to be stained by some expressed personal juice; with the desire to be loved, to be held close to the other shape; to put off the veil of darkness and see burning eyes.

Then a light is struck; in it appears a sunburnt face, lean, blue-eyed, and the arrow flies as the match goes out:

'He beats her every Saturday; from boredom, I should say; not drink; there's nothing else to do.'

The moment runs like quicksilver on a sloping board into the cottage parlour; there are the tea things on the table; the hard windsor chairs; tea caddies on the shelf for ornament; the medal under a glass shade; vegetable steam curling from the pot; two children crawling on the floor; and Liz comes in and John catches her a blow on the side of her head as she slopes past him, dirty, with her hair loose and one hairpin sticking out about to fall. And she moans in a chronic animal way; and the children look up and then make a whistling noise to imitate the engine which they trail across the flags; and John sits himself down with a thump at the table and carves a hunk of bread and munches because there is nothing to be done. A steam rises from his cabbage patch. Let us do something then, something to end this horrible moment, this plausible glistening moment that reflects in its smooth sides this intolerable kitchen, this squalor; this woman moaning; and the rattle of the toy on the flags, and the man munching. Let us smash it by breaking a match. There—snap.

And then comes the low of the cows in the field; and another cow to the left answers; and all the cows seem to be moving tranquilly across the field and the owl flutes off its watery bubble. But the sun is deep below the earth. The trees are growing heavier, blacker; no order is perceptible; there is no sequence in these cries, these movements; they come from no bodies; they are cries to the left and to the right. Nothing can be seen. We can only see ourselves as outlines, cadaverous, sculpturesque. And it is more difficult for the voice to carry through this dark. The dark has stripped the fledge from the arrow—the vibrations that rise red shiver as it passes through us.

Then comes the terror, the exultation; the power to rush out unnoticed, alone; to be consumed; to be swept away to become a rider on the random wind; the tossing wind; the trampling and neighing wind; the horse with the blown-back mane; the tumbling, the foraging; he who gallops for ever, nowhither travelling, indifferent; to be part of the eyeless dark, to be rippling and streaming, to feel the glory run molten up the spine, down the limbs, making the eyes glow, burning, bright, and penetrate the buffeting waves of the wind.

'Everything's sopping wet. It's the dew off the grass. Time to go in.'

And then one shape heaves and surges and rises, and we pass, trailing coats, down the path towards the lighted windows, the dim glow behind the branches, and so enter the door, and the square draws its lines round us, and here is a chair, a table, glasses, knives, and thus we are boxed and housed, and will soon require a draught of soda-water and to find something to read in bed.

Gas[1]

IT is not necessary, perhaps, to dwell upon the circumstances. There can be few people who have not at one time or another had a tooth out under gas. The dentist stands very clean and impersonal in his long white overcoat. He tells one not to cross one's legs and arranges a bit under one's chin. Then the anæsthetist comes in with his bag as clean and impersonal as the dentist and only as black as the other is white. Both seem to wear uniform and to belong to some separate order of humanity, some third sex. The ordinary conventions lapse, for in ordinary life one does not after shaking hands with an unknown man at once open one's mouth and show him a broken tooth. The new relation with the third sex is stony, statuesque, colourless, but nevertheless humane. These are the people who manage the embarkations and disembarkations of the human spirit; these are they who stand on the border line between life and death forwarding the spirit from one to the other with clean impersonal antiseptic hands. Very well, I resign myself to your charge, one says, uncrossing one's legs; and at your command I cease to breathe through the mouth and breathe through the nose; breathe deep, breathe quietly, and your assurance that one is doing it very nicely is a parting salute, a farewell from the officer who presides over the ritual of disembarkation. Soon one is beyond his care.

With each breath one draws in confusion; one draws in darkness, falling, scattering, like a cloud of falling soot flakes. And also one puts out to sea; with every breath one leaves the shore, one cleaves the hot waves of some new sulphurous dark existence in which one flounders without support, attended only by strange relics of old memories, elongated, stretched out, so that they seem to parody the world from which one brought them, with which one tries to keep still in touch by their means; as the curved glass at a fair makes the body seem tapering and then bloated. And as we plunge deeper and deeper away from shore, we seem to be drawn on in the wake of some fast flying always disappearing

[1] Written in 1929

black object, drawn rapidly ahead of us. We become aware of something that we could never see in the other world; something that we have been sent in search of. All the old certainties become smudged and dispersed, because in comparison with this they are unimportant, like old garments crumpled up and dropped in a heap, because one needs to be naked, for this chase, this pursuit; all our most cherished beliefs and certainties and loves become like that. Scudding under a low dark sky we fly on the trail of this truth by which, if we could grasp it, we should be for ever illuminated. And we rush faster and faster and the whole world becomes spiral and like wheels and circles about us, pressing closer and closer until it seems by its pressure to force us through a central hole, very narrow through which it hurts us, squeezing us with its pressure on the head, to pass. Indeed we seem to be crushed between the upper world and the lower world and then suddenly the pressure is lessened; the whole aperture widens up; we pass through a gorge, emerge into daylight, and behold a glass dish and hear a voice saying, 'Rinse the mouth. Rinse the mouth,' while a trickle of warm blood runs from between the lips. So we are received back by the officials. The truth that was being drawn so fast ahead of us vanishes.

Such is a very common experience. Everybody goes through it. But it seems to explain something that one observes very often in a third-class railway carriage for example. For it is impossible not to ask some questions as one looks down the long narrow compartment where so many different people sit facing each other. If they begin originally like that, one muses, looking at a child of three, what is the process that turns them into that? And here one looks at a heavy old man with a despatch box; or at an overdressed red-faced woman. What has made that extraordinary change? What sights, what experiences? For except in some very rare cases it seems as if the passing of sixty or seventy years had inflicted a most terrible punishment on the smooth pink face, had imparted some very strange piece of information, so that, however the features differ, the eyes of old people always have the same expression.

And what is that piece of information? one asks. Is it probably that all these people have been several times under gas? Gradually they have been made to think that what passes before them has very little substance. They know that they can be rid of it for a small sum. They can then see another thing, more important, perhaps drawn through the water. But what hardly any of them knows is whether he or she wishes to be rid of it. There they sit, the plumber with his leaden coil, the man with his despatch box, the middle-class woman with her parcel from Selfridges, revolving often unconsciously the question whether there is any meaning in this world compared with the other, and what the truth is that dashed ahead through the water. They woke before they had seized it. And the other world vanished. And perhaps to forget it, to cover it over, they went to the public house, they went to Oxford Street and bought a hat. As one looks down the third-class carriage, one sees that all the men and women over twenty have often been under gas; it is this that has done more than anything to change the expression of the face. An unchanged face would look almost idiotic. But, of course, there are a few faces which look as if they had caught the thing that dashes through the water.

Fishing

WHILE there is a Chinese proverb which says that the fisherman is pure at heart 'as a white sea-shell', there is a Japanese poem, four lines long, which says something so true but at the same time so crude about the hearts of politicians that it had better be left in its original obscurity. It may be this contradiction—Major Hills, says his publisher, 'has been a member of the House of Commons for thirty years. . . . Throughout his long parliamentary life he has remained faithful to his favourite sport' —which has produced a collision in his book; a confusion in the mind of the reader between fish and men.

All books are made of words, but mostly of words that flutter and agitate thought. This book on the contrary, though made of words, has a strange effect on the body. It lifts it out of the chair; stands it on the banks of a river, and strikes it dumb. The river rushes by; a voice commands: 'Stand absolutely motionless. . . . Cast up and slightly across. . . . Shoot the line out. . . . Let the flies come well round. . . . On no account pull. . . . Do not be in a hurry to lift. . . .' But the strain is too great, the excitement too intense. We have pulled—we have lifted. The fish is off. 'Wait longer next time,' the voice commands; 'wait longer and longer.'

Now, if the art of writing consists in laying an egg in the reader's mind from which springs the thing itself—whether man or fish—and if this art requires such ardour in its practitioners that they will readily, like Flaubert, give up all their bright spring mornings to its pursuit, how does it come about that Major Hills, who has spent thirty years in the House of Commons, can do the trick? Sometimes at four in the morning, in the early spring dawn, he has roused himself, not to dandle words, but to rush down to the river—'the exquisite river, with its vivid green wooded banks, its dark rose-coloured sandstone rocks, its rushing crystalline water', and there he has stood with his rod. There we stand too.

Look at the rod. It was bought of Strong of Carlisle and cost one pound. 'It consisted of a piece of whole bamboo with a lancewood top spliced on. . . . Never have I had a rod sweeter to cast with and throwing a longer line.' It is not a rod; it is a tool, more beautiful than a Persian pot, more desirable than a lover. '. . . A friend broke it . . . and I could never get another like it . . . and I grieved sorely, for bamboo cannot be mended.' What death or disaster could be more pungent? But this is no time for sentiment. There deep under the bank lies the old male salmon. What fly will he take? The grey turkey, with a body of violet silk, the archdeacon in fact, number one? The line is cast; out it floats; down it settles. And then? '. . . The fish went perfectly mad, overran my reel . . . jammed it, and broke my twisted gut trace. It all happened in a few seconds. . . .' But they were seconds of extraordinary intensity, seconds lived alone 'in a world of strong emotion, cut off from all else'. When we look up Corby's walks have changed. 'The trees had their young light leaves, some of them golden, the wild cherry was covered with drifts of snow and the ground was covered with dog mercury, looking as though it had been newly varnished. . . . I felt receptive to every sight, every colour and every sound, as though I walked through a world from which a veil had been withdrawn.'

Is it possible that to remove veils from trees it is necessary to fish?—our conscious mind must be all body, and then the unconscious mind leaps to the top and strips off veils? Is it possible that, if to bare reality is to be a poet, we have, as Mr. Yeats said the other day, no great poet because since the war farmers preserve or net their waters, and vermin get up? Has the deplorable habit of clubs to fetter anglers with ridiculous restrictions, to pamper them with insidious luxuries, somehow cramped our poets' style? And the novelists—if we have no novelist in England today whose stature is higher than the third button on Sir Walter's waistcoat, or reaches to the watchchain of Charles Dickens, or the ring on the little finger of George Eliot, is it not that the Cumberland poachers are dying out? 'They were an amusing race, full of rare humour, delightful to talk to. . . . We often had chats on the banks and they would tell me quite openly of their successes.' But now 'the old wild days are over'; the poachers are gone. They catch trout, commercially, innumerably, for hotels. Banish from fiction all poachers' talk, the dialect, the dialogue of Scott, the publicans, the farmers of Dickens and George Eliot, and what remains? Mouldy velvet; moth-eaten ermine; mahogany tables; and a few stuffed fowls. No wonder, since the poachers are gone, that fiction is failing. . . . 'But this is not catching trout,' the voice commands. 'Do not dawdle. . . . Start fishing again without delay.'

It is a bad day; the sun is up; the trout are not feeding. We fail again and again. But fishing teaches a stern morality; inculcates a remorseless honesty. The fault may be with ourselves. 'Why do I go on missing at the strike? . . . If I had more delicacy in casting, more accuracy, if I had fished finer, should I not have done better? And the answer is—Yes! . . . I lost him through sinning against the light. . . . I failed through obstinate stupidity.' We are sunk deep in the world of meditation and remorse. 'Contradiction lies at the root of all powerful emotions. We are not ruled by reason. We follow a different law, and recognize its sanctions. . . .' Sounds from the outer world come through the roar of the river. Barbarians have invaded the upper waters of the Eden and Driffield Beck. But happily the barbarians are grayling; and the profound difference that divides the human race is a question of bait—whether to fish with worms or not; some will: to others the thought is unutterably repulsive.

But the summer's day is fading. Night is coming on—the Northern night, which is not dark, for the light is there, but veiled. 'A Cumberland night is something to remember', and trout—for trout are 'curious pieces of work'—will feed in Cumberland at midnight. Let us go down to the bank again. The river sounds louder than by day. 'As I walked down I heard its varied cadence, obscured during sunlight, at one moment deep, then clamorous, then where thick beech trees hid the river subdued to a murmur. . . . The flowering trees had long since lost their blossoms, but on coming to a syringa bush I walked suddenly into its scent, and was drenched as in a bath. I sat on the path. I stretched my legs. I lay down, finding a tuft of grass for pillow, and the yielding sand for mattress. I fell asleep.'

And while the fisherman sleeps, we who are presumably reading—but what kind of reading is this when we see through the words Corby's trees and trout at the bottom of the page?—wonder, what does the fisherman dream? Of all the rivers rushing past—the Eden, the Test, and the Kennet, each river different from the other, each full of shadowy fish, and each fish different from the other; the trout subtle, the salmon ingenious; each with its nerves, with its brain, its mentality that we can dimly penetrate, movements we can mystically anticipate, for just as, suddenly, Greek and Latin sort themselves in a flash, so we understand the minds of fish? Or does he dream of the wild Scottish hill in the blizzard; and the patch of windless weather behind the rock, when the pale grasses no longer bent but stood upright; or of the vision on top—twenty Whooper swans floating on the loch fearlessly, 'for they had come from some land where they had never seen a man'? Or does he dream of poachers with their whisky-stained weather-beaten faces; or of Andrew Lang, drinking, and discussing the first book of Genesis; or of F. S. Oliver, whose buttons after a meal 'kept popping off like broom pods in autumn'; or of Sparrow, the hunter, 'a more generous animal never was seen'; or of the great Arthur Wood and all his bees? Or does he dream of places that his ghost will revisit if it ever comes to earth again—of Ramsbury, Highhead, and the Isle of Jura?

For dream he does. 'I always, even now, dream that I shall astonish the world. An outstanding success. . . .' The Premiership is it? No, this triumph, this outstanding success is not with men; it is with fish; it is with the floating line. 'I believe it will come. . . .' But here he wakes 'with that sense of well-being which sleep in the open air always engenders. It was midnight, moonless and clear. I walked to the edge of the flat rock. . . .' The trout were feeding.